Automated Lighting

Automated Lighting

The Art and Science of Moving Light in Theatre, Live Performance, Broadcast, and Entertainment

Richard Cadena

ELSEVIER

AMSTERDAM • BOSTON • HEIDELBERG • LONDON
NEW YORK • OXFORD • PARIS • SAN DIEGO
SAN FRANCISCO • SINGAPORE • SYDNEY • TOKYO

Focal Press is an imprint of Elsevier

Focal
Press

Acquisitions Editor: Cara Anderson
Project Manager: Dawnmarie Simpson
Marketing Manager: Christine Degon Veroulis
Cover Design: Eric DeCicco

Focal Press is an imprint of Elsevier
30 Corporate Drive, Suite 400, Burlington, MA 01803, USA
Linacre House, Jordan Hill, Oxford OX2 8DP, UK

 Recognizing the importance of preserving what has been written, Elsevier prints its books on acid-free paper
whenever possible.

Library of Congress Cataloging-in-Publication Data
Cadena, Richard.
   Automated lighting : the art and science of moving light in theatre, live performance, broadcast &
entertainment / Richard Cadena.
      p.   cm.
   Includes index.
   ISBN-13: 978-0-240-80703-4 (pbk. : alk. paper)
   ISBN-10: 0-240-80703-0 (pbk. : alk. paper)   1. Stage lighting.   2. Television—Lighting.   I. Title.
   PN2091.E4C33 2006
   778.5'343—dc22

                                                                                                2006009198

British Library Cataloguing-in-Publication Data
A catalogue record for this book is available from the British Library.

ISBN 13: 978-0-240-80703-4
ISBN 10: 0-240-80703-0

For information on all Focal Press publications
visit our website at www.books.elsevier.com

06 07 08 09 10   10 9 8 7 6 5 4 3 2 1

Printed in China.

This book is dedicated to Noe Cadena, an extraordinary father, husband, little league coach, marathon runner, and engineer, who gave of his mind, body, and spirit to provide for his family and give them every opportunity he could. Dad, you are my inspiration.

Contents

Preface

Automated Lighting: The Art and Science of Moving Light in Theatre, Live Performance, Broadcast, and Entertainment covers the history, the science, and the art of automated lighting, including the mechanical, electromechanical, electrical, electronic, and optical principles of operation as well as aspects pertaining to lighting design, programming, and implementation. It contains practical information about the principles of operation of an automated luminaire as well as information about how it is used and some of the issues that designers will face. The book is divided into sections, starting with the history of automated lighting and a systems overview, then moving on to electricity and electronics, electromechanical and mechanical systems, optical systems, communications, maintenance and troubleshooting, digital lighting, automated lighting programming, lighting design with automated luminaires, and the future of automated lighting. Within those sections are the basics of DC and AC electricity, electronics, power supplies, digital electronics, electromechanical systems, optical systems (including dichroic filters, reflectors, lenses, and more), lamp technology, lighting effects (including color mixing, glass gobos, and more), data distribution systems, DMX, RDM, ACN, DMD, DLP, LCD, a range of design issues, and a discussion of the future of the technology. The text is illustrated, to the extent possible, with drawings and photographs to augment and reinforce the written material. My hope is that I have presented enough material to sufficiently address the important aspects of automated lighting, especially those that will help you attain your career goals.

This book is intended to be a guided course in automated lighting technology, from the basics to application, and most everything in between. Although it does mention specific products and brand names for illustrative purposes, it is not intended to be product specific. Knowledge of electricity and electronics is helpful, but there should be enough information presented herein to guide the more ambitious beginner to understand the principles involved.

My desire is that the material presented in this book will provide a solid foundation for aspiring lighting professionals as well as reinforce and add to the knowledge of more experienced lighting professionals. As the industry grows and matures, more and more opportunities are opening up and becoming available, in tech support, sales, engineering, design, management, and many other fields. In order to make the most of these opportunities, it pays to be well prepared and to learn as much as you can about every aspect of the industry. I hope that you will find this book educational, informative, and motivating enough to help you catapult your career in the entertainment lighting industry.

Richard Cadena

Acknowledgments

The book that you now hold in your hands is the result of many early mornings spent writing when I should have been exercising, many late nights when I should have been sleeping, many weekends when I should have been tending my lawn, and many holidays when I should have been relaxing or recreating with my family. Now that I'm a little fatter, I have bags under my eyes, my lawn is overgrown, my sailboat is neglected, and my family doesn't recognize me without my laptop, I'm most pleased to offer over 100,000 words and more than 250 photographs and illustrations about the one thing that seems to make it all worthwhile: automated lighting technology. But if you think this book is about the nuts and bolts of moving lights, then you're missing the big picture. It's really not about automated lighting so much as it is about the irrepressible ingenuity of the human mind and our insatiable hunger for a deeper understanding of the universe and how to experience it. It's about how art and science can transform one another; how the nonnegotiable (science) and the negotiable (art) can combine to create the unimaginable. It's a book about life as seen through the filter of science, art, and technology. I hope that by illuminating some of the dark corners of the mind, it will serve to illustrate just how vast the darkness is and to pique your interest about the potential discoveries that may lie ahead.

I have many people to thank for helping to make this book possible. I was fortunate enough to be in the right place at the right time when the company I went to work for in the mid-1980s, Blackstone Audio Visual, became a manufacturer of automated lighting called High End Systems. Due to the foresight, hard work, and dedication of Richard Belliveau, Lowell Fowler, and Bob Schacherl—the three original owners—as well as numerous employees and countless customers, the company went on to become one of the world's foremost automated lighting manufacturers. I am grateful to have been a part of it. Later, when I went to work for Martin Professional, and then when I started a manufacturer's rep firm, and again when I became the editor of *PLSN*, I was fortunate enough to share the company of many industry luminaries, visit numerous manufacturing facilities and production companies, and attend way too many shows, trade shows, and events around the world, each of which has contributed significantly to the body of information in these pages.

I would be remiss if I didn't mention those people who enable me to write and learn about the industry, provide the opportunity to do what I love best, and make it worthwhile to get out of bed each day and face the stacks of "work" that await me. I especially want to thank Noe and Yolanda Cadena, a.k.a. dad and mom, who unselfishly gave their love and encouragement, among other things; Lisa and Joey Cadena, a.k.a. my wife and daughter, who give me the motivation to strive for excellence and who keep me young at heart; Cara Anderson, Diane Wurzel, and all the fine people at Focal Press; Mike Wood, industry uber-guru, without whom this book would be a mess; and the countless people who were there to answer my endless questions, some of whom include:

Daniel W. Antonuk, Electronic Theatre Controls, Inc.
Richard Belliveau, High End Systems
Scott Blair, High End Systems
Rusty Brutsche, PRG/VLPS
Michael Callahan, Variable-Parameter Fixture Corporation
Jack Calmes, Syncrolite
Christian Choi, freelance programmer
Andy Collier, Technical Marketing Ltd.
Gil Densham, Cast Software
Harry Donavan, Rigging Seminars
Michael Fink, Magical Designs
Jules Fisher, Fisher Dachs, Associates
Doug Fleenor, Doug Fleenor Designs
Kirk Garreans, ALP Design & Production, Inc.
John Gott, SLS Loudspeakers
Breck Haggerty, Diagonal Research
Mitch Hefter, Design Relief
Chas Herington, Zenith Lighting
Bill Hewlett, Hubbell Lighting
Matthias Hinrichs, Martin Professional
James D. Hooker, Osram-Sylvania
Anne Hunter, Rosco
John Glen Hunter, freelance farmer

Scott Ingham, firmware engineer
Steve Irwin, freelance programmer
George Izenour, Yale School of Drama (retired)
Mats Karlsson, Barco
Maribeth Linden, TLC International
Debi Moen, High End Systems
Robert Mokry, Lightparts.com
Jim Moody, lighting designer
Joel Nichols, Apollo Design Technology
Paul Pelletier, Martin Cananda
Richard Pilbrow, Theatre Projects Consultants
Don Pugh, Lightparts.com
Jeff Ravitz, Visual Terrain
Scott Riley, freelance automated lighting programmer
Karl Ruling, ESTA
Luciano Salvati, Techni-Lux
Brad Schiller, High End Systems
Arnold Serame, production designer
Woody Smith
David Snipp, Stardraw.com Ltd.
Bill Strother, William Strother Design
Dany Tancou, Cast Software
Ermanno Tontoni, SGM
Howard Ungerleider, Production Design International
Teddy Van Bemmel, Altman Lighting
Rufus Warren, Design & Drafting
Steve Warren, Avolites
and so many, many more.

SECTION 1

Introduction to Automated Lighting

CHAPTER 1
Automated Lighting in the Global Village

I will prepare and someday my chance will come.—Abraham Lincoln

It's an exciting time to be involved with automated lighting. The palette of effects and features has never been richer, nor has there ever been a wider selection of automated fixtures from which to choose. Increased global competition is putting downward pressure on pricing, and it has never been less expensive to buy into the technology. Manufacturers are finding ways to make automated lighting fixtures smaller and lighter, with ever-increasing light output. The optics are getting better and more efficient, while a number of third-party manufacturers have formed a cottage industry based on supplying high-resolution glass gobos for projection and effects. Lamp manufacturers are making strides in increasing lamp performance with longer life and better quality light. Life in the world of automated lighting is good.

State-of-the-art automated lighting instruments embody a wide range of disparate technologies in the convergence of optics, mechanics, robotics, and electronics, mixed with a bit of artistic ingenuity and a flair for design. Few products combine this level of sophistication and complexity in one package. In automated lighting fixtures, high-current devices like lamp circuitry reside in close proximity to high-speed, microelectronic components and circuits like communications transmitters and digital signal processors. Voltages inside the fixture range from a few volts for the electronics and motor drive circuits to thousands of volts in the lamp starting circuit. The internal operating temperature can reach 1832°F (1000°C) in the optical path of a typical automated lighting fixture, yet the electronics are sensitive enough to require a reasonably cool environment to perform reliably. These fixtures regularly cycle between room temperature and operating temperature, placing great stresses and strains on the interfaces between glass, ceramics, metal, and plastics. At the same time, many of these fixtures are designed to withstand the rigors of being shipped all over the world in freighters, airplanes, and trucks. They are often subject to daily handling from stagehands, physical shock from being bounced around on moving trusses, and thermal shock from cycling on and off. They are truly an amazing blend of modern machinery, computer wizardry, and applied technology.

The number of available automated lighting products has risen dramatically in the past few years. One of the best ways to see these products is to attend one of several entertainment lighting trade shows around the world. At the Entertainment Technology Show/Lighting Dimensions International (ETS-LDI) trade show (www.ets-ldi.com) alone, there are at least two dozen different automated lighting manufacturers and distributors represented, largely from the top-tier manufacturers; about a dozen and a half automated lighting console manufacturers; and all variety of manufacturers of gobos, road cases, lamps, design software, and more. At trade shows such as the SIB International Exhibition in Rimini, Italy (www.sibinternational.com), PLASA in London (www.plasa.org), Siel in Paris, and Musicmesse in Frankfurt, there are many more European lighting manufacturers exhibiting their wares. Italy alone is home to at least a dozen well-known entertainment lighting manufacturers. There are many more emerging manufacturers in Europe and Asia who exhibit at trade shows all around the world. The supply side of the industry is thriving, much to the benefit of the automated lighting consumer.

The technology has advanced to the point where today's automated lighting fixtures are about half the size and weight, with about twice as much light output, as an equivalent fixture of 10 years ago. Manufacturers are learning how to design and build more efficient power supplies and optics, making better use of light and electricity. Many are switching to high-tech plastic housings and components to save weight, labor costs, and manufacturing costs (provided they can exceed the break-even point of the heavy cost of tooling). At the same time, the price of automated lighting is falling. Today, you can buy an automated lighting fixture for less than half the price (adjusted for inflation), for twice the light output, and with many more features than you could in the late 1980s and early 1990s.

The design of automated lighting requires the cooperation of several disciplines that coordinate their efforts to bring a finished product to market. Designers draw from disciplines as diverse as physics, electrical and electronics engineering, software and firmware engineering, mechanical and chemical engineering, thermal engineering, and aesthetic design. These designers are under constant and intense pressure to innovate and leapfrog the competition before they are out-innovated. Every year, dozens of manufacturers and distributors compete for the business of thousands of prospective buyers at dozens of trade shows around the world. These trade shows put an incredible amount of pressure on manufacturers to bring finished products to the market, sometimes at the expense of perfecting the product. Millions of dollars are at stake when a new product is under development, and the faster a product comes to market, the better the return on the investment. Conversely, the longer it takes a manufacturer to get a new product to market, the more money it takes and the better the chance that another manufacturer will beat them to market. As a result, manufacturers sometimes launch a product prematurely in their rush to meet the market demand. It's a big stakes game. Manufacturers who can give customers what they want are the ones who will survive another year and have a chance to compete again.

To make matters more interesting, increased global competition is changing the entertainment lighting industry. Recently there has been a flood of inexpensive imported products coming from places like China and the Czech Republic. These products are built with cheap labor, and they are designed to be extremely cost-competitive. Many years ago products coming out of developing countries were decidedly inferior to the products of more industrialized nations. No longer is that the case. Contrary to what some may believe, many of these products are very well designed and manufactured and are surprisingly robust. The technology and resources to manufacture quality products are available to anyone with access to labor and the ability to obtain investment capital to buy machinery and equipment. It has become easier to compete in the automated lighting manufacturing arena because the barrier to entry has fallen considerably as components are becoming more readily available. In the early days of automated lighting, manufacturers often had to customize certain components. For example, stepper motors were adapted for automated lighting by developing specialized grease, custom magnets, custom rotors, customer windings, and custom insulation. Today, suitable stepper motors are available off the shelf.

In 1995, I caught a glimpse into the future of Chinese manufacturing at the Pro Audio, Lights, and Music (PALM) trade show at the Beijing International Exhibition Center in Beijing, China. There were many automated lighting manufacturers and distributors from around the world exhibiting at the show, hoping to generate interest in the rapidly developing Asian economy. Rows and rows of exhibit booths were filled with animated lighting displays, and crowds of people wandered from booth to booth examining the wares. In one long hall toward the back of the convention center, there was an entire section devoted exclusively to Chinese lighting manufacturers. It was both stunning and amazing to find over a dozen displays showing exact replicas of the most popular products of the day. Several fixtures wore the trademark red stripe of the Martin Roboscan. Another was an exact copy of a Lightwave Research Trackspot. I examined the imitation Trackspot very closely, and I even opened one up to have a look inside. I found circuit boards that had apparently been reverse engineered, and every feature, inside and out, was copied exactly. The sole exception was on the trademark silver label on the side of the fixture. The manufacturer had copied the lettering exactly as it appeared, except that they apparently knew better than to print "U.S.A." Instead, they replaced those letters with the word "China." So the new label read, verbatim, "Trackspot, Lightwave Research, Austin, TX China" (Figure 1-1).

It truly is a global village.

Figure 1-1 Imitation Trackspot made in "Austin, TX China." (Photograph courtesy of High End Systems [retouched photo].)

CHAPTER 2

The Foundation of the Automated Lighting Industry

If I have been able to see further, it was only because I stood on the shoulders of giants.—Sir Isaac Newton, scientist and philosopher (1642–1727)

In the relatively short period of time from 1981 to the present, automated lighting has gained tremendous popularity in the entertainment and "architainment" lighting industries. What began mostly as a concert and touring phenomenon quickly gained acceptance in nightclubs and discotheques throughout the world, where technology is often embraced and nurtured. Once it was proven that automated lighting could meet certain criteria for noise, intensity, and reliability, it slowly found applications in Broadway, off-Broadway, and other theatre applications across the spectrum. Now automated lighting has permeated almost every aspect of theatrical lighting, including television and film, cruise ships, houses of worship, and retail environments.

The Genesis of the Automated Lighting Industry

The concept of mechanized lighting can be traced at least as far back as 1906 when Edmund Sohlberg of Kansas City, Missouri, was issued a patent for a remote-controlled spotlight. The fixture had a carbon-arc source, an electromechanical color changer, and a series of cords and pulleys that allowed an operator to remotely change the pan, tilt, and zoom by manually adjusting the cords. The idea was to locate the operator in a hidden location while the light was perched on the balcony rail, and the operator could move it at will.

In 1925, Herbert F. King of Newtonville, Massachusetts, filed a patent application for an "automatic spotlight" with motorized pan and tilt. On August 14, 1928, U.S. patent number 1,680,685 was issued in his name for "a light projector which may be moved automatically to cause the stream of beams to move through a predetermined path and spot successively a plurality of objects and hold the spot for an interval on at least one of said spots." His patent describes successively spotlighting items in a store window; however, it appears that it might be one of the earliest uses of electric motors for motorizing the pan and tilt in a luminaire.

A couple of years later, on November 30, 1927, Charles Andreino of Montreal, Quebec, Canada, filed a Canadian patent for an "adjustable projector," and on November 29, 1928 the same patent was filed in the U.S. patent office. The U.S. patent, number 1,747,279, was issued on February 18, 1930 for a projector with a remote control that facilitated pan and tilt as well as remote focus.

Later on, in the 1930s, Robert Snyder applied for a U.S. patent related to "improvements . . . on spotlights which are remotely controlled." Patent number 2,097,537 was applied for on June 7, 1933 and was issued on November 2, 1937. Almost simultaneously, Joseph Levy was also thinking about a remotely controlled spotlight. Levy worked for Century Lighting, which was eventually bought by Strand Lighting, and he was the coinventor of the Leko, the name of which is a combination of Levy and (Edward) Kook. In 1936 Levy received patent number 2,054,224 for a motorized pan and tilt unit on which a mirror or a luminaire could be mounted and which was controlled by a joystick. It used self-synchronizing or "selsyn" motors to precisely control the pan and tilt position.

Also in the 1930s, a contemporary of Levy, George Izenour, began conceptualizing a lighting fixture with remote control of the pan, tilt, focus, beam angle, and color. He was employed by the Federal Theatre Project working repertory theatre when he realized the flexibility that such a system might afford. But the complexity of the system and the available technology at the time made it virtually impossible to realize his concept.

By the end of 1949, Cecil B. DeMille was working on a movie for Paramount Pictures called *The Greatest Show on Earth*, and he wanted a remotely operated lighting fixture that they could mount high under the big top. Century Lighting was brought in as a collaborator and, along with Paramount, built a remote-controlled fixture for the movie. In 1954, 2 years after *The Greatest Show on Earth* was released, Lou Erhardt of Century Lighting succeeded in building a remotely controlled 1000-watt Fresnel fixture. It was a modified version of the popular Century FeatherLite 8" Fresnel with servo motors driving the pan and tilt. Izenour, working as a consultant to Century, developed the mechanical dimming system in order to keep the color temperature constant through the dimming curve; this system is still in use today in the Wybron Eclipse II double irising dimmer (www.wybron.com). By 1960, literature from Century Lighting was advertising a "large variety of remote control devices for positioning and varying spotlight distributions," all of which were "assembled to special order." They offered "motorized drives for vertical or horizontal movement," a motorized iris in a Leko, or a motorized focus screw in a Fresnel, in any of their products up to 750 watts (Figure 2-1). Motorized FeatherLite Fresnel units were installed in NBC's Studio 8H at Rockefeller Center in New York City sometime in the late 1950s or early 1960s. According to Izenour, the lights were sabotaged by stage hands who feared for their jobs. They reportedly put sand in the gear boxes, which ended their useful life only a couple of years after they were installed. In 1971, the lights were donated to the Pennsylvania State University Stage Lighting Archives, where they remain to this day.

When Izenour became an associate professor at Yale University School of Drama in the 1950s, he developed two prototypes of a remote-controlled 2K Fresnel fixture. The first attempt did not work, but the second, which was a refined version of the first, was more successful. The working prototype used three servo motors driven by a null-seeking signal bridge circuit using electron tube push–pull servo amplifiers. But the potentiometers used in the feedback circuit lacked the precision to provide accurate repeatability.

Izenour attempted to build another remote-controlled fixture in 1969. The moving mirror fixture was built around a 1K ellipsoidal, and it had to be water cooled to prevent the motor-driven iris from seizing up. The mirror was panned and tilted by means of a self-synchronous (selsyn) drive motor and the douser was solenoid driven. Another selsyn-driven motor controlled the remote focus. Only two production models were ever manufactured; they were operated at Milwaukee Repertory Theatre for a short period, but it was never a commercial success.

Synchronicity

Often times when an inventor in one part of the world begins working with one idea, other inventors simultaneously and independently develop similar ideas. This happened with the inventions of calculus (Leibnitz and Newton) and the electric light bulb (Edison and Swan). Psychiatrist Carl Jung defined this phenomenon as synchronicity and described it as "meaningful coincidence." So it seems that the idea of using remote control of the

REMOTE CONTROL SPOTLIGHTS

Century Lighting manufactures a large variety of remote control devices for positioning and varying spotlight distributions. They are assembled to special order to permit greatest adaptability in each individual installation. These range from an iris Lekolite to serve as a followspot in a night club to an entire system of retractable Fresnelites for swift changes covering an entire performance area. The savings in rehearsal and operational time can effect substantial long range economies in such installations.

CENTROLITE SYSTEM

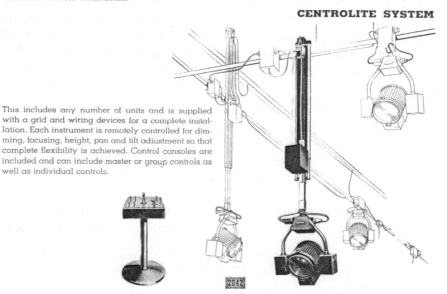

This includes any number of units and is supplied with a grid and wiring devices for a complete installation. Each instrument is remotely controlled for dimming, focusing, height, pan and tilt adjustment so that complete flexibility is achieved. Control consoles are included and can include master or group controls as well as individual controls.

REMOTE CONTROL CARRIAGE

This unit contains motorized drives for vertical or horizontal movement. The iris of the Leko or the focus screw of the Fresnelite may be motor driven for control of the beam spread. Any Lekolite up to 750 watts or Fresnelites up to 8" lens diameter can be accommodated. A control panel is included. Drive speeds are variable and are controlled by the distance the levers are moved.

SEE CENTURY LIGHTING DATA SHEETS FOR DETAILED INFORMATION

Figure 2-1 A 1960 Century Lighting catalog offers "motorized drives for vertical or horizontal movement," a motorized iris in a Leko, or a motorized focus screw in a Fresnel, in any of their products up to 750 watts. (Catalog courtesy of Bob Schiller, who started with Century Lighting in 1950 and retired from Strand Lighting in 1992.)

pan, tilt, and focus (PTF) of a spotlight came into the collective consciousness of the lighting industry in the early 1960s. It was then that a young lighting designer named Jules Fisher had been pondering the problem of lighting a musical production of *Peter Pan* in the round.

"I was working at the Casa Mañana arena theatre in Fort Worth, Texas," he said. "Faced with the problem of how to do 'Tinkerbell' in the round got me thinking of a remote control instrument. I knew of Century [Lighting's] work with remote positioning instruments that were in development for the television studios and a remote positioning mirror device for the ANTA theatre in Washington Square. George [Izenour], I believe, was involved with these as well as Stanley McCandless. They were both under a contract arrangement with Century. I was working with a theatre technician/sound designer, Garry Harris, and he suggested using [synchro] motors to drive the motion. [Synchro] motors of all sizes were available on Canal Street at surplus stores as they were a staple to the armed forces to move everything in planes and ships."

Fisher designed, patented, and built the remote-controlled lights with a 120-watt PAR 64 12-volt lamp with a very narrow beam (Figure 2-2).

Figure 2-2 Fisher's patented 120-watt remote-controlled PAR 64.

On September 28, 1965, U.S. patent number 3,209,136 was issued in his name for a "remote control movement system including a unit for variably positioning a light source device and controller therefor." The fixture panned 360 degrees and tilted 270 degrees using selsyn motors. It had a chain drive for the tilt and a worm gear for the pan. It was manually controlled by an operator who turned a pair of selsyn motors built into the remote. The motors in the remote (transmitters) and the motors in the fixture (receivers) were wired together and moved in tandem. When the operator moved the potentiometer on the controller, the motor in the fixture followed it. Because the two motors were a quarter of a degree out of synch with each other, the operator could feel increased resistance when the pan and tilt dials were turned, which provided a feel for the inertia of the system.

"In a [synchro]," Fisher explained, "being an analogue device, the motion is extremely smooth. Stepper motors, although easier to index, introduce increments [steps] to the motion. Roger Morgan, my assistant at that time, suggested we bake the paint on in my kitchen stove, which we did. It was first used in Texas for that production of *Peter Pan*. Mounting it in the center of the grid over the circular stage the light could move anywhere on the stage as well as all over the audience in 360 degrees. I added a variable-speed, motor-operated micro switch in series [with the lamp] so [it] had a blinking quality [and] appeared to 'breathe.' Tinkerbell had a heart. As he grew weaker or stronger with the audience applause the blinking rate decreased and increased."

Fisher built several of these fixtures, which were used in various capacities, including the showroom of an antique dealer. Ultimately, he had a difficult time convincing lighting manufacturers of the commercial feasibility of the fixture. According to him, they "didn't quite see the future for such a unit."

Meanwhile, across the Atlantic Ocean in Vienna, Austria, Pani Projection and Lighting were helping to mechanize the lighting in some of the German opera houses. The PTF functions were mechanically linked and motor driven, not so much for effects during a show, but for the changeovers between shows. Many times the lighting positions were difficult to reach, and shows were coming in and out so quickly that there was precious little time to refocus. The phenomenon was fairly limited to that part of Europe, since the opera houses were among the few who could afford the high price tag.

But in England, a different approach to motorized lighting was in its infancy. It was there that a young lighting designer was by his own admission engaged in an "obsession with mirrors," which began after he saw a version of the camera obscura (a primitive pinhole camera from the 1700s) as a child in Bristol, England. Peter Wynne Willson went on to become one of the first lighting designers for an English band called Pink Floyd.

"In 1968," he related, "for a Pink Floyd gig at the Round House in Chalk Farm, London, we ran the entire lightshow from [1000-watt slide] projectors, which I had fitted with long [300 mm] lenses and resiliently articulated mirrors [at rest, the mirrors returned to a home position]. In the gate were progressive gobos, an iris diaphragm, variable speed color [gel filter applied to an acrylic disc], and flicker wheels. With dexterity, the units could be spotlights, follow-spots, laser-simulators and 3D gobo projectors."

A few years later, in the 1970s, his company, the Light Machine Company, designed, manufactured, and sold luminaires, both static and with motorized mirror attachments. They were marketed as the Light Machine Gun system.

Also in the late 1960s, a design competition for a new performing arts center was held in Basel, Switzerland. An architect enlisted the help of a friend named Dr. Fritz von Ballmoos to help with the design. Dr. von Ballmoos, who was a trained physicist and an opera buff, had no background in entertainment or in lighting; he owned a company that built custom electronics and electromechanical systems. But his research led him to the idea of building an automated lighting system, which was proposed along with the design for the performing arts center. Theirs was the winning proposal, and in the early 1970s they fabricated and installed 200 automated lights in the center. The lights had the ability to pan, tilt, change color, change the size of the beam, and dim remotely. The color changer consisted of two color wheels mounted on the same axis, each of which had an open position for no color. The controller had memory for the storage of cues, and the entire system remained in use for 20 years. Dr. von Ballmoos received patents for this system in six countries, and he sought to promote the concept among manufacturers. He found no takers.

By the early 1970s, the idea of motorized PTF fixtures was slowly taking root in opera houses and television studios. Jim Moody, in his book *Concert Lighting: Techniques, Art and Business*, reports seeing motorized lighting in

Japan's NKH television studios, in the BBC studio in London, and in Germany in the early 1970s.

In the United States at about the same time, lighting designer Stefan Graf and production electrician Jim Fackert were touring with the popular rock and roll band Grand Funk Railroad. It was before the advent of truss towers and flown rigging, so they had to rely heavily on followspots. They were playing in a different venue every night, with different followspot operators provided by the local facility. Graf grew increasingly frustrated with the followspots and operators, and he often spoke to Fackert about it. Fackert, who was an inventor and tinkerer, came up with the idea of putting a servo-controlled mirror on the followspots and operating them remotely. When he mentioned the idea, Graf thought it was completely outlandish. Nevertheless, he provided the seed money to build the units. Fackert succeeded in building four units, which they dubbed the Cyklops (Figure 2-3 and Figure 2-4). Grand Funk Railroad toured with the Cyklops

Figure 2-3 Cyklops fixture, circa 1972.

Figure 2-4 Grand Funk Railroad on stage, lit by the Cycklops.

fixtures for several years before they were placed in Graf's rental company, Fantasee Lighting (www.fantaseelighting.com), where they were used for many other tours and productions.

"If We Can Make It Change Color . . ."

One of the shows that Grand Funk Railroad played was in Dallas, Texas. The company that provided the sound for that show was called Showco, which was owned and operated by Rusty Brutsche, Jack Maxson, and Jack Calmes. Showco watched the Cyklops with interest. A few years later, Showco got into the lighting business, with great success. They landed several big-name concert tours, including Led Zeppelin, the Who, the Rolling Stones, Wings, Eric Clapton, and Genesis. They hired several lighting designers, technicians, engineers, and support personnel.

In response to the demand for lighting, Showco's engineering department developed lighting equipment that they could use in their rental operation. At that time, very few lighting manufacturers made the type of equipment they needed, so they built their own. In 1978, they began work on a color-changing PAR can. The PAR was the main instrument of choice for concert lighting at the time. They tried a number of different ideas, including a high-speed semaphore mechanism to move the gel frames and a system of pneumatic powered cylinders using compressed air to move the gel frames. Another attempt used a liquid dye system with three chambers, each with a different color dye. It varied the amount of dye in a chamber to vary saturation and change the color. None of these ideas proved to be practical.

Jim Bornhorst was the head of Showco's audio engineering department in 1980, when Brutsche assigned him to the project. He was soon joined by Showco engineers Tom Walsh, John Covington, and Brooks Taylor. Bornhorst familiarized himself with a new light source, the GE MARC 350 metal halide arc lamp, which John Tedesco of Phoebus Lighting had been using in his Ultra Arc followspots since 1977. The 350-watt discharge lamp had an integral dichroic glass reflector that reflected visible light but not infrared light. As a result, the projected light was significantly lower in temperature than a PAR lamp. Still, when a gel filter was placed in the optical path, it quickly evaporated. So Bornhorst started looking for another color medium. His interest in photography led him to try dichroic filters, which are coated glass color filters used in photographic enlargers. Bornhorst and his team ordered some samples from Edmund Scientific and began experimenting with them. Much to their delight, they discovered that the dichroic filters could handle the heat from the MARC 350, and they did a great job of coloring the light. Bornhorst and the others felt that they could build a color-changing mechanism based on dichroic filters, and they soon developed two approaches. The first was to build a series of three color wheels, each with a family of dichroic filters mounted in them. By using the filters individually or in series, they could create a wide range of colors. (This design was later used in the VL1, VL2, and VL6 luminaires.) The second design used three pivoting dichroic filters that gradually cross-faded from one color to another. (This design was later used in the VL3, VL4, and VL5 luminaires.) They built a prototype of the cross-fading design, and it proved to work well (Figure 2-5).

One day, a group of Showco employees including Brutsche, Bornhorst, Walsh, Covington, Maxson, and Tom Littrell went to lunch at Salih's Barbeque in Dallas. They were discussing the new color-changing light when out of the blue, Maxson said, "You know, if we can make it change color, we should also make it move."

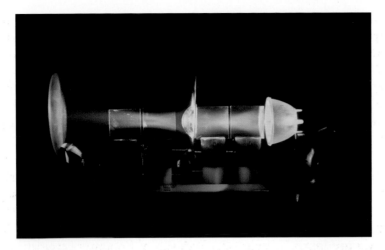

Figure 2-5 Prototype of the first Vari-Lite on the optical bench.

According to Brutsche, "We all stopped eating, like that EF Hutton ad, and said, 'Of course; what an obvious thing to do.'"

Before they left the restaurant that day, they decided that, in addition to adding a pan and tilt yoke, they would add dimming and an iris and that they would use computer control. They went back to the shop and started building a prototype using handmade and model airplane parts. In 12 weeks they had a working prototype, which they later named VL0 (Figure 2-6). Walsh designed and hand-built a controller that used a single microphone cable to transmit a serial digital data signal, and Taylor wrote the software (Figure 2-7 and Figure 2-8). It could store 16 cues.

Flush with the success of the working prototype, the company set out to market it. One of their clients, Genesis, prided themselves on using cutting-edge technology, so Brutsche thought they would be the ideal partner to launch the new product. He called Tony Smith, the band's manager, told him about the prototype, and asked if he could show it to him. Smith and the band agreed.

On December 15, 1980, Brutsche and Bornhorst flew to London and went to the recording studio where Genesis was working on their next album, *Abacab*. The album was to be released in the summer of 1981, and they were planning a major world tour to promote it. The studio was located in the

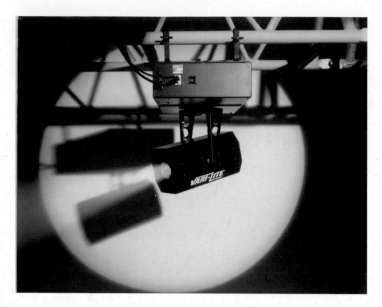

Figure 2-6 The first Vari-Lite fixture.

Figure 2-7 The first Vari-Lite console.

Figure 2-8 The Vari-Lite engineering development team standing around the first Series 100 console. They are, left to right, John Covington, Jim Bornhorst, Brooks Taylor, and Tom Walsh. Covington and Bornhorst designed the VL1 luminaire, Taylor wrote the software, and Walsh designed the digital hardware. The circuit boards were handmade by Walsh using wire wrap technology. The console communicated with the VL1 luminaires over a serial data link that Walsh and Taylor developed. Taylor wrote the software and loaded it into the console using paper punch tape from a teletype machine. The console used five RCA 1802 processors and operated 32 channels. This is the console that was used on the 1981 Genesis tour where the first Vari-Lite system was introduced to the world on September 27, 1981 in a bullring in Barcelona, Spain.

English countryside (Figure 2-9), and when they arrived the temperature was near freezing. Smith suggested that they set up the prototype in an old barn that stood next to the studio.

"The barn was nearly 300 years old and the oak beams in the ceiling were like steel," Brutsche said. "We had difficulty securing the prototype luminaire to the beams. It was cold [and we had] no heat in the barn. When we first fired the unit up, it was so cold that none of the parts would move. But as the bulb heated the unit up it started to work. We programmed four cues, the beam shooting to each of the four walls in a different color."

Figure 2-9 The English country house where the Vari-Lite was demonstrated to Genesis.

With the light rigged and programmed, Brutsche and Bornhorst were ready to unveil the prototype to the band. They asked Smith and the band to come to the barn for the demonstration. While everyone stood shivering in the cold, they executed the four cues.

Mike Rutherford, the band's bass player, broke the silence. "By Jove," he said, "I didn't know it was going to move!"

Smith and the band were very impressed, and they all went inside to negotiate a deal to use the lighting system in the upcoming *Abacab* tour. The band agreed to use a system of 55 lights. In the process of closing the deal, Brutsche told Smith that they were trying to think of a name for the new lighting system. Smith blurted out, "How about Vari-Lite?" Thus was born the name and a new era in entertainment lighting.

Rehearsals for the tour were scheduled to begin in August, 1981. From the time Brutsche and Bornhorst signed an agreement to deliver the lights they had a little over 6 months in which to build all 55 lights and the controller, including the software, from scratch. On March 2, 1981 Bornhorst filed a patent for a "computer controlled lighting system having automatically variable position, color, intensity, and beam divergence."

In July, they assembled the system for the first time and turned it on (Figure 2-10). What they saw was not what they had expected.

"When we first conceived Vari-Lite," said Brutsche, "we thought we were building a system of color changing lights that were repositionable. When we fired the system up the first time and saw the light beams move in unison under the control of the computer, we were astounded at the visual impact of the effect. The whole idea of the kinetic and visual effect of the moving light beams was not preconceived; it was an unexpected result of the system. It was the beam movement and the instantaneous dichroic color changing that made Vari-Lite such a sensation in the industry."

On September 25, 1981, the *Abacab* tour kicked off, with its first show in a bullfighting ring in Barcelona, Spain. It was there that the first system of Vari-Lites was unveiled to the public.

While Showco were in the early stages of attempting to build a color-changing PAR can, Peter Wynne Willson began producing a moving mirror fixture called the PanCan. In 1979, the first units were sold. The PanCan

Figure 2-10 The "magic moment." The first Vari-Lite system in operation.

was a programmable moving mirror that could be retrofitted to theatre spotlights and PAR cans. The first units used an analog open-loop system with a joystick for pan and tilt. The second-generation system, introduced in September 1982, was a digital system with stepper motors and computer control. System III was a closed-loop servo system. It was sold and used in many parts of Europe and the United States, primarily in nightclubs and discotheques. One of the units was purchased by Bruno Dedoro, the owner of an Italian theatrical lighting manufacturer named Coemar. In a few years he would design and build an automated moving mirror fixture called the Coemar Robot.

Also in 1979, the same year that the PanCan appeared on the market, a company in France named Cameleon, led by Didier LeClercq, started building a remote followspot that LeClercq called the Telescan. It was a moving mirror fixture built specifically for the hire market. By 1981, the first Telescan Mark 1 fixture with a 1200-watt HMI lamp had been built. It was a very large fixture that resembled a followspot with a moving mirror attachment, originally built as a remote followspot for the theatre and opera. Later on, the Telescan Mark 2 became popular in the touring market with large music productions (Figure 2-11).

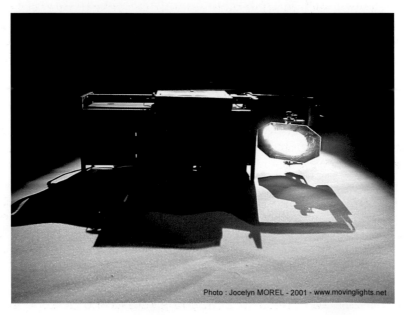

Photo : Jocelyn MOREL - 2001 - www.movinglights.net

Figure 2-11 The Telescan Mark 2. (Photograph by Jocelyn Morel, 2001, www. movinglights.net.)

The early 1980s was a heady time for touring production and automated lighting. Showco were building a following with their new moving yoke creation and was touring around the world with different bands. Several production companies saw or heard about the new technology and decided to follow suit by building their own moving lights. One of those companies was Morpheus Lights, as Dan English explains.

"We were doing a Journey show in Seattle. It was J. R. (John Richardson), his brother Bruce and myself on the lighting crew. We were subbing in the lights because their lights were out with somebody else. Ken Mednick, who was their lighting designer, was driving us over to the show, and he said, 'I just heard about this show in Europe with Vari-Lites!' He had all these ideas about prism lighting and we thought, 'What is this guy talking about?' In the meantime, J. R. was thinking, 'Hmmm, I think I can do that.' And by the time I got back from the tour, Bruce already had a light moving around."

The Richardson brothers had started Morpheus as a production company after attending engineering college at Berkeley; they knew their way around electronics. After they heard about Vari-Lite, they dissected and studied the optics of several short throw followspots. Within about 6 months of the Vari-Lite debut, they built their own servo-driven yoke fixtures out of sheet metal that "looked kind of like a shoe box." It was dubbed the Pana-Spot. The color change was accomplished by solenoids tripping a boom with gel colors, and the lamp source was a MARC 350 with the power supply in a separate enclosure. Rather than build their own controller, they used a Kliegl Performer, using one channel for each attribute.

The first time the Pana-Spots were used was when six units were sent out on a Jimmy Buffett show. Soon to follow were a Paul Anka show in Las Vegas and a tour with Devo.

"That was pretty startling because people weren't used to seeing these lights. The show was set up with a lot of symmetry, and, of course, with Devo it was pretty dramatic. It was a great looking show. Candace Brightman (lighting designer for the Grateful Dead) and I saw that show and that's when she went, 'Oh yeah, I'll take those.'"

By October 1982, Morpheus were building the second generation of the Pana-Spot with a single gobo and seven colors. That December, English was operating the lights on the Grateful Dead tour.

The Black Hole

The atmosphere was no less charged about automated lighting in Europe than it was in North America. In 1980, a special effects company called Cause & Effects Limited was started in response to a need for 21 fiberglass cannons that were to be used on an AC/DC tour. At that time, the only automated fixture commonly used in Europe was the PanCan. The owner of the company, Nick Lynch, had the idea to mount a standard "Thomas" PAR 64 in a moving yoke driven by DC motors and controlled with a pulse-width modulated signal. One of the idiosyncrasies of the fixture was that once it reached its final destination the motors would power down and relax the tension in the gear system. The unit would then relax and fall away from position by a couple of degrees, then the sensor would pick this up and reenergize the motor, pushing it back into position. This series of actions would cause the lamp to oscillate. According to former employee Steve Warren, this is where the term "nodding buckets" (a popular collo-quialism in Europe) originated. The problem was addressed by the addi-tion of an electrical braking device. The company produced approximately 50 units, which were used in various tours, most notably a Gary Newman tour. Some of the fixtures were installed in the London Hippodrome, a famous nightclub. Since there were no moving light consoles available at the time, the company was forced to design and manufacture a controller, the complexity of which contributed to the dissolution of Cause & Effects Limited in 1984.

Other European companies enthralled with automated lighting were slightly more long lived. Shortly after the Vari-Lite took off, another English company called Tasco entered the automated lighting business. They began by producing a moving yoke fixture called the Starlite. They found early success in Europe and opened an office in the United States shortly after-ward. Before it was all over they had built five generations of the Starlite, and their controller was very advanced; it had a voice recognition system and a visualizer much like today's visualization programs. But their ambi-tious attempt to produce such an advanced controller for moving lights ultimately proved to be their undoing. The company was eventually bought by David Snipp, and today they manufacture a software product called StarDraw.

Because the original Vari-Lites toured both Europe and North America, their influence was far reaching. Dyna-Might Sound and Light in

Springfield, Missouri, were one of the companies that was quick to follow. While touring with bands such as Huey Lewis, Pat Benatar, Alabama, Talking Heads, and Chicago, John Gott, the owner, saw something that got his attention.

"I saw some Vari-Lites at an early Genesis show," Gott said, "when they were first starting to come onto the market in the early '80s. We were getting excited about what we were doing with little portable lighting systems and I said, 'This is going to be the future of lighting.' So I started figuring out how to dump lots more big money down a black hole [laughs]."

Dyna-Might had about half a dozen employees at that time, and they started building prototypes of moving lights.

"We started off with a yoke, and I contracted a satellite dish company to do some of the original engineering design. We used DC servo motors with analog control. Then we built a controller that had joysticks and memory positions that were analog sets—you'd set trim pots to a position and you'd move the joystick and it would go to a position and stop there. You had limit settings, basically, left and right, up and down."

Their first production run was a PAR 64-based moving yoke light called a Moto-Yoke. They built and sold 500 units. Next came an ellipsoidal-based unit, built around a Times Square 1000-watt ellipsoidal, and eventually they built an arc source fixture called the Moto-Arc.

"Probably 70% of our product went out of the country. They went to Europe and Asia—we had guys flying in here and wiring in hundreds of thousands of dollars trying to get product. We were growing like crazy. We had 35 people by '87 just cranking out product like crazy."

And there were more companies who recognized the opportunity. In the mid-1980s, Summa Technologies began manufacturing a moving yoke fixture called the Summa HTI (Figure 2-12). It was the first moving yoke fixture to use the DMX512 control protocol. At the time, there were some people who believed that it was unsuitable for controlling automated lighting.

Despite the growing competition, Vari-Lite were intent on protecting their market share by protecting their intellectual property. On July 5, 1983, U.S.

Figure 2-12 The Summa HTI was the first automated light to use DMX.

patent 4,392,187 was issued to Vari-Lite, Ltd. The abstract of the patent (www.uspto.gov) describes the system in broad terms:

> A lighting system is disclosed which includes a control panel for operating a plurality of lights by means of a single two conductor signal cable and a power cable. Two embodiments of lights are provided for use in the present lighting system. In the first embodiment, the light includes four dichroic filters mounted for pivotal motion on axes passing through the light path formed by light emanating from a lamp. The dichroic filters may be aligned with the light path, thereby eliminating the effect of the filters. The dichroic filters may be singly or in combination pivoted so that the light in the light path is incident on the dichroic filter at a predetermined angle to transmit a preselected color therethrough. Four primary color dichroic filters are employed. An integrating lens is provided for homogenizing the color of the light. A projection lamp may be employed with an elliptical mirror which reflects light to converge at a focus. A collimating lens

is then used to align the light for passage through dimmer and douser units and a focusing lens. The second embodiment of the light includes two color wheels each having 32 apertures formed in their outer periphery. Thirty one of the apertures are filled with dichroic filters to permit a preselected color to be transmitted therethrough with one aperture left open for passing white light. A gobo wheel and an intensity wheel may also be provided. A zoom lens may be provided. The lighting system permits the color, intensity, divergence and pan and tilt of each of the lights to be adjusted from the control panel for each cue in a show. The settings for each cue during a show may be stored in a memory and recalled to set the variable functions of each light when desired.

As more and more competitors entered the field, Vari-Lite clung stubbornly to a big share of the market. They also stuck to their rental-only policy and closely guarded their intellectual property. Vari-Lite technicians literally worked behind cloaked areas to prevent prying eyes from taking ideas.

For Sale: Automated Lighting

In 1986, an Italian lighting manufacturer named Coemar built a moving mirror fixture they called the Robot. The first incarnation of the fixture used a MARC 350 arc lamp and Airtronics servo motors, both of which proved to be problematic. The U.S. distributor for Coemar at the time was an Austin-based company named High End Systems. Richard Belliveau, one of the three owners of High End and the de facto technology officer, experimented with the Robot lamp and power supply and found that an HTI 400 with a magnetic ballast was brighter and much more reliable. So High End began modifying the fixtures and reselling them.

Another issue with the Coemar robot at the time was the dedicated controller. It could only control one address even though the fixtures were individually addressable. As a result, every fixture under its control would always pan, tilt, and change color and gobo together. A small company in the UK called WB Lighting, which was the distributor for Coemar in the UK at the time, built a computer-based controller that could individually address each fixture. It was the first moving light controller to use a mouse and icons with a visual display. The developer of the software, Mike Wood (now of Mike Wood Consulting) had to reverse engineer the communication protocol because "Coemar refused to tell me."

A short time later, another Italian lighting manufacturer, Clay Paky, began shipping a moving mirror fixture called the Golden Scan. This fixture had a HMI 575 lamp and condenser optics, which yielded a far more uniform beam and better center-to-edge focus. It also had another technology that rendered it far more reliable than the Coemar Robot: it had stepper motors instead of servo motors.

High End Systems, interestingly enough, were also the distributor for Clay Paky at the time, and the improvements of the Golden Scan were not lost on Belliveau. In 1989, High End and Clay Paky had a falling out, and as a result Belliveau designed and built a moving mirror fixture called the Intellabeam (Figure 2-13). High End then put their manufacturing operation into high gear, shifting their focus from distribution to manufacturing. Because of High End's background as a distributor of European lighting equipment, the Intellabeam was initially perceived by much of the professional lighting community as a "disco" light. But Belliveau was determined to change the market perception. One day, he copied the Upcoming Tours page from *Performance Magazine*, a now-defunct trade publication dealing with concert tours, and scribbled "$1000" across the top of it. He made several copies and handed them out to the staff. I was one of those staffers.

Belliveau emphatically offered a $1000 cash reward to the first person who could get at least 24 Intellabeam fixtures placed on any of the half dozen

Figure 2-13 High End Systems Intellabeam 700.

upcoming tours listed on the page. After several unsuccessful attempts to contact the lighting designers through artist's management over the course of 2 weeks, I temporarily gave up out of frustration and set aside the photocopy. A few days later I received a call from a man with an English accent asking for a High End Systems dealership. He was designing and installing a lighting system at a club in Bali and he had heard about the Intellabeams. Because we had semi-exclusive dealer arrangements and because we commonly received several calls per week asking for a dealership, I was reluctant to grant him a dealership. But he was very persistent, refusing to hang up the phone. Instead, he played every card he could, finally mentioning that he was the lighting designer for Dire Straits. That immediately set off an alarm in my head, and I madly scrambled through the stack of papers on my desk looking for the $1000 photocopy. I found it and confirmed that Dire Straits was one of the target tours. I quickly reversed course and invited him to Austin at the company's expense.

Chas Herington, Dire Straits' lighting designer, arrived in Austin in the fall of 1990 to investigate the possibility of using Intellabeams on the band's upcoming tour. He spent 2 days looking at the Intellabeam and talking to everyone in the company, particularly Richard Belliveau, who is a very persuasive man. By the time he left, he had agreed to specify Intellabeams on Dire Straits' *On Every Street* tour in 1990–1991. Knowing Belliveau as I do, I firmly believe that he was so bound and determined to capture this tour that he would not have let Herington leave without agreeing to use the fixture—he would have sat on him if he had to. Fortunately, no one had to resort to physical restraint, and Herington ended up using a system of 64 Intellabeams plus a plethora of other High End gear. His faith in Belliveau and the untried gear was rewarded with a spectacular show, thanks to his superb lighting design skills and the tenacity of a High End System tech named Bill McCarty, whom the company sent on the road with the gear. By the time the tour ended, High End Systems had gained a reputation as a manufacturer of reliable touring gear. Their policy of selling gear rather than exclusively renting it did much to change the concert and touring lighting industry. High End Systems went on to garner market share and develop many more automated lighting systems, including the Cyberlight, Studio Color, Studio Spot, Studio Beam, Technobeam, and x.Spot.

Around the same time, a small Danish company called Martin was building smoke machines. Soon they graduated to building moving light scanners they called Roboscans. Over the years they expanded their product line and vastly improved the reliability of their automated lighting. Today, they are among the world's largest automated lighting manufacturers with annual sales in excess of $120M worldwide.[1] Their line of MAC fixtures includes the MAC 2000 Profile, Wash, and Performance fixtures, which are among the most specified automated lights in the concert and touring industry.

Today, the competition in the automated lighting market is intense. The stalwarts of the industry such as Vari-Lite, Martin, High End Systems, Morpheus, Coemar, and Clay Paky are facing increasing competition from relative newcomers such as SGM (www.sgm.it), Pearl River, Robe Show Lighting, and many more. There are more Chinese manufacturers going into lighting manufacturing, and distributors such as American DJ and Elation Professional are increasingly bringing better quality, affordable goods into the marketplace. ETC, one of the world's largest dimming and controls manufacturers, have recently jumped into the automated lighting business with their Source Four Revolution, an automated Source Four fixture. There are many more manufacturers and distributors, far too many to name, but suffice it to say that there is no shortage of choices for the discriminating lighting designer and specifier.

Sue Me, Sue You Blues

The landscape of the automated lighting industry has been shaped by innovations and the protection of the intellectual property that resulted from hard work and long hours of research. Over the years the Vari-Lite Corporation have brought litigation on at least five separate occasions, against companies including Syncrolite, Summa Technologies, High End Systems, Clay Paky, and Martin Professional. In all of the cases, Vari-Lite either won or settled out of court, and in the case of Summa, the lawsuit was enough to shut down the company.

Vari-Lite might have more successfully limited their competition if it wasn't for their prior patent, which had been issued to Dr. von Ballmoos, and their failure to either acquire or license that patent. When Vari-Lite originally applied for its patent, the European Patent Office rejected its broad claims on the basis of the prior art established in 1972 by the von Ballmoos patent.

---

[1] Aktieselskabet Schouw & Co. Annual Report 2002 (www.schouw.dk).

Vari-Lite's patent claims were said to "lack novelty." The patent Vari-Lite did finally receive was limited in scope, allowing them to protect specific features of its system.

Prior to this, a company called Variable-Parameter Fixture Development Corporation had acquired the rights to the von Ballmoos patent in order to clear the way for them to develop automated luminaires and automated features in followspots. In 1984, Variable-Parameter sent Vari-Lite a letter raising the question of apparent infringement on the von Ballmoos patent based on information available at the time. Vari-Lite inquired about licensing fees, but instead of pursuing licensing they filed suit against Variable-Parameter, seeking to have the von Ballmoos patent declared invalid and/or not infringed. After years of discovery and with the case heading to trial, Vari-Lite filed a request for a reexamination of the von Ballmoos patent in the U.S. Patent Office, saying that several earlier patents were not considered when the von Ballmoos patent was originally filed. Along with the reexamination, they requested a delay in the original lawsuit pending the outcome of the reexamination. After considering Vari-Lite's documentation and additional material submitted by Variable-Parameter, the Patent Office announced that it would recertify the von Ballmoos patent as valid. Vari-Lite decided to settle out of court. In July, 1988, Variable-Parameter and Vari-Lite entered into a consent decree by which Vari-Lite accepted the von Ballmoos patent as ". . . duly and legally issued . . . good, valid and enforceable . . ." and that Vari-Lite's Model 100 and Series 200 systems were ". . . adjudged covered by said patent." Vari-Lite paid Variable-Parameter $1,000,000 for a limited covenant not to be sued under the patent.

Next, Variable-Parameter sought to license the patent to Morpheus Lights, who refused to enter into discussions. Like Vari-Lite, Morpheus then sought to have the patent examined a second time, hoping to have the U.S. Patent Office declare it invalid. Instead, the patent was once again certified as valid. Still, Morpheus refused to go to trial or to settle out of court. In the end, the court entered a default judgment against the company's owner. The court found that the owner ". . . personally knew of the patent and was personally informed by his engineers, as well as his patent counsel, that the manufacture and lease of the . . . [accused] systems was an infringement." As a result, the court awarded Variable-Parameter $12M on $30M in sales. Before a similar judgment could be entered against Morpheus, the secured creditor sought to impose a receiver and the company filed a Chapter 11 bankruptcy. The creditor then forced out the owner and installed a CEO of their own choosing, and the company operated in bankruptcy.

The assets of the company were then sold to another company in which the patent holder held substantial interest. They have since revitalized their new product development, resulting in a new 1200-watt Pana-Beam wash fixture.

The Future of Automated Lighting

At a private showing in a hotel room across the street from the LDI trade show in 1998, there was a prototype of a digital lighting fixture that offered a peek into the future of the technology. The Icon M, designed and built by Lighting and Sound Design, a subsidiary of PRG (www.prg.com), was an automated light with a digital engine enabling the projection of "soft" gobos. The digital engine was a Digital Mirror Device, or DMD, made by Texas Instruments, that has an array of microscopic mirrors controlled by a digital signal. The signal orients each individual mirror so that it either reflects or doesn't reflect incident light from the internal light source. The result is a projected image with a resolution matching the number of mirrors, each mirror acting as a single pixel. The content could be an animated image or a static image that could be designed on a computer or captured by a camera or scanner. This particular fixture stored the images in the onboard memory and held 1000 soft gobos. The next year it was debuted on the trade show floor at LDI, and it was a real paradigm shift for the industry. Many people were amazed by the demonstration of animated projection and a seemingly endless palette of gobos.

Alas, the fixture never made it to mass production, although a limited number of fixtures were produced that did see limited touring action on a Korn tour and a couple of others. However, the story does not end there.

On November 23, 1999, U.S. Patent 5,988,817 was issued to a group of inventors, including executives of Active Vision Co., Ltd. of Tokyo, Japan. The patent covered a plural of projectors "being provided independently with a pan driving device and a tilt driving device so that the direction of projection can be freely changed; and having at least one of functions of changing the direction of projection, the position of a projected image, the synthesis, shape or arrangement of an image and/or the size of an image and displaying each image in a flying state to constitute a screen image system harmonized with lighting in a representation space." The company was the first to build a computer-controlled video projector with pan and tilt capability, dubbed the Active Vision System. But it was primarily marketed in Japan and received little international attention.

The digital lighting market began to heat up at LDI 2001, when High End Systems picked up the "digital lighting" mantel and trotted out the Catalyst Media Server and orbital mirror head. The media server provides the digital content that is fed to a video projector, and the orbital mirror head that is attached to the projector provides the beam movement. The combination is a digital lighting system that offers colored animation and an unlimited palette of soft gobos and effects. The key to the system is the DMX interface that allows it to be controlled by any DMX lighting controller, thus marrying the video and lighting imagery.

At LDI 2003, High End upped the ante by unveiling a self-contained digital light called the DL-1. It is a moving yoke fixture with a 4500 ANSI lumen LCD projector in a stylized housing. Critics of the light are skeptical of the intensity, and the fixture is among the highest-priced luminaires. But many lighting professionals, including Christian Choi, who has used Catalyst on numerous productions including the Super Bowl halftime show and many concert tours, believe that media servers will change the television and lighting industries. If the current trend of smaller, lighter, brighter, and cheaper lighting continues, and there's no reason to think it won't, then it's only a matter of time before digital lighting and media servers play side by side with conventional lighting, both moving and static.

But regardless of where the technology takes us, one thing is certain: what the future holds for the industry is more and better automated lighting, and along with it, a growing demand for designers, programmers, technicians, engineers, and sales and marketing personnel. The technology will become increasingly complex, and those who have a firm grasp of the fundamental principles behind it will have the best opportunity for meaningful work in the field.

CHAPTER 3

Automated Lighting Systems

The future of art is light.—Henri Matisse (1869–1954), French painter and sculptor

Automated lighting systems range from small systems with a few luminaires running preset programs in a master/slave configuration with no external controller to extremely large systems with multiple fixture types and multiple controllers running simultaneously on a network. One of the larger automated lighting systems was used in the taping of the HBO special *Britney Spears, Live from Las Vegas* in 2001. It had a total of 618 automated lights, including 12 different models from four different manufacturers. The automated lighting alone, not including any conventional lighting, consumed about two-thirds of a megawatt and had a retail value of well over $5 million, not counting the power distribution, rigging hardware, transportation, and labor.

Most lighting designers spend their entire career building a good portfolio and never come close to having an opportunity to design a lighting rig of that size and scope. But regardless of whether an automated lighting system is small, medium, large, or mega large, there are common systems, practices, and elements that should be familiar to the designer, programmer, operator, technician, or stagehand. Learning about how these systems go together and work together will help you prepare for the eventuality of handling an automated lighting system of any size.

Systems Overview

From a systems standpoint, every automated lighting system has certain common elements, including the following:

- Rigging system

- Power distribution system

- Data distribution system

- Control system

- Luminaires or fixtures

Figure 3-1 illustrates the five major components of an automated lighting system.

Rigging Systems

From a safety standpoint, the rigging system and the power distribution system are the two most important aspects of any lighting rig. The purpose of a rigging system is to provide a safe and convenient structure on which to hang production equipment including lighting, sound, video, scenic elements, and equipment. Automated lighting fixtures tend to be very heavy compared to conventional lighting and require the utmost care in rigging and in the prevention of rigging accidents. The internal components, and sometimes external components, of automated lighting, such as large chokes and transformers, tend to increase the size and weight of automated lighting. The higher in power, the larger and heavier they tend to be. A typical 1200-watt automated lighting fixture can weigh up to 100 pounds (45 kg) or more. Consider that a typical lighting rig might have at least a dozen or more fixtures for a small- to medium-sized rig, so the weight of the entire system can be measured in tons. Because these rigs are typically hanging over the heads of performers and very often the audience as well, it's crucial to use the proper rigging hardware and techniques and to emphasize safety and caution when rigging. While rigging practices are beyond the scope of this book, suffice it to say that a qualified rigger should be involved in rigging any structure on which you are planning to rig a lighting system.

There are many ways to rig automated lighting systems. In concerts and touring and special events, typical rigging systems are flown aluminum truss structures, ground supported truss structures, or a combination thereof. In the theatre, automated lighting is typically rigged on a

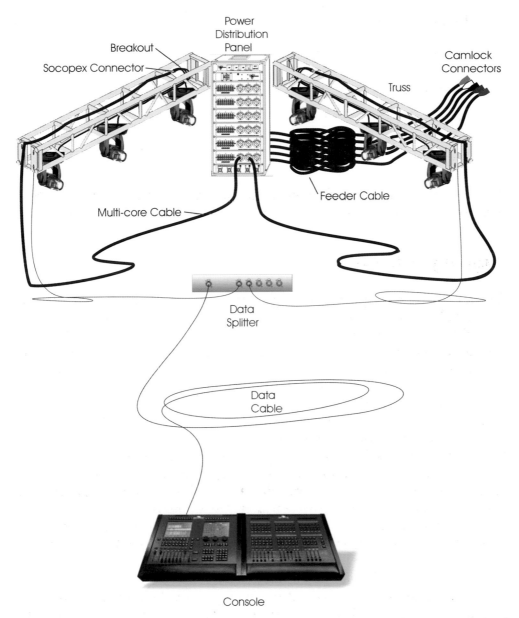

Figure 3-1 A typical automated lighting system comprises the following: a rigging system on which to hang the luminaires; a power distribution system, which safely distributes electricity among the luminaires; a data distribution system, which distributes the control signal to each luminaire; a control system, which generates the control signals; and the luminaires.

counterweight rigging system or on a motorized line-shaft system. For smaller portable systems, motorized lighting towers, crank towers, and lighting trees can also be used for rigging automated lighting. Of course, automated lighting is sometimes placed on flat surfaces, such as on the ground, on a stage, on a riser, or in a set without any rigging at all.

Aluminum Structures

Portable rigging built from modular sections of aluminum truss are commonly used for temporary structures in entertainment lighting. They are lightweight, are relatively quick and easy to assemble, and can be configured in a variety of different structures by as few as two people.

Sections of truss (Figure 3-2) are not made from pure aluminum because it is not strong enough for structural support. Therefore, the raw material is commonly mixed with other metals, usually copper, magnesium, manganese, silicon, and zinc, to produce the alloys from which aluminum truss is made. The amount of other metals used in the alloy gives it certain desirable characteristics, such as hardness, corrosion resistance, light weight, and bright finish. In North America, the alloy 6061-T6 is commonly used for truss, and in Europe 6082-T6 is more commonly used.

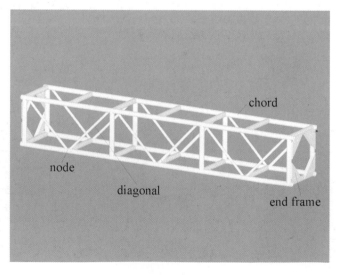

Figure 3-2 The parts of a typical section of truss.

Truss is commonly classified as light-duty, medium-duty, and heavy-duty, depending on the dimensions. Light-duty truss is usually 12 inches (30.48 cm) by 12 inches or 18 inches, medium-duty truss is 20.5 inches (52 cm) square, and heavy-duty truss is 20.5 inches (52 cm) by 30 inches (76.2 cm). The main chords of a typical section of truss are typically 2 inches in (outer) diameter.

Each class of truss can come in ladder (two main chords), triangular (three main chords), or box truss (four main chords), and they can be either spigoted or plated. Spigoted truss is assembled using short sections of aluminum inserts called spigots that link sections of truss together. Plated truss is assembled by bolting the end plates of two or more sections of truss together.

Every truss is rated according to the maximum allowable point load and the maximum allowable uniformly distributed load (UDL) (Figure 3-3).

ALLOWABLE LOAD DATA

MEDIUM DUTY TRUSS 20.5" x 20.5" PLATED

Span ft. (mtrs)	MAXIMUM ALLOWABLE UNIFORM LOADS			MAXIMUM ALLOWABLE POINT LOADS							
				CENTER POINT			THIRD POINT			QUARTER POINT	
	Load #/ft.	Load lbs (kgs)	Max Defl. in.	Load lbs (kgs)		Max Defl. in.	Load lbs (kgs)		Max Defl. in.	Load lbs (kgs)	Max Defl. in.
Single Camloc through 3/8" gusset plates											
10 (3.04)	658	6580 (2985)	0.06	3292 (1493)		0.05	2469 (1120)		0.06	1646 (747)	0.06
20 (6.09)	157	3140 (1424)	0.24	1580 (717)		0.19	1185 (538)		0.24	790 (358)	0.23
30 (9.14)	65	1950 (885)	0.53	980 (445)		0.44	735 (333)		0.54	490 (222)	0.51
40 (12.21)	32	1280 (581)	0.93	658 (298)		0.80	493 (224)		0.97	329 (149)	0.91
50 (15.24)	17	850 (386)	1.43	447 (203)		1.28	335 (152)		1.50	223 (101)	1.43
Two Camlocs through 3/8" gusset plates											
10 (3.04)	839	8390 (3806)	0.08	5336 (2420)		0.08	4002 (1815)		0.10	2668 (1210)	0.09
20 (6.09)	260	5200 (2359)	0.38	2602 (1180)		0.31	1951 (885)		0.39	1301 (590)	0.36
30 (9.14)	110	3300 (1497)	0.86	1661 (753)		0.70	1246 (565)		0.88	831 (377)	0.82
40 (12.21)	58	2320 (1052)	1.52	1169 (530)		1.26	876 (397)		1.56	584 (265)	1.46
50 (15.24)	34	1700 (771)	2.38	856 (388)		2.01	642 (291)		2.43	428 (194)	2.30
5/8" Diameter Grade 8 bolts with standard washers through 3/8" gusset plates											
10 (3.04)	839	8390 (3806)	0.08	4744 (2152)		0.07	3558 (1614)		0.09	2372 (1076)	0.08
20 (6.09)	230	4600 (2087)	0.34	2306 (1046)		0.27	1729 (784)		0.35	1153 (523)	0.32
30 (9.14)	97	2910 (1320)	0.76	1464 (664)		0.62	1098 (498)		0.78	732 (332)	0.73
40 (12.21)	51	2040 (925)	1.36	1021 (463)		1.13	765 (347)		1.39	510 (231)	1.30
50 (15.24)	29	1450 (658)	2.10	737 (334)		1.80	553 (251)		2.16	369 (167)	2.05

Note: Deflections reported in the above tables are maximum expected for full loadings (indoors only). All loads are based on 10'-0" sections. Other section lengths are available.
Load tables are reprinted from engineering reports developed by Parkhill, Smith & Cooper, Inc., structural engineers, and apply to truss fabricated after December, 1989.

Figure 3-3 Typical truss loading table. (Courtesy of Tomcat.)

Most truss manufacturers supply data for each type of truss they offer, showing the deflection for a given span of the truss with a given point load and UDL. If the truss system is ground supported by truss towers, each tower also has a maximum load and a maximum height.

Theatrical Rigging

The vast majority of theatres use a counterweight system to rig lighting and set pieces (Figure 3-4). A counterweight system normally uses a series of pipes and a system of lines, blocks, and counterweights to balance the weight of the load on each pipe and bring them to equilibrium. In North America, 1.5-inch schedule 40 black iron pipe, commonly referred to as a "batten," is typically used, while in Europe, a 75-mm OD (outer diameter) pipe is used to rig scenery and a 48-mm OD pipe, commonly referred to as a "barrel," is rigged underneath for lighting and electrics. Incidentally, a 48-mm OD pipe is the same dimension as a 1.5-inch (actually 1.61-inch inner diameter, ID) schedule 40 pipe. A motorized line-shaft system is similar to a counterweight rigging system except it uses electric winches instead of counterweights.

Rigging Hardware

Lighting instruments, whether automated or conventional, normally have a yoke onto which a clamp or a half-coupler can be bolted in order to rig it on a rigging system. Automated lighting is, in most cases, very big and heavy; it is often rigged with two clamps or half-couplers (Figure 3-5). Dual clamps also provide more stability for moving lights and help prevent rotation from torque. In some cases three clamps are used for more mounting stability.

There are many different types of clamps and couplers, including cast iron c-clamps, but half-couplers offer the most security. Regardless of which type of clamp or coupler is used, a safety cable should always be used with lighting instruments (Figure 3-6).

Power Distribution Systems

Like a rigging system, a well-designed power distribution system is a key component for the safe operation of a lighting rig. The job of a power

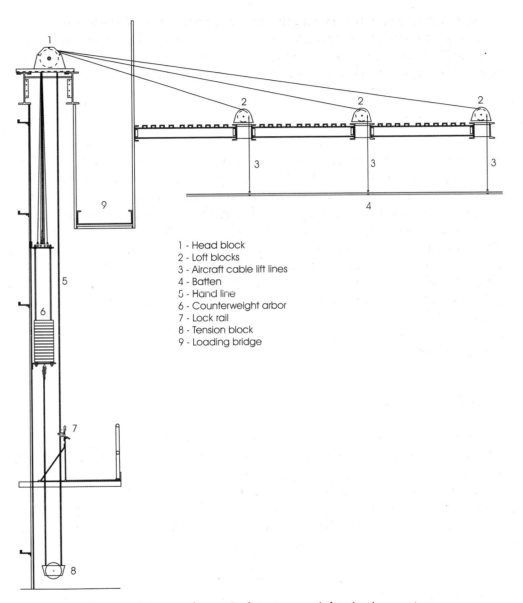

1 - Head block
2 - Loft blocks
3 - Aircraft cable lift lines
4 - Batten
5 - Hand line
6 - Counterweight arbor
7 - Lock rail
8 - Tension block
9 - Loading bridge

Figure 3-4 Parts of a typical counterweight rigging system.

distribution system is to safely and reliably distribute power to each electrical load in the system while at the same time providing protection from overloading and short circuits. Because of the dangers involved in working with and around high voltage, only qualified personnel should design, configure, or connect power distribution equipment. It is beyond the scope

Figure 3-5 Many automated luminaries are rigged with two half-couplers.

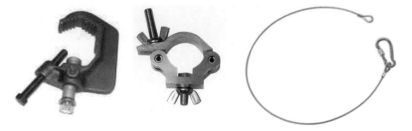

Figure 3-6 Left to right: cast iron c-clamp, half-coupler, safety cable.

of this book to cover power distribution system design in detail; however, there are some very important basic principles with which every lighting professional should be familiar.

Every power distribution system (power distro, or PD) should have certain common elements (Figure 3-7), including the following:

• Disconnect switch

• Feeder cables

- Distribution panel with overload protection (circuit breakers)

- Branch circuits

- Connectors

In addition, some, but not all, PDs also have dimmers and dimmer circuits. The majority of automated lighting uses arc lamps (although more incandescent models are being introduced), which can only be dimmed mechanically; therefore, a lighting system with only automated lighting has no need for dimmers or dimmer circuits. However, most automated lighting systems have at least some conventional lighting, which is mostly incandescent lighting and requires dimming circuits.

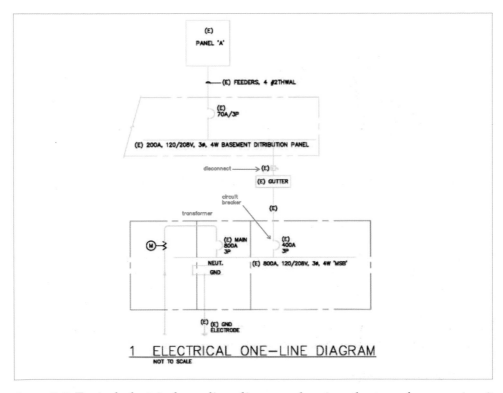

Figure 3-7 Typical electrical one-line diagram showing the transformer, circuit breakers, disconnect switch, and distribution panel.

Disconnect Switch

A disconnect switch or a mains disconnect switch is a dry contact closure switch that, in the off state, completely isolates one side so that a portable power distribution system can be tied in (Figure 3-8). Before a portable PD is tied in or wired into the mains circuit, the disconnect should be placed in the off position and locked out. In the case of a multiconductor system, such as a three-phase power system (also known as a five-wire system), the disconnect isolates all "poles" of the switch with the throw of a single lever. In a theatre, the disconnect switch is sometimes known as a company switch because it is provided as a courtesy to a visiting company.

Feeder Cable

Feeder cable is the largest cable in a power distribution system, and its job is to feed current to the rest of the system. The size of the feeder cable needed for any particular job is based on the total connected load of the

Figure 3-8 A disconnect switch allows the feeder cable to be safely tied in.

entire system. According to the *NFPA 70: National Electrical Code 2005 Edition*, feeder cable for theatres, performance areas, and similar locations must be listed for "extra hard usage," meaning type SC, SCE, SCT, or W cable. It must also be fused or have a circuit breaker that is plainly marked as such, and it must have sufficient ampacity to carry the total connected load. The Entertainment Standards & Technical Association (ESTA, www. esta.org) is developing a standard called BSR 1.18, Entertainment Technology—Recommended practice for the selection, installation, use, and maintenance of single-conductor portable power feeder cable in the entertainment industry. The standard is intended as a guide to selecting, installing, using, and maintaining single-conductor portable power feeder cables in order to promote safety and compatibility in the equipment and practices used in live performance, film, and video production in North America.

The ampacities of the allowed cable types (SC, SCE, SCT, and W) are listed in Table 3-1. The ratings are based on an ambient temperature of 86°F (30°C). The three columns identify the temperature ratings of the cable.

It's a good idea to allow for at least 20% overhead. It's also important to note that excess cable should never be coiled because it can act as a huge inductor and impede the flow of energy, producing excessive heat in the process and possibly melting the feeder cable. Instead, stack the excess cable in a figure eight, which alternates the magnetic field and cancels it out.

Most modern facilities in North America operate on a three-phase, five-wire "wye" system, which has three hot legs or phases (red, blue, and

Table 3-1 Feeder cable ampacities.

Size (AWG or kcmil)	140°F (60°C)	167°F (75°C)	194°F (90°C)
2	140	170	190
1	165	195	220
1/0	195	230	260
2/0	225	265	300
3/0	260	310	350
4/0	300	360	405

Ampacity of cable types SC, SCE, PPE, G, G-GC, and W (portable, extra hard usage) based on ambient temperature of 30°C (86°F). Reprinted with permission from NFPA 70-2005, the National Electric Code® Copyright ©2004, National Fire Protection Association, Quincy, MA 02169. National Electric Code® and NEC® are registered trademarks of the National Fire Protection Association, Quincy, MA 02169.

black), one neutral (white), and one ground (green). The phase-to-phase voltage is 208 V, and the phase-to-neutral voltage is 120 V at 60 Hz. Most of Europe operates on either 220 V single-phase, 380 V three-phase or 230 V single-phase, 400 V three-phase at 50 or 60 Hz, but since 1988, the harmonized standard in Europe allows a range of voltages from 216.2 V to 253 V (230 V + 10%/−6%). Australia operates on 240 V/415 V and Japan uses a 100 V/200 V power grid. The color code for European countries was harmonized in 2004, but the old colors could have been used until April 2006. The color codes are shown in Table 3-2.

The feeder cable in a portable power distribution system (Figure 3-9) is normally tied into the mains circuit by a qualified electrician. The discon-

Table 3-2 European color standards for three-phase systems.

	Old Color	New Color
Earth (ground)	Green/yellow striped	Green/yellow striped
Neutral	Black	Blue
Live/phase 1	Red	Brown
Phase 2	Yellow	Black
Phase 3	Blue	Grey

Figure 3-9 Excess feeder cable should be stacked in a figure 8. (Photograph courtesy of Dadco.)

nect switch should always be turned off and locked out before the feeder cable is tied in. In the rare event that there is no disconnect switch, then the feeder cable might have to be tied in live, or "hot," which is a very dangerous task that should only be undertaken when there is no other option, and then only by qualified personnel with the proper equipment, including a rubber matt, rubber-soled boots, rubber gauntlets, and a face shield.

Distribution Panels and Portable Power Distribution Units (PPDUs)

A distribution panel is typically the next component of a power distribution system after the feeder cable. It serves two purposes: it houses the overcurrent protection equipment (circuit breakers) and it serves to divide the incoming power into branch circuits. In a permanent installation like in a night club or a church, the distribution panelboards, or circuit breaker panels, are normally housed in a wall-mounted enclosure with a hinged door. In a U.S.-style breaker panel, the breakers are arranged in two columns with up to 21 breakers per side, and they are numbered left to right, then top to bottom. Each row represents a different phase, so that rows 1, 4, 7, etc. are phase X, rows 2, 5, 8, etc. are phase Y, and rows 3, 6, 9, etc. are phase Z. In a UK-style breaker panel, the breakers are arranged in two columns, but they are numbered from top to bottom in the left-hand column, and then from top to bottom in the right-hand column.

In a portable power distribution unit (PPDU) (Figure 3-10), the circuit breakers are typically built into a rack-mounted enclosure and mounted in a flight case with casters (wheels). The feeder cables are usually connected with a cam-type connector, such as a Crouse-Hinds Cam-Lok or equivalent. The outputs are typically configured with any one of a variety of connectors, depending on your preference. They can be Edison, twist-lock, stage pin, or terminal strip connectors. They often have many accessories, such as LED indicators and built-in ammeters.

Overcurrent Protection

Overcurrent protection devices are designed to protect life, limb, and property from the hazards of electrical faults. In a power distribution system they are normally fuses and/or circuit breakers (Figure 3-11), and they are

Figure 3-10 Portable power distro unit showing Cam-Lok inputs and outputs with double neutral (bottom), Socapex connector outputs (middle and top), twist-lock connectors (top), and Edison connectors (top).

rated by the maximum current at the rated voltage. Most household circuit breakers in North America are thermal breakers. They sense current by means of a bimetallic strip that flexes due to the differences in the thermal properties of each side of the strip. When current flows through it, one side expands faster than the other, and if enough current flows through it, then it flexes enough to trip the shutoff mechanism. Thermal circuit breakers are influences by the ambient temperature, and in hot environments they trip sooner than they should. In addition, they gradually lose their calibra-

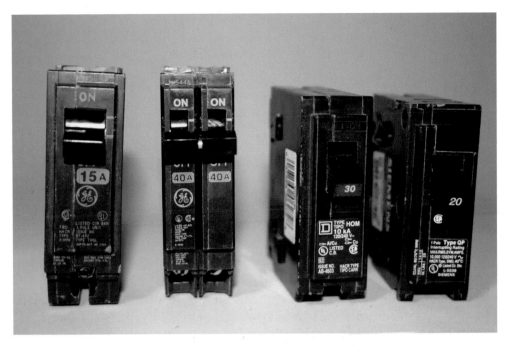

Figure 3-11 Circuit breakers are available in a variety of configurations. LR: GE 15A single pole; GE 40A double pole; Square D 30A single pole; Siemens 20A single pole.

tion every time they trip, and they eventually become too weak to operate properly. In Europe, and in many PPDUs, magnetic circuit breakers are much more common. They measure the current flow by sensing the magnetic field around a conductor in direct proportion to the current. They trip much faster and more accurately than thermal breakers. In the United States, circuit breakers for 14, 12, and 10 AWG circuits should have an interrupt rating of no more than 15, 20, and 30 amps, respectively.

Dimmers

Conventional lighting like PAR cans and Lekos typically have no built-in electronics or dimming; they rely on outboard dimmers, whose job it is to control the light level of the lighting instruments connected to it. Most automated luminaires have mechanical dimming or onboard electronic dimming, but some, like the Vari-Lite VL1000, require external dimmers.

Branch Circuits

A branch circuit is the set of wires (hot, neutral, and ground in a three-wire system) that carries power from the last overcurrent protection device to one or more electrical loads. Every branch circuit must have its own overload protection, and it can have as many receptacles or outlets as necessary as long as the connected load does not exceed the rated current of the circuit. In practice, it is a good idea to allow a 20% overhead by loading a circuit only 80%. For example, a 20-amp circuit should only be loaded to 16 amps.

In a permanent installation, branch circuits are normally run through electrical metallic tubing (EMT) or "conduit," which helps protect the insulation on the wires from nicks and cuts. The more conductors are in a single conduit, the higher the overall temperature, and thus the ampacity of each conductor has to be de-rated according to the total number of circuits.

In portable power distribution systems, branch circuits are often run in multicore cable, a single cable with several individually insulated wires. The most common configurations of multicore cable for entertainment applications are 19-conductor, 14-conductor, and 7-conductor cable. They are commonly terminated on either end with a Socapex-type 19-pin (Figure 3-12) or 7-pin connector.

When branch circuits are run a long way and/or when the wire gauge is small, the resistance in the wire causes a voltage drop, which should be taken into account in larger systems with long runs. The National Electrical Code (NEC) allows for a 3% voltage drop across a branch circuit and another 2% across the feeder circuit, or a total voltage drop of 5%. For a 120 V circuit, that's a maximum voltage drop of 6 volts. The maximum length of a branch circuit for a maximum 3% voltage drop in a 120 V/60 Hz single-phase circuit with 100% power factor (purely resistive load) at 80% of full load is given in Table 3-3.

A multicore cable is typically terminated at the load by using a breakout assembly, which splits a multicore cable from a single connector to individual branch circuits (Figure 3-13).

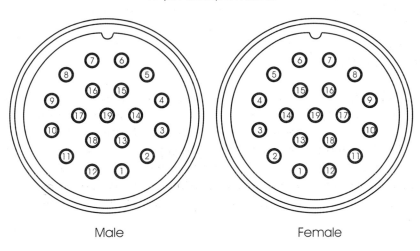

Male   Female

Number			
1	Pin 1	Pin 2	Pin 13
2	Pin 3	Pin 4	Pin 14
3	Pin 5	Pin 6	Pin 15
4	Pin 7	Pin 8	Pin 16
5	Pin 9	Pin 10	Pin 17
6	Pin 11	Pin 12	Pin 18

Figure 3-12 Nineteen-pin Socapex pinout and their associated circuits shown from solder side. Pin 19 is not connected.

Table 3-3 Maximum allowable length for branch circuits.*

Wire gauge	3% drop
#14	49.2'
#12	58.8'
#10	62.4'

*Maximum allowable voltage drop based on NEC 2005 210.19 FPN No. 4.

Figure 3-13 Socapex to IEC breakout. (Photograph courtesy of Rhyner Event Renting.)

Figure 3-14 Left to right: Locking connector, stage pin connector, Edison connector, CEE connector, and IEC connector.

Connectors

There are many types of connectors with which to connect an electrical load to a branch circuit (Figure 3-14). Depending on the voltage, the application, and the geographical area, there are a handful of connectors that are more common in entertainment lighting and automated lighting. For small 120VAC loads in North America such as consoles and rack-mounted gear, the Edison plug is very common. For 120VAC and 208VAC automated lighting, twist-lock-type connectors work well because they lock on connection, but stage pin connectors are more common in the theatre. In Europe, CEE connectors in a variety of sizes are very common.

Worldwide Electrical Safety and Wiring Codes

The invention of the electric light bulb near the end of the nineteenth century spawned the widespread use of electricity, resulting in a rapid increase in the number of fires reported. The NEC is the set of codes and standards governing the installation and operation of electrical equipment in the United States. It was first written in 1897 after it was recognized that a need existed for it. The NEC is updated regularly, and it is used not only in the United States and its territories, but also in several other countries.

Many other countries have their own set of codes and regulations. In Canada, the Canadian Standards Association has the *Safety Standard for Electrical Installations,* while in the UK, the Institute of Electrical Engineers has the *Requirements for Electrical Installations: IEE Wiring Regulations.* Other European countries use portions of the IEC *Electrical Installations for Buildings* standard.

Although the codes are used a guide, the overriding authority belongs to the authorities in the local jurisdiction. Local codes and laws vary quite a bit from location to location, but aside from the omission of sections and the addition of codes in some places, the codes normally carry the force of law.

Most municipalities have a local electrical inspector whose job it is to interpret and enforce the sometimes confusing local codes in an effort to protect the safety and well-being of the general public. They have the authority to shut down or "red tag" any construction project that does not meet local codes or ordinances according to their interpretation of them. In addition, the local fire marshal has the ability to stop a show if they feel there are certain unsafe conditions, such as a fire hazard due to the improper use of power distribution equipment.

Many performance facilities employ a full-time house electrician or master electrician (ME) whose job it is to accommodate the power distribution needs of a visiting show. In those instances, the local ME has authority over visiting electricians in the case of a dispute over the safety of the system. In most cases, the ME is very helpful and will do most anything, as long as it's deemed safe, to ensure that the show will go on.

Compliance

In certain applications of entertainment lighting, particularly permanent installations, any equipment in a lighting system that uses electricity is expected to comply with regulations regarding the manufacture of electrical and electronic equipment. There are testing laboratories called Nationally Recognized Testing Laboratories (NRTLs) that specialize in compliance testing and listing equipment, the most common of which are Underwriters Laboratories (UL), Intertek Testing Services NA, Inc. (ITSNA, formerly ETL), Canadian Standards Association (CSA), and TUV. When equipment is in compliance, it is listed with an NRTL and issued a compliance sticker that must be visible on the unit. In some cases companies are allowed to self-certify. In Europe, it is a requirement that all lighting products sold in the European Economic Area, Turkey, and Switzerland carry the CE mark of compliance.

Requirements and enforcement vary from location to location, but many inspectors strictly require compliance on any electrical equipment, including automated lighting, that is installed in new construction. In portable concert and touring applications and in most theatres, compliance is rarely enforced but should be encouraged.

Wire Gauges

Wires and cables are sized according to standards that define the cross-sectional diameter of the conductors. The ampacity (how much current they can safely carry under specified conditions) is a factor of the wire size, the ambient temperature, and the temperature rating of the insulation covering the conductor. For example, THHN wire is commonly used in North America for permanent installations in commercial buildings and it is rated at 194°F (90°C).

The American Wire Gauge (AWG) is the standard by which wire and cable is manufactured and used in North America; the smaller the gauge, the larger the diameter of the wire. In most other parts of the world, wire is specified by the area of its cross-section in square millimeters. For example, 4/0 cable (pronounced four-ought, also designated as 0000) is 107.22 mm^2. Table 3-4 shows the ampacity of THHN wire with no more than two or three conductors in a multiconductor cable with an ambient temperature of 86°F (30°C).

Table 3-4 Ampacity of THHN wire in free air.

AWG	Diameter (mm)	Diameter (inches)	Square (mm²)	Resistance (ohms/1000 m)	Ampacity with 194°F (90°C) insulation in free air
14	1.63	0.064	2.0	8.54	21
13	1.80	0.072	2.6	6.76	27
12	2.05	0.081	3.3	5.4	36
10	2.59	0.10	5.26	3.4	48
8	3.25	0.13	8.30	2.2	65
6	4.115	0.17	13.30	1.5	89
4	5.189	0.20	21.15	0.8	102
2	6.543	0.26	33.62	0.5	119
1	7.348	0.29	42.41	0.4	137
0	8.252	0.33	53.49	0.31	163
00 (2/0)	9.266	0.37	67.43	0.25	186
000 (3/0)	10.40	0.41	85.01	0.2	214
0000 (4/0)	11.684	0.46	107.22	0.16	253

Data Distribution Systems

The purpose of a data distribution system is to reliably deliver high-speed digital data from a control system to every receiving device in the system (Figure 3-15). The system can be as simple as a single controller with one data line running to a single receiving device such as an automated light, or it can be very complex, with multiple sources of data, distribution splitters, and amplifiers and several isolated output links. The system may be composed of any or all of the following elements:

- Data cables

- Data splitter

- Data distribution amplifier

- Data converter

- Data terminator

- A/B switch

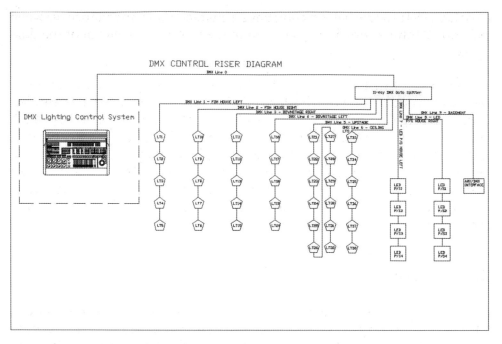

Figure 3-15 Typical control riser diagram.

The majority of data distribution systems in existence today are built for the DMX512 standard, a 256 K baud serial digital signal encoded with commands and data. But an increasing number of manufacturers are preparing for and incorporating Ethernet or TCP/IP protocols. In the instances where Ethernet is used but is not the native protocol, there are a number of protocol converters and proprietary adaptations of TCP/IP such as ArtNet, ETCNet, and Strand Net that are used to convert back and forth between the two protocols.

Data Cables

Data cables are purpose-built low-impedance cables designed to efficiently transmit digital signals with minimal signal degradation. Microphone cables are high-impedance cables and are not suitable for data transmission and therefore should not be used in lieu of data cables. Data cables such as Belden 9841 (www.belden.com) have a characteristic impedance between 100 and 120 ohms, which helps maintain the original waveform of the data signal.

For permanent installations, CAT5 shielded twisted pair (STP) cable has been tested and proven reliable for DMX512 transmission. A report entitled *DMX512 Over Category 5 Cable—Task Group Report* was published by ESTA (www.esta.org) and is available on their website. For portable applications, ordinary CAT5 cable is not durable enough to withstand the rigors of touring. Certain products such as Dura-Flex DMX control cable (Figure 3-16) or ProPlex data cable are made specifically for portable data distribution applications, with more durable jackets and larger conductors.

Data Splitters

A data splitter takes a single input and retransmits it to several outputs. The number of outputs varies by manufacturer and model. The purpose of a data splitter is to increase the number of devices that can be connected to a single data line and to isolate branches of a data distribution system to increase reliability of the system and to facilitate faster troubleshooting.

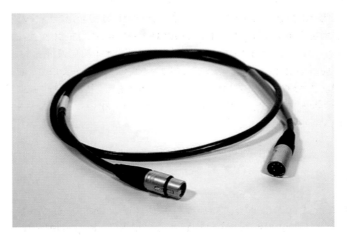

Figure 3-16 DMX data cable with 5-pin XLR connectors. (Photograph courtesy of Creative Stage Lighting.)

Any RS-485-type data transmission system such as DMX512 is limited to 32 devices per line. If, for example, more than 32 automated lights are connected to a single data line, the signal will be too weak to properly drive them, and they will behave erratically. Because a data splitter retransmits the incoming signal to several outputs, each output is capable of driving up to 32 devices. For example, a one-input, five-output data splitter is capable of driving 160 individual devices.

A data splitter also makes it easier to troubleshoot a data distribution system because each output is isolated from the input. For example, without a data splitter, if there are 32 devices connected to a single data line and one of them is malfunctioning by shorting the data line, then every device on that data link is susceptible to erratic operation or complete inoperability. If, on the other hand, a data splitter is used to split the data line into four output data links, then a malfunction of one device will be isolated to one of eight devices instead of 32.

The use of a data splitter (Figure 3-17) is recommended wherever a group of devices is isolated. For example, if there are four truss structures, one upstage, one downstage, one stage left, and one stage right, then it is a good practice to use a data splitter to run individual data lines to each truss structure instead of running a single data line to and from each truss structure.

Data Amplifiers

The purpose of a data amplifier (Figure 3-18) is to boost a data signal. Any RS-485-type data transmission system such as DMX512 is limited to a

Figure 3-17 DMX 11-way splitter with five-pin XLR connectors. (Photograph courtesy of Doug Fleenor Design.)

Figure 3-18 DMX four-channel isolated amplifier. (Photograph courtesy of Doug Fleenor Design.)

maximum transmission length of 1000 m (3281 feet), but the recommended practice is to limit it to a maximum of 500 m (1541 feet).[1] For applications in which the combined data links (excluding outputs from a data splitter) exceed the recommended maximum, a data amplifier should be used to boost the signal and ensure the integrity of the data.

Since a data splitter retransmits the incoming signal, it is by definition an amplifier as well as a data splitter. But there are some data amplifiers that are not data splitters.

Data Converters

In the world of entertainment lighting, there is one dominant protocol, DMX512, but there are a few other protocols that were formerly in use or were used in proprietary systems. In addition, there are new protocols being developed all the time. For that reason, protocol converters are sometimes necessary, particularly in systems that integrate legacy equipment. Various protocol converters, such as analog-to-DMX and DMX-to-Ethernet, are available from a variety of manufacturers, such as Doug Fleenor Designs, Interactive Technologies, Pathway Connectivity, Artistic Licence, and Goddard Design.

---

[1] *Recommended Practice for DMX512—A Guide for Users and Installers,* by Adam Bennette (© PLASA 1994).

Data Terminators

A data terminator (Figure 3-19) should always be inserted at the end of every DMX512 data link. The purpose of a data terminator is to match the impedance of the line in order to prevent signal reflections that interfere with the signal propagation. A data terminator is a simple device that plugs into a data connector and places a 120-ohm resistor across the two individual conductors in a data line. If a data link is not terminated, the equipment connected to that line will behave erratically or will not operate at all. In the event that a data splitter is used or if multiple outputs from a console are used, then all of the data lines require termination. The larger the data distribution system, the longer the data runs; the more devices that are connected to the data line, the more likely a missing terminator will cause problems. Some people falsely believe that it is okay to build a data distribution system without data termination because they have gotten away with it on smaller system without any problems. But it is a good practice to always use termination to avoid problems.

Figure 3-19 DMX512 data terminator. (Photograph courtesy of Doug Fleenor Design.)

A/B Switches

In some data distribution systems there might be redundant backup systems to ensure operability in the event of a failure of the primary system. In such systems, an A/B switch is necessary to provide for the manual selection of the active data source (Figure 3-20). Most A/B switches are simple devices with a provision for two inputs, one output, and a manual rotary switch.

Figure 3-20 A/B switch for DMX512 data.

Data Connectors

The type of connector used on a data cable depends on the type of data signal and the manufacturer's choice of connector. The DMX512 and DMX512-A standards call for a five-pin XLR connector, and many production companies stock five-pin cable exclusively. However, some automated lighting manufacturers use three-pin XLR connectors, despite the fact that they do not conform to DMX protocol, because the fourth and fifth pins in the DMX512 standard are unused. They are, however, used in the new DMX512-A control protocol. The newly released standard calls for the use of the fourth and fifth pins as a second "universe" of DMX512 channels or for bidirectional communication between the console and the devices on the data line. Therefore, it is a good practice to use five-pin XLR connectors on all DMX512 data cables to ensure compatibility in the future.

Many automated lighting manufacturers are now providing Ethernet connectors in addition to XLR connectors on their products. Ethernet can be used as a transport that carries DMX512 data or it can be used in the future with a new protocol called Architecture for Control Networks (ACN). As of this writing, ESTA is in the long process of writing a new standard for a digital protocol, ACN, that will eventually supplant DMX512. That doesn't mean that DMX512 will be obsolete, but it will likely not be the most prevalent protocol in the future. The ACN protocol does not define the physical layer, and the connector type will depend on the network media, for example, wired Ethernet, wireless Ethernet, Firewire, or fiber. Consoles and automated luminaires will likely make extensive use of RJ-45 connectors, the same connectors that are used for networking computers. Standard plastic RJ-45 connectors are not suited for portable data distribution applications, but ruggedized RJ-45 connectors such as the Neutrik EtherCon connector are being marketed for this purpose. Ruggedized connectors have a diecast aluminum shell, much like the shell of an XLR cable, around a standard RJ-45 connector.

The output of a device is always a female connector and the input is always a male connector, except in the case of patch cables, which typically use male connectors on both ends. This is important to remember, because it is a huge waste of time to run cable the wrong way. This standard is easy to remember if you consider that a live cable would be easy to short if its output were male; therefore, a female output protects against shorts.

Control Systems

Control systems can be very simple or very complex. In its simplest form, a control system is a single controller connected to a data distribution system. On the other extreme, a control system may have multiple controllers, redundant backup, storage and playback units, media servers, remote focus units, and preset stations, all linked together through Ethernet and/ or DMX512.

Automated Lighting Controllers

Automated lighting controllers come in many sizes, shapes, and forms. The earliest controllers were dedicated consoles and controllers with proprietary protocols or direct analog control of multiple parameters.

Today, virtually every automated lighting console uses DMX512 protocol, although they differ in many ways to suit different budgets and applications.

Automated Lighting Consoles

The vast majority of automated lighting controllers today are consoles or desks. Consoles range from entry-level models that operate a dozen or more fixtures to the very upper range models that can operate hundreds or thousands of fixtures. The more popular consoles in the touring world and in most other applications are the MA Lighting grandMA, the Martin Maxxyz, and the Flying Pig Systems WholeHog (Figure 3-21). In theatre applications the ETC Expression and the Strand 520 are very popular.

The more high-end consoles have many features that help speed the programming process, particularly with very large automated lighting systems. Among these features are fixture libraries, effects generators, offline editors, and visualizers.

PC-Based Controllers

There are a growing number of automated lighting controllers that are nothing more than a software program that runs on an ordinary laptop or desktop computer. They are sold with a dongle or widget that converts the

Figure 3-21 Automated lighting consoles. Left to right: MA Lighting grandMA, Martin Maxxyz, and High End Systems WholeHog III.

computer's USB or RS-232 output to DMX512. They often have many of the features that are found in more expensive consoles, and some even share the same software as their full-console versions.

Dedicated Controllers

In the early days of automated lighting before DMX512 was introduced, all automated lighting controllers were dedicated to a certain brand and model fixture. They used either a proprietary multiplex digital signal or analog control signals and individually run cables for every fixture. Today, dedicated controllers are seldom manufactured, but they can still be found in older systems. Examples of popular dedicated controllers are the Intellabeam LCD controller and the Martin 3032.

Playback Units

A playback unit is storage device that records and plays back DMX512 information (Figure 3-22). They are used in applications in which a repeatable light show can be preprogrammed and played back without the need to make changes on the fly. For example, a DMX512 playback unit might be used on a dark ride at an amusement park where an event, like a passing car, would trigger the start of the show. They are also sometimes used as an emergency backup unit in the event of a failure of the primary controller.

Figure 3-22 Automated lighting replay unit. (Photograph courtesy of MA Lighting.)

Remote Focus Units

A remote focus unit (RFU) is usually a small handheld accessory to a console that allows the programmer to stand on the stage or in a remote location to more easily focus the lights. The RFU usually has limited functions that allow for the selection of individual fixtures, intensity, and focus control.

Preset Stations

A preset station is a remote panel that either calls up cues remotely from a separate console or stores a limited number of cues that can be played back at will. In permanent installations they are often used by nonlighting personnel to have limited control of house lights and stage lighting for various purposes. For example, the pastor of a church might use it to set the light levels for a baptism or a choir rehearsal. They are also used in the theatre at the stage manager position to turn on work lights or to control the house lights. Preset stations sometimes output DMX512 and sometimes work on a proprietary protocol (Figure 3-23).

Media Servers

Video is increasingly playing a part in productions of every type. As a result, there have been an increasing number of media servers on the market that can call up digital files and trigger them from any DMX512 lighting console (Figure 3-24). These media servers take a DMX512 input and output a variety of video signals that are then routed to a video display device.

Redundant Backup Systems

In live performance applications, having a redundant backup system is highly recommended. A backup system is very often a scaled-down version of the primary controller, or even a PC-based version of the controller (Figure 3-25). For true redundancy, the backup controller should have the same show file running on the same version of software, and the two controllers should be synchronized through MIDI, SMPTE, MIDI Show

Figure 3-23 Wall-mount preset station with 10 presets. (Photograph courtesy of Doug Fleenor Design.)

Control, or some other time-coded system. The outputs of the two controllers should be connected to an A/B switch that can be switched in the event of a failure or malfunction of the primary controller.

Luminaires

At the heart of every automated lighting system are the fixtures themselves. Automated lighting fixtures come in a vast array of sizes and shapes, and new models are introduced every year. They can be classified, with very few exceptions, as moving mirror fixtures or moving yoke fixtures. They can be further classified according to whether they have an incandescent lamp source or an arc lamp. If they have an arc lamp, then they can be further classified by the type of power supply they have, either a magnetic ballast power supply or an electronic switching power supply. Still, regardless of the type of automated light fixture, there are more commonalities than disparities between fixture types.

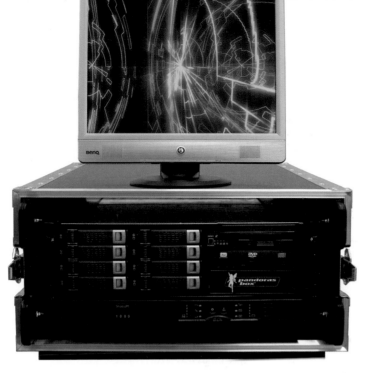

Figure 3-24 A DMX512-controlled media server stores and plays back graphic files that are fed to a display device such as a projector or LED display. Pandora's Box is one example of such a media server.

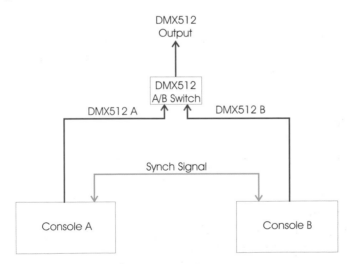

Figure 3-25 A redundant backup system can provide security for the control system in show mode. Two consoles are locked in synchronization with MIDI, SMPTE, MIDI Show Control, or some other signal. If one console crashes, then the operator can throw the A/B switch to divert the DMX512 output from the backup console to the lighting system.

Every automated light fixture, regardless of the type, has the following systems in common (Figure 3-26):

- Electrical system

- Electronic system

- Electromechanical system

- Mechanical system

- Optical system

Electrical Systems

The electrical system has two main functions: to supply the power for the lamp circuit and to supply low-voltage power to the electronics systems and electromechanical systems. The input to the electrical system is always at the connector at the end of the power cord and usually encompasses the lamp power supply and lamp, as well as the circuitry that drives the IC (integrated circuit) chips and motor drivers. Some incandescent automated luminaires have two power cables, one for the lamp and one for the electronics.

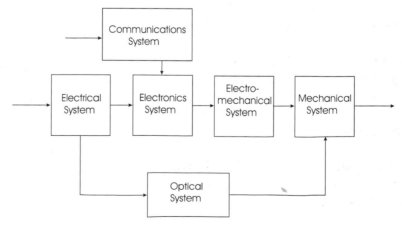

Figure 3-26 Block diagram of an automated luminaire.

Electronics Systems

The primary function of the electronics system is to take the control signal input, translate it to computer code, and execute commands in the form of motor movements or, in the case of electronic dimming, lamp voltage. The main components in the electronics system are the following:

- Control signal transmitters and receivers

- Microprocessors or microcontrollers

- Memory

- Digital-to-analog converters

- Motor drivers

- Position-sensing circuitry

Electromechanical Systems

The electromechanical system consists of components that convert electrical energy to movements. The main electromechanical components in automated lights are motors, usually stepper motors but sometimes servo motors, and solenoids.

Mechanical Systems

The mechanical system is made up of the moving parts such as gears, belts, bearings, axles, and the chassis.

Optical Systems

The optical system comprises the following:

- Reflectors

- Lamps

- UV and I/R filters

- Color Media

- Gobos

- Lenses

- Effects

Communications Systems

When a fixture receives a control signal, the communications circuitry in the automated lighting fixture amplifies it and feeds it to the processor, where it is deciphered and acted upon. Some communications circuits also provide electrical isolation from the data line.

In the early history of automated lighting before DMX512, there was no standard communications protocol. Some automated lighting used analog control with one control wire (plus a common) for each parameter, i.e., pan, tilt, color, gobo, etc. Other fixtures used proprietary digital multiplexed control signals that were similar, from a physical standpoint, to DMX. When the United States Institute for Theatre Technology (USITT) developed the DMX512 in 1986, it was a huge step forward, though it was not ideally suited for automated lighting. It was originally intended for dimming only, and the fact that it lacks a timing signal and data packets are sent sporadically made it difficult to manage smooth cross-fades and movements. Automated lighting manufacturers were left to their own devices in order to make their products pan and tilt smoothly. As a result, many automated luminaires now use schemes that only respond to changes in position, and/or they use starting and ending points from the console and let the processor on the luminaire calculate the intermediate positions.

Today, DMX512/1990 is the de facto standard for controlling automated lighting, and DMX512-A will soon become more prominent. But the digital landscape is rapidly changing. There are no less than three new standards making their way or that have made their way through the approval process: DMX512-A, RDM, and ACN. In March of 2004, the Control Protocols Working Group of the ESTA Technical Standards Program voted to accept USITT DMX512-A Asynchronous Serial Data Transmission Standard for Controlling Lighting Equipment and Accessories. The Technical Standards Committee, the ESTA Board, and the American National Standards Institute (ANSI) Board of Standards Review approved the measure on November 8, 2004, and it is now ANSI E1.11-2004. It provides for a optional second data link in the same cable and connector set. The uses for the second data link range from adding a second "universe" of 512 data channels to adding bidirectional communication from the fixture in either half-duplex or full-duplex mode. RDM, or Remote Device Management, will allow for bidirectional communication in half-duplex mode on the first data link to be implemented in legacy fixtures.

In the next section, we will learn about these systems in more detail. Most of the material under discussion will focus on the underlying principles behind the technology, that which does not change from manufacturer to manufacturer and model to model. As the technology evolves there will be improvements in size, weight, efficiency, cost, and effects. Barring a major technological revolution in the industry, an event that rarely happens but is often claimed, then the principles you will learn in the following pages will serve you throughout your professional lighting career.

SECTION 2

Electricity and Electronics

CHAPTER 4

DC Electricity

Benjamin Franklin proved an important scientific point, which is that electricity originates inside clouds. There, it forms into lightning, which is attracted to the earth by golfers. After entering the ground, the electricity hardens into coal, which, when dug up by power companies and burned in big ovens called "generators," turns back into electricity, which is sent in the form of "volts" (also known as "watts," or "rpm" for short), through special wires with birds sitting on them to consumers' homes, where it is transformed by TV sets into commercials for beer, which passes through the consumers and back into the ground, thus completing what is known as a "circuit."—Dave Barry

One of the keys to understanding automated lighting, or any lighting, for that matter, is to follow the flow of energy from the input to the output. A fundamental law of nature is that energy can be neither created nor destroyed; it can only change forms. Electricity is one form of energy, and the job of any lighting system is to take electrical energy and efficiently convert it to light energy. In the real world, only a fraction of the energy put into a lighting system comes out as visible light. Most is lost to heat, some is lost to mechanical energy, and some is converted to invisible light waves.

The process of converting electrical energy to light can be as simple as passing a current through a filament to heat it up to the point where it gives off light, or it can be a much more complicated process involving electronic switching power supplies with voltage regulation, current regulation, and arc lamps. In automated lighting, you will come across both of these scenarios, and it is imperative that you understand them both. In each case, understanding begins with the concept of direct current, or DC, electricity.

The Flow of Electrons

In simple terms, electricity is nothing more than the flow of electrons (Figure 4-1). A single electron is an extremely small particle that carries a negative electrostatic charge. Whether it is at rest or in motion, it is a charged particle. An electron is a subatomic particle that is so small that it takes millions and millions of them to produce any significant amount of electricity.

The Relative Size of Electrons

Because an electron is so small, it is sometimes difficult to grasp the simple concept of electricity. Because we can't see electrons flowing with the naked eye, nor can we see electrostatic attraction, it is impossible to learn by direct observation. To give you an idea of the scale we're talking about, let's suspend our belief momentarily and pretend that we can shrink down to the atomic level. Now, take a look at the period at the end of this sentence and you will find that we can fit something on the order of 6.25 trillion atoms within the circumference of it. Atoms vary in size according to their type, but a simple carbon atom is approximately 0.1 nm, or 0.0000000001 m, in diameter, and the vast majority of it is empty space. If the nucleus of an atom were half a centimeter in diameter, then you would have to walk about a mile to find the orbit of the outermost electrons. The electrons orbiting the nucleus of the atom are much smaller than the nucleus— approximately one-billionth of a nanometer in diameter, perhaps even smaller; no one knows for sure. Given the dimensions we are dealing with, it's no wonder we sometimes find it difficult to grasp the concept of electricity (Figure 4-2).

The Electron Drift Theory

Still, the flow of electrons is a relatively simple concept that becomes clear when you understand what happens when you apply a voltage to a

Figure 4-1 An electron is an electrostatically charged particle. Ele ctricity is the flow of electrons.

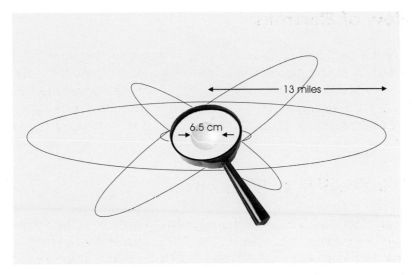

Figure 4-2 If the nucleus of an atom were the size of a tennis ball, the orbit of the outermost electron would be about 13 miles away.

conducting material. The nucleus of an atom is made up of positively charged protons and uncharged neutrons. Since opposite charges attract, the electrostatic attraction between the positively charged protons in the nucleus and the negatively charged electrons orbiting the nucleus is the main force that holds an atom together. The residual attraction of neighboring atoms binds them together to form molecules, of which the entire world is made. Under normal circumstances, the total number of electrons and protons in an atom is exactly the same, producing a net charge of zero (neither positively or negatively charged).

When a voltage is applied to a conductor, the more loosely bound electrons in the outermost orbit of the atom are pulled from their orbit and follow the path of least resistance toward the higher voltage potential. When one electron is pulled away from an atom, it leaves a "hole," and that atom now carries a net positive charge in the absence of the electron. The free electron will "drift" toward the higher potential, colliding with atoms along the way. Each collision the electron encounters takes away some of its kinetic energy and converts it to heat energy. As the kinetic energy of the traveling electron is lost it slows down. The more it slows down, the more likely it is to "fall" back into the orbit of another atom that has lost its outer electrons (Figure 4-3). This is known as electron drift. Billions and billions of

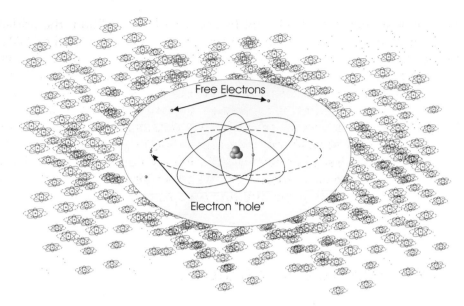

Figure 4-3 When a voltage is applied to a conductor, electrons are pulled from the outermost orbit of the atoms. The free electrons move toward the higher potential, colliding with atoms along the way. As the electrons collide, they lose energy and eventually "fall" back into the orbit of an atom with a missing electron.

these interactions are going on at lightning speed, creating the massive flow of energy due to the motion of the electrons. This is what we know as electricity. More specifically, we refer to the flow of energy through the motion of the electrons as current.

Friction

In the process of the mass migration of electrons, the collisions between free electrons and the larger molecules produce friction that heats up the conducting material. For a given amount of current, the amount of friction produced is directly proportional to the resistance of the conducting material.

$$\text{Heat} \sim \text{Resistance}$$

Friction is lost energy that will not be recovered. In addition, the added thermal load in the venue due to lost heat energy contributes to the HVAC (heating, ventilation, and air conditioning) requirements for the building, which drives up the cost of operating lighting systems. As we will see later on, there is a simple way to calculate the heat load in BTUs (British thermal units) or in joules based on the inefficiency of a power distribution and lighting system. This should be taken into consideration in the design phase of a lighting system for permanent installation. In touring situations it is much less of an issue because the building architects have most likely already taken into consideration the HVAC requirements under normal show conditions, including the building occupancy and the lighting and electrical loads.

Conductive Properties of Materials

In order for current to flow, there must be a conducting medium such as a wire or cable. Some materials are better conductors than others because their molecules contain atoms that more readily give up electrons. These materials are known as good conductors, and they offer little resistance to the flow of electrons. Copper, gold, silver, aluminum, and other metallic elements are good conductors and have a very low resistance value (Table 4-1). Other materials such as carbon, wood, paper and rubber are poor conductors of electricity. They are considered good insulators because they inhibit the flow of electricity. Still others, such as germanium and silicon, will conduct electricity under certain conditions and are known as semiconductors.

Current Convention

When we think of the direction of the flow of DC electricity, we tend to think in positive terms. For example, if a current flows from left to right, then we tend to think of some ethereal substance traveling from left to right. But electrons are negatively charged. Therefore, when an electron travels from left to right, the standard convention is that the current is flowing in the opposite direction (Figure 4-4). Only the U.S. Navy refers to the direction of current flow as the same direction as the flow of electrons.

Table 4-1 Resistivity and temperature coefficient at 20°C.

Material	Resistivity (ρ) (ohm m)	Conductivity (σ) $\times 10^7$ (/ohm m)
Silver	1.59×10^{-8}	6.29
Copper	1.68×10^{-8}	5.95
Aluminum	2.65×10^{-8}	3.77
Tungsten	5.6×10^{-8}	1.79
Iron	9.71×10^{-8}	1.03
Platinum	10.6×10^{-8}	0.943
Lead	22×10^{-8}	0.45
Mercury	98×10^{-8}	0.10
Nichrome (Ni, Fe, Cr alloy)	100×10^{-8}	0.10
Constantan	49×10^{-8}	0.20
Carbon (graphite)	$3 \times 10^{-5} - 60 \times 10^{-5}$	. . .
Germanium	$1 \times 10^{-3} - 500 \times 10^{-3}$	. . .
Silicon	0.1–60	. . .
Glass	$1 \times 10^9 - 10000 \times 10^9$	. . .
Quartz (fused)	7.5×10^{17}	. . .
Hard rubber	$1 \times 10^{13} - 100 \times 10^{13}$	. . .

Source: Giancoli, Douglas C., *Physics*, 4th ed., Prentice Hall (1995).

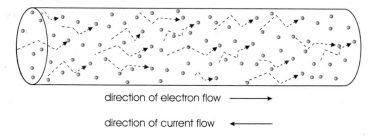

direction of electron flow ⟶

direction of current flow ⟵

Figure 4-4 The direction of current is opposite the direction of the flow of electrons because electrons carry a negative charge.

Voltage, Current, and Resistance

In the study of DC electricity, it is important to have a firm grasp of at least three basic concepts: voltage, current, and resistance. Those three parameters are closely related in an electric circuit. You already have a basic understanding of current, which is the flow of electrons, and resistance, which is the resistance to the flow of electrons.

Voltage is sometimes referred to as potential because, like gravity, it has the potential to cause something to happen. Gravity has a potential to make something fall, thereby giving it kinetic energy; electricity has the potential to make electrons flow, thereby producing electrical energy. In both cases, there is potential energy available.

Water and Electricity—Bad Mix, Good Analogy

To better understand the concept of electricity flowing in a circuit, it is sometimes easier to consider an analogy between water and electricity. In the water–electricity analogy, water pressure is analogous to voltage; it is the force that causes water to flow. Without water pressure, water will not flow. Without voltage, current will not flow. A water pipe is analogous to a conductor. The bigger the pipe, the easier the water flows. The smaller the pipe, the less water can flow. A very small pipe, then, is analogous to a small conductor with a high resistance and a large pipe is analogous to a large pipe with low resistance.

A complete water distribution system, then, is analogous to an electric circuit (Figure 4-5). The water stored in a reservoir is like a battery that stores a charge. The dam that holds back the water has a tremendous amount of water pressure at the bottom. That water pressure is like the voltage in the battery, ready to deliver the water or electricity on demand. The pipe that carries the water to the subdivision is like the feeder cables that carry electricity from the power generation station to the houses in the subdivision. Along the way there are switches and valves that turn the water and electricity on and off. When the tap is on, the water flows. When the light switch is on, the current flows.

The DC Circuit

A simple DC circuit is shown in Figure 4-6. The battery provides the voltage that makes the current flow when the circuit is completed. The wiring provides a path for the flow of electricity, and it completes the circuit. The resistor prevents the current from becoming too large and destroying the entire circuit. The load, in this case, is a light bulb, but it might just as well be a motor, a fog machine, or anything that uses electricity.

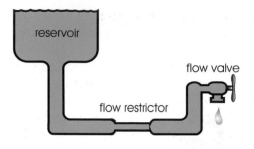

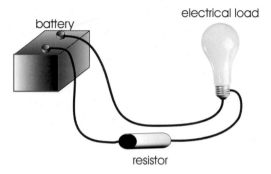

Figure 4-5 Top: The water pressure from the reservoir forces water through the pipe, the flow restrictor limits the amount of flow, and the flow valve turns the flow on and off. Bottom: The voltage supplied by the battery drives current through the wires, the resistor limits the flow of electricity, and the light bulb draws the current.

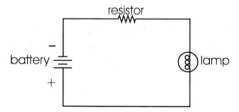

Figure 4-6 Schematic diagram of a DC circuit.

Units of Measure—Current, Voltage, Resistance, Power

In the International System of Units (*Système International d'Unitès*, or SI units), there are base units and derived units. A base unit is one that is standardized by agreement, such as the standard unit of one meter. Derived units are characterized as those that can be derived using base units and a formula. For example, a cubic meter is a derived unit.

The unit of measure of current, the ampere or amp (A), is a base unit in the SI system of units. One ampere is defined as "that constant current which, if maintained in two straight parallel conductors of infinite length, of negligible cross-section, and placed one meter apart in a vacuum, would produce between these conductors a force equal to 2×10^{-7} newtons per meter of length." (Source: International Bureau of Weights and Measures (BIPM) website—http://www.bipm.fr/en/si/si_brochure/chapter2/2-1/2-1-1/ampere.html) The original definition of an amp was one coulomb of charge moving past a point in one second. It takes 6.24×10^{18} electrons to produce one coulomb of charge. Current is usually represented in an equation by the letter I.

Voltage is a derived unit in the SI system. It is usually represented in an equation by the letter V, though sometimes it is referred to electromotive force, or EMF. It describes the potential for current to flow and it is measured in volts (V).

Resistance is also a derived unit in the SI system. It is measured in ohms, represented by the Greek letter Ω (omega). Although resistance is always represented in a schematic diagram as a separate entity, it is sometimes a characteristic of a component such as a wire or a motor. The math symbol for resistance is R.

A watt, as defined by the SI system, is a measure of power defined as one joule per second. Power is usually represented in an equation by the letter P, and it is measured in watts (W) or kilowatts (kW). A kilowatt is 1000 watts.

The Resistor Color Code

A resistor is a component used as a building block for electronic circuits. They are sometimes integrated in chips (integrated circuit chips, or IC chips) and sometimes used as discrete components (Figure 4-7). Discrete component resistors in through-hole circuit boards are normally cylindrical in shape, and most are approximately a half inch long and about a

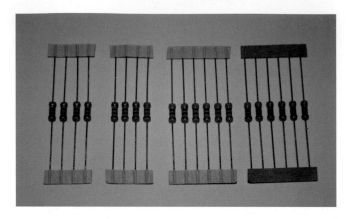

Figure 4-7 Discrete resistors.

quarter of an inch in diameter. Newer surface-mount technology resistors are typically rectangular.

Resistors vary in value depending on the requirements of the circuit design. The value is determined in the manufacturing process, during which they are color-coded with their designated value. The color code consists of four bands printed on the cylindrical body of the resistor. By deciphering the color code of each band, the value of the resistor can easily be determined.

The bands are read from left to right, with the resistor oriented so that the tolerance band (typically gold or silver and usually separated from the other three bands by a space) is on the right. Each resistor value has two digits and a multiplier. The first band represents the first digit of the value. The second band represents the second digit, and the third band represents the multiplier (Table 4-2).

By looking at the values of the first two bands and the multiplier represented by the third band, the value of the resistor can be calculated. For example, if a resistor has a brown band, a black band, and a red band, the first band (brown) represents the digit 1. The second band (black) represents the digit 0. Together, they represent the two-digit number 10. The third band (red) represents a multiplier of 100. Therefore, the value of the resistor is 10×100, or 1000 ohms.

Table 4-2 Resistor color code.

Color	Digit	Multiplier
Black	0	×1
Brown	1	×10
Red	2	×100
Orange	3	×1000 or 1 k
Yellow	4	×10,000 or 10 k
Green	5	×100,000 or 100 k
Blue	6	×1,000,000 or 1 M
Violet	7	Silver: divide by 100
Gray	8	Gold: divide by 10
White	9	Tolerances
		Gold = 5%
		Silver = 10%
		None = 20%

The fourth band is the tolerance band. It represents the guaranteed accuracy of a resistor. A gold band states that the resistor will be within 5% of its stated value. A silver band represents 10% tolerance, and if there is no fourth band then the resistor has a tolerance of 20%.

Resistor Wattage

In addition to having a resistance value, resistors also have a wattage rating that should not be exceeded. The wattage is normally stated on the packaging, and in general, the bigger the resistor, the higher the wattage rating. The wattage rating is important because it determines the maximum amount of power that the resistor can handle before destructing.

Series Resistance

When a series of resistors are connected in a circuit end to end, then the total value of resistance is the sum of the individual resistors. They are said to be connected in series.

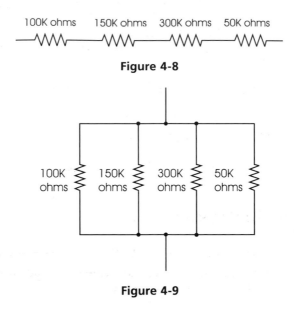

100K ohms   150K ohms   300K ohms   50K ohms

Figure 4-8

Figure 4-9

Example: In the resistor network shown in Figure 4-8, the total resistance can be calculated by adding the value of each resistor in series.

$$R_{total} = 100\,k + 150\,k + 300\,k + 50\,k$$

$$R_{total} = 100{,}000 + 150{,}000 + 300{,}000 + 50{,}000$$

$$R_{total} = 600{,}000\,ohms = 600\,k\,ohms$$

Parallel Resistance

When two or more resistors are connected to common nodes, they are said to be connected in parallel. To find the value of resistors in parallel, use the following formula:

$$\frac{1}{R(T)} = \frac{1}{R1} + \frac{1}{R2} + \cdots,$$

where R(T) is the total resistance.

Example: In the resistor network shown in Figure 4-9, find the value of the total resistance.

$$\frac{1}{R(T)} = \frac{1}{R1} + \frac{1}{R2} + \frac{1}{R3} + \frac{1}{R4}$$

$$\frac{1}{R(T)} = \frac{1}{100k} + \frac{1}{150k} + \frac{1}{300k} + \frac{1}{50k}$$

$$\frac{1}{R(T)} = \frac{24}{600k}$$

$$R(T) = 25,000 = 25\,k\,ohms$$

Series/Parallel Resistance

If a circuit has resistors connected in both series and parallel, the total resistance can be found by calculating the value of the parallel components and adding them to the series components.

Example: Find the total value of resistance in the circuit shown in Figure 4-10.

> Step 1: Calculate the value of the parallel resistor network. From the previous example, we know the total resistance is 50k ohms.
> Step 2: Replace the parallel resistor network with a single resistor of the same value and redraw the network, as shown in Figure 4-11.
> Step 3: Sum the series resistors. A: 650k ohms.

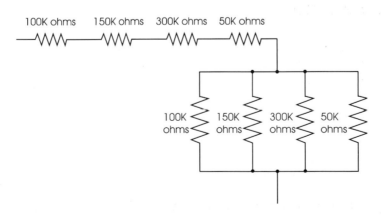

Figure 4-10

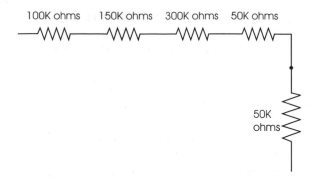

Figure 4-11

Ohm's Law

Ohm's law is one of the most important fundamental relationships in electronics. It describes the mathematical relationship between the voltage, current, and resistance.

$$V \text{ (volts)} = I \text{ (amps)} \times R \text{ (ohms)}$$

According to Ohm's law, for a constant resistance, the current is directly proportional to the voltage in a circuit; the higher the voltage, the higher the current. Alternatively, for a constant voltage, the current is inversely proportional to the resistance; the higher the resistance, the lower the current.

Example: In a 12-volt DC circuit, how much current does a 150-ohm resistor draw?

$$V = I \times R$$

$$12 \, \text{volts} = I \times 150 \, \text{ohms}$$

$$I = 12 \, \text{volts}/150 \, \text{ohms} = 0.08 \, \text{amps}$$

Example: How much current does a 150-ohm resistor draw in a 24-volt DC circuit?

$$V = I \times R$$

$$24 \text{ volts} = I \times 150 \text{ ohms}$$

$$I = 24 \text{ volts}/150 \text{ ohms} = 0.16 \text{ amps}$$

Practice Problems

1. In a 24-volt circuit, a lamp draws 6.25 amps. What is the effective resistance of the lamp? A: 3.84 ohms.
2. A 12-volt circuit has a 3-amp fuse. How much resistance is required to keep the fuse from blowing? A: 4 ohms or more.
3. If 10 amps is flowing through a 150-ohm resistor, what is the voltage drop across the resistor? A: 1500 volts.
4. If a 9-volt battery is connected to a circuit and it draws 100 milliamps (a milliamp is 0.001 amps), what is the resistive load on the circuit? A: 90 ohms.
5. A 24-volt circuit is connected to a 150-ohm resistor. How much current will flow? A: 0.16 amps.
6. Five amps is flowing through a circuit with a 9-volt battery. What is the resistance in the circuit? A: 1.8 ohms.

DC Power

In a DC circuit, the power in watts is equal to the voltage times the current.

$$P \text{ (watts)} = V \text{ (volts)} \times I \text{ (current)}$$

Example: A 12-volt DC circuit draws 10 amps. How much power is consumed?

$$P = V \times I$$

$$P = 12 \text{ volts} \times 10 \text{ amps} \times 120 \text{ watts}$$

Example: A 12-volt battery is connected across a light bulb with a resistance of 24 ohms. What is the wattage of the lamp?

$$V = I \times R$$

$$12 \text{ volts} = I \times 24 \text{ ohms}$$

$$I = 12\,\text{volts}/24\,\text{ohms} = 0.5\,\text{amps}$$

$$P = V \times I$$

$$P = 12\,\text{volts} \times 0.5\,\text{amps} = 6\,\text{watts}$$

Practice Problems

1. A 12-volt bulb is drawing 10 amps. What is the wattage of the bulb?
   A: 120 watts.
2. How many amps will a 150-watt lamp draw in a 12-volt circuit?
   A: 12.5 amps.
3. How much current does a 250-watt lamp draw in a 24-volt circuit?
   A: 10.4 amps.

CHAPTER 5

Electricity and Magnetism

[Electricity, heat, and magnetism] are all by one and the same dynamical action.—Lord Kelvin, British scientist who developed a mathematical analysis of electricity and magnetism

As a kid, did you ever play with magnets? If you did, you probably know that a permanent magnet has a north pole and a south pole. You may not have known what they were called, but you most likely observed that one end of a bar magnet is attracted to the opposite end of another bar magnet. If you put them side by side with the wrong ends touching each other, they would flip around and right themselves so that the north pole of one magnet was stuck to the south pole of the other and vice versa.

Magnetism is an integral part of electricity. Wherever you find electricity, you will find magnetism. To fully understand how electricity is generated and distributed, how motors work, and how sensors detect things like yoke positions, color wheel positions, and gobo wheel positions, it's imperative to understand how electricity and magnetism relate to each other.

Magnetic Lines of Flux

If you think about the two poles of a permanent magnet and the magnetic field around it, you will realize that there is a path from one pole to the other on which the strength of the magnetic field is constant. If you pick a point that is a fixed distance from the magnet and follow the path along which the magnetic strength remains the same, then you are following a line of flux. It is similar to an isobar on a weather map.

Lines of flux, of course, are not visible. But if you took a magnet and put it under a glass table, then sprinkled iron filings on the table top, they

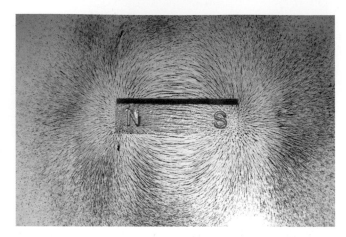

Figure 5-1 A line upon which the strength of the magnetic field is constant is called a line of flux.

would align themselves along the lines of flux, enabling you to "see" the magnetic lines of flux flowing around the magnet (Figure 5-1).

Electromagnetic Induction

Magnets figure prominently in the generation of electricity and in electric motors, as we will soon see. But permanent magnets are not the only source of magnetism. When electricity flows, it also produces a magnetic field around the flow. In the case of a current passing through a conductor, a magnetic field is induced in such a manner that the lines of flux wrap around the circumference of the conductor in a predictable direction. The right-hand rule is a good way to remember the direction of the lines of flux flowing around a current-carrying conductor. If you wrap the fingers of your right hand around the conductor (if you try this at home, make sure it's an insulated conductor!) and stick out your thumb in the direction of the flow of conventional DC current, then your fingers indicate the direction of the lines of flux (Figure 5-2).

The strength of the magnetic field is inversely proportional to the square of the distance from the conductor. The farther away from the source, the weaker the field. The phenomenon of inducing a magnetic field by the flow of current is known as electromagnetic induction; thus, an electromagnet is a temporary magnet produced by a coil of current-carrying wire wrapped around an iron core.

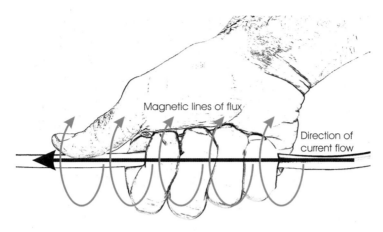

Figure 5-2 A magnetic field is induced around a current-carrying conductor in the direction of your fingers if you wrap the fingers of your right hand around the conductor and stick out your thumb in the direction of the flow of current.

Inducing Current

We know that a current-carrying conductor induces a magnetic field, but did you also know that a magnet can induce a current in a conductor? If a conductor passes through a magnetic field in such a way as to "cut" the lines of flux, then the magnetic attraction of the electrons in the conductor causes them to move, and it induces a flow of current in the conductor (Figure 5-3). But the conductor has to move across the lines of flux, not move parallel to them, in order to produce a current (Figure 5-4). That's not to say that it has to move exactly perpendicular to the lines of flux; if it is moving at an angle to the lines of flux, then only the perpendicular component of the movement will generate a current (Figure 5-5). For example, if a conductor moves at a 45-degree angle to a magnetic field at a rate of two inches per second, then that is equivalent to moving perpendicular to the magnetic field at a rate of 1.414 inches per second (the square root of 2).

A current can be induced in a conductor as long as there is relative movement between the two and the movement has some component of perpendicular travel relative to the magnetic lines of flux. It makes no difference if the magnet is moving and the conductor is stationary or vice versa as long as one is traveling relative to the other. The magnitude of the current is directly proportional to the speed of travel: the faster the travel, the greater the current.

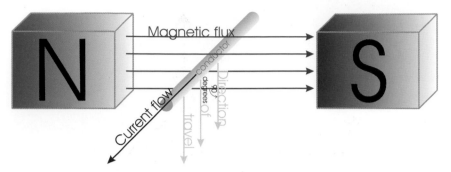

Figure 5-3 Moving a conductor in a direction perpendicular to magnetic lines of flux will induce a current in the conductor.

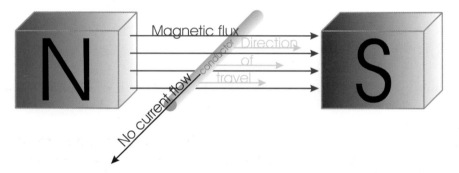

Figure 5-4 Moving a conductor in a direction parallel to magnetic lines of flux induces no current in the conductor.

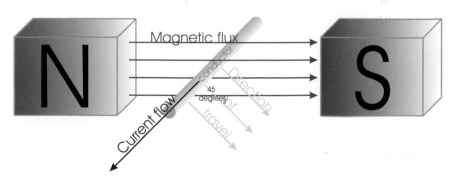

Figure 5-5 Moving a conductor at an angle relative to magnetic lines of flux will induce a current due to the perpendicular component of movement.

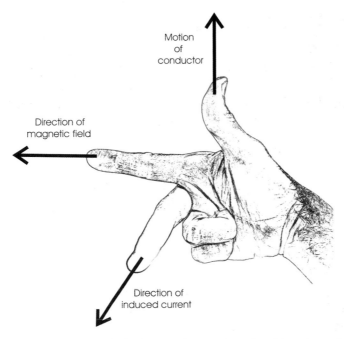

Figure 5-6 The right-hand rule helps to determine the direction of an induced current.

There is another right-hand rule that can be used to determine the direction of the induced current. If you take your right hand, stick out your thumb in the direction of travel for the conductor, extend your index finger in the direction of the magnetic flux (north to south) and hold your middle finger out so that it is perpendicular to both your index finger and your thumb, then your middle finger will indicate the direction of the flow of induced current (Figure 5-6). The mnemonic MFC can help you remember the orientation:

thuMb = Motion of conductor

First finger = magnetic Flux

seCond finger = Current

Alternating Current

The principle of induced current is the basis of AC generation. Once we have established that we can induce a current by moving a conductor through the magnetic lines of flux, building a generator is a simple matter of configuring a rotor with windings that spin about an axis suspended in a magnetic field. As the rotor spins, the windings rotate through the flux and generate a current.

To illustrate, let's build an imaginary generator. We'll start with an axle, around which we will place a loop of wire so that it can rotate about the axis. To simplify things, we'll fashion the loop in a rectangle so that two sides of the loop will cut the lines of flux as it rotates and two sides will not. Then we'll place the axle and wire in the center of two poles of a magnet.

As the rotor spins, the two sides of the conductor that cut the lines of flux rotate 360 degrees to complete a full cycle. The instantaneous direction of travel of the conductors is tangential to the circle of travel. During one cycle, there are four critical points of interest (Figure 5-7). At the top of the circle, the conductors are traveling parallel to the lines of flux, so no current is generated. At the 90-degree point, the conductors are traveling at a right angle to the flux and generate the peak current. At 180 degrees, the conduc-

	Position	Degrees	Unit Current Value
(A)	 ◯	0	0
(B)	 ↘	90	1
(C)	 ↩	180	0
(D)	 ↺	270	-1

Figure 5-7 (A) At 0 degrees, the conductors are traveling parallel to the magnetic flux and generate no current. (B) At 90 degrees, the conductors travel at right angles to the flux and generate the peak current. (C) At 180 degrees, the conductors are traveling parallel to the flux and the current falls back to zero. (D) At 270 degrees, the conductors travel at right angles to the flux but in the opposite direction. The current that is generated is the negative peak.

tors are traveling in the opposite direction from the start of travel and parallel to the flux. Then at 270 degrees, they are traveling at a right angle and opposite in direction from the 90-degree point, thereby generating a negative peak current.

The illustrations in Figure 5-7 show the unit current values at specific points along the path of the conductors as they travel in a circular path through the magnetic field. Obviously, there are many points in between the four points that are plotted. Each point along the way generates a unique value of current flow in direct proportion to the perpendicular component of travel. For example, at 45 degrees the wire has a perpendicular component and a parallel component of travel of equal magnitude. The parallel component contributes nothing to the current, but the perpendicular component is traveling at 0.707 times the speed of the wire. Therefore, it generates 0.707 times the peak current.

If we were to plot the value of the current for each of the 360 degrees in one cycle, we would see a curve taking shape. We refer to the curve as a waveform. A full plot of the waveform produces a sine wave (Figure 5-8).

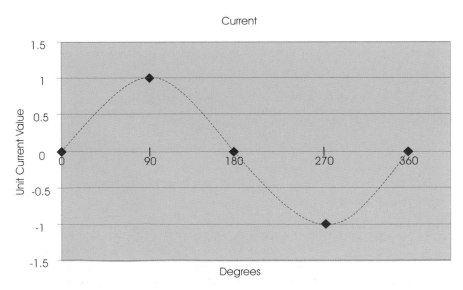

Figure 5-8 Plot showing the unit values of the current generated at the four points around a circle. A full cycle of the current waveform produces a sine wave.

You may remember sines and cosines from your high school trigonometry classes. In abstract form, trigonometry can be challenging, but in real-world applications it's a lot easier to visualize the relationship between periodic motion, such as that of a spinning rotor and trigonometric functions. In fact, the single revolution of the rotor in the generator that we just described is closely related to trigonometry. In the study of automated lighting, it is helpful to know a little bit about sine waves. It is especially applicable when we are dealing with alternating current and the beam angle of lighting fixtures.

CHAPTER 6

AC Electricity

*George Westinghouse was, in my opinion, the only man on this globe who
could take my alternating-current system under the circumstances then existing and win the battle against prejudice and money power. He was a pioneer
of imposing stature, one of the world's true noblemen of whom America may
well be proud and to whom humanity owes an immense debt of gratitude.*
—Nikola Tesla, inventor of the alternating current generator

The sine wave that we dissected in the previous chapter is an example of
a periodic function, or a function that repeats. When current alternates
periodically between positive and negative values it is known as alternating current, or AC. AC electricity has some very unique properties that we
will soon learn about.

The Alternating Current Generator

The generator we "built" in the previous chapter is a simplified example
of a more complex machine (Figure 6-1). An actual generator would have
a coil of wire wrapped around each pole of the rotor, and the magnetic
field is usually generated by a pair of electromagnets.

But the principles are the same. As a generator spins, it produces a current
if there is a complete circuit. If the circuit is open (not a complete path for
electricity to flow), then it has the potential for current to flow, otherwise
known as voltage. In a two-pole generator, the speed of rotation coincides
with the speed at which one complete sine wave is generated; if the generator is spinning at one revolution per minute (rpm), then the sine wave
will take 1 minute to complete. The speed of rotation is proportional to the
frequency of the sine wave. Frequency is an important concept of AC electricity; it is measured in cycles per second or, more commonly, as Hertz
(Hz).

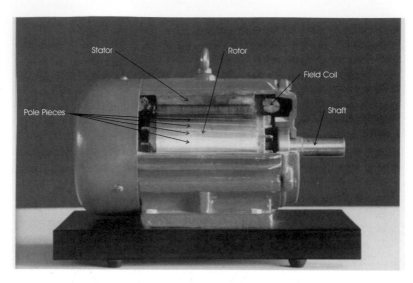

Figure 6-1 An AC generator showing the major components.

Speed of rotation of generator (rpm) ~ frequency (Hz)

In the United States, Canada, and parts of Mexico, the frequency of the power grid is standardized at 60 Hz. That means that the voltage from a common household electrical outlet is always going to be generating 60 complete sine wave cycles every second. In a two-pole generator, 3600 rpm, or 60 revolutions per second, produces a 60-Hz sine wave. In real life, most generators have multiple poles and run at slower speeds. A 12-pole generator, for example, generates 60 Hz power when it spins at 600 rpm.

> Example: In Europe and many parts of the world, the standard frequency is 50 Hz. What is the rotational speed of a two-pole generator producing 50 Hz? A: 3000 rpm.

Most automated lighting luminaires, with the exception of those with an auto voltage-sensing power supply, have a multi-tap transformer that allows it to be tapped for various voltage and frequency combinations. If the voltage is set properly but the frequency is not, the luminaire will not behave according to specification.

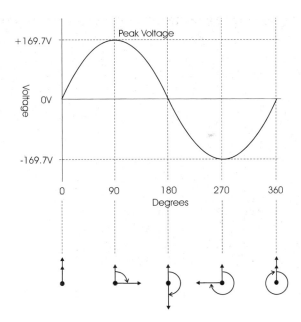

Figure 6-2 The sine wave varies between its positive and negative peak values.

Peak Value

Until now we have avoided referring to any specific values in the AC waveform by referring to the unit current value. The unit to which we are referring is the peak value of the waveform. If, for example, the peak is 170 volts, then the AC voltage fluctuates between 170 volts and −170 volts (Figure 6-2).

Average Value

Because the positive half cycle and the negative half cycle of a sine wave are perfectly symmetrical, the average value over the entire cycle is zero. But intuitively, we know that if we were to touch a "live" wire with 170 volts peak value, we would instantly recognize that the average value doesn't convey enough information! A much more meaningful measure of the average value of a period function like a sine wave is something called the root mean squared, or RMS, value.

RMS literally means the square root of the average, or mean, squared. That simply means that if you take each value along the time line and square it, then find the average of those numbers and take the square root of the result, you would have something that represents a good average. The formula works because when you square a number, the result is always a positive value regardless of its sign to begin with. By squaring it, then taking the square root, you are assured of getting a positive result. In essence, you are inverting the negative half cycle and averaging it with the positive half cycle.

For a sine wave, if you did the math you would find that the RMS value is 0.707 times the peak value.

$$\text{Average voltage (RMS)} = \text{peak voltage} \times 0.707$$

In North America, the standard wall outlet produces a peak voltage of 169.7 VAC or 120 VAC RMS. When it is not specified whether we are referring to peak voltage or RMS voltage, it is assumed that we are referring to the average or RMS value (Figure 6-3).

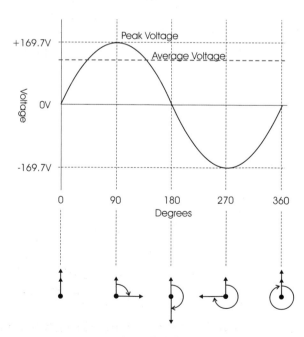

Figure 6-3 The "average" or RMS value of a sine wave is 0.707 times the peak value.

The Inductor

A magnetic field can induce current to flow in a conductor, but it can also impede the flow of current under certain circumstances. If a length of wire is wrapped around a cylinder to form a coil, then the flow of current through the wire will set up a strong magnetic field through the center of the coil (remember the right-hand rule?). Each turn in the coil strengthens the magnetic field and reinforces the flux (Figure 6-4).

In a DC circuit, a coil of wire with current passing through it produces a strong magnetic field, but it is of little consequence to the flow of current. It is in essence still just a length of wire. Once the coil is energized and the magnetic field reaches full strength, the circuit sees the coil as nothing more than a dead short, just as if it were not coiled.

On the other hand, in an AC circuit—remember, the current is constantly changing directions—it's a different story. During the positive half cycle of the sine wave, the current sets up a strong magnetic field in a specified direction. During the negative half cycle when the current changes direction, the magnetic field that was set up by the positive half cycle will oppose the change of direction in the current. It acts as to "choke" the current. After a short while, the magnetic field collapses and sets up in the opposite direction. Both the current and the magnetic field are constantly changing directions and the current is constantly impeded.

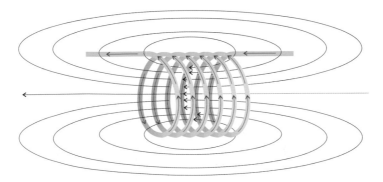

Figure 6-4 A coil of wire with current flowing through it generates a strong magnetic field through the center of the coil.

This coil of wire is known as an inductor (Figure 6-5). It is sometimes referred to as a choke because it chokes the current. In our water–electricity analogy, an inductor may be thought of as a large paddle wheel in a channel of water. When the water flows, it starts the paddle wheel turning, giving it momentum. If the water current suddenly changes direction, the paddle wheel will resist it because it's turning the other way. Once the reverse current overcomes the momentum of the wheel it will begin to turn the other way. But it initially resists the change in direction until the momentum is overcome. The same is true of an electrical current. The magnetic field of the inductor is like the momentum in the paddle wheel.

Inductance is measured in henrys, after the American scientist Joseph Henry. The henry is a very large value; therefore, it is more common for inductors to be measured in millihenries (10^{-3} henries or 0.001 henries). Many components in an automated light have some inductance, for example, motors, transformers, ballasts, and even lamp filaments, to a small degree.

The exact value of inductance in an inductor can be calculated based on the wire gauge, the diameter of the coil and the number of turns. The mathematical symbol for an inductor is L.

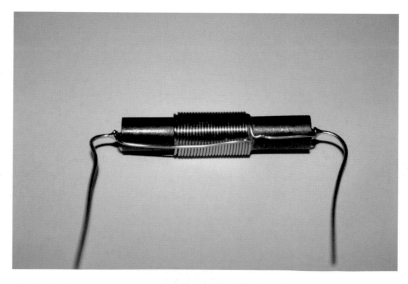

Figure 6-5 An inductor opposes the flow of AC electricity but acts as a short in a DC circuit.

In a DC circuit, an inductor is seen as a dead short. To an AC circuit, however, an inductor resists the flow of current in direct proportion to the frequency and the inductance. The resistance to the flow of current in an inductor is called inductive reactance, X_L and it is measured in ohms.

$$X_L \text{ (ohms)} = 2\pi f L,$$

where X_L is the inductive reactance, π is pi (3.14), f is the frequency, and L is the inductance in henries (Figure 6-6).

Example: What is the inductive reactance of a load with an inductance of 250 millihenries at a frequency of 60 Hz?

$$X_L = 2\pi f L,$$
$$X_L = 2 \times \pi \times 60 \times 0.250 = 94.25 \text{ ohms}$$

The Capacitor

A capacitor is a charge storage device (Figure 6-7). It stores an electrostatic charge temporarily by collecting electrons on a pair of plates separated by an insulating material. It is similar to a battery except that a battery

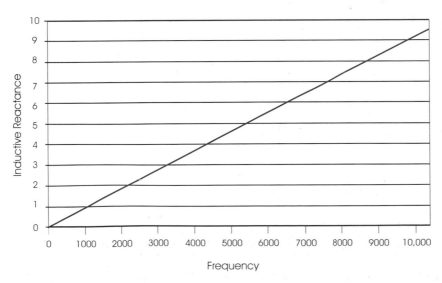

Figure 6-6 The higher the frequency, the higher the inductive reactance.

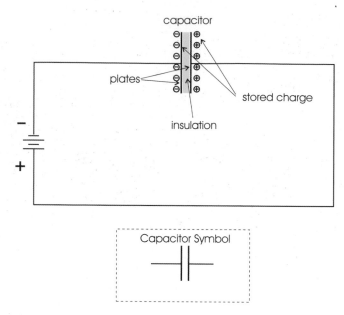

Figure 6-7 A capacitor stores a charge by collecting electrons and holes on two plates separated by an insulating material.

produces a charge through a chemical reaction, while a capacitor only stores a charge from an external source.

In our water–electricity analogy, a capacitor can be thought of as a water tower that temporarily stores water from a reservoir until it is needed. It cannot generate new water; it can only take on water that is pumped from the reservoir. It holds the water at elevation so that the water pressure assures delivery on demand.

The value of a capacitor is measured in farads, after Michael Faraday, a British physicist and chemist who discovered electromagnetic induction. A farad is a very large quantity, so most capacitors have a value in micro-farads (0.000001 farads or 10^{-6} farads) or smaller.

The classic capacitor is a discrete component made from two layers of foil separated by an insulating film, mica, or paper (Figure 6-8). The foil collects the charged electrons when a voltage is applied to the two leads, and it discharges them when it finds a path for the flow of electrons.

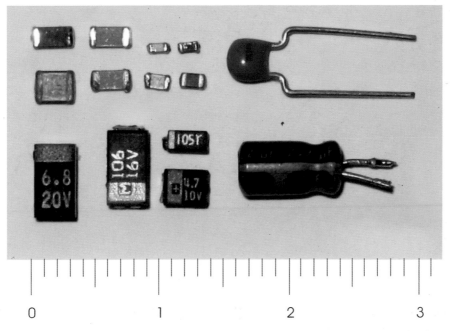

Figure 6-8 A capacitor is a charge storage device. The devices on the left half of the photo are surface mount technology (SMT) capacitors; in the upper right is a tantalum capacitor, and in the lower right is an electrolytic capacitor. The scale shown is in inches. (Photograph courtesy of www.wikipedia.org.)

Because the two plates in a capacitor are separated by an insulating material, a capacitor acts like an open circuit to a DC source once it is charged. To an AC circuit, however, a capacitor resists the flow of current in inverse proportion to the frequency and the capacitance. The resistance to the flow of current in a capacitor is called capacitive reactance, X_C, and it is measured in ohms.

$$X_C = \frac{1}{2\pi f C},$$

where X_C is the capacitive reactance, f is the frequency, and C is the capacitance in farads (Figure 6-9).

Example: What is the capacitive reactance of a load with a capacitance of 250 microfarads at 150 kHz?

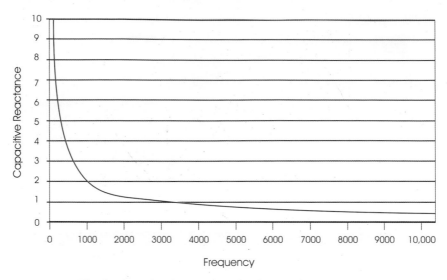

Figure 6-9 The higher the frequency, the lower the capacitive reactance.

$$X_C = \frac{1}{2\pi f C}$$

$$X_C = \frac{1}{2 \times \pi \times 150,000 \times 0.00025}$$

$$X_C = \frac{1}{235.5} = 0.00425 \text{ ohms}$$

Phase Relationships

In a purely resistive load, current flows instantaneously when voltage is applied to a circuit. There is no lag time between the applied voltage and the current flow; the voltage and current are always in phase with each other. In a pure inductor, however, there is a 90-degree shift between the voltage and the current. The current lags behind the voltage because the energy flowing to the inductor has to first set up a magnetic field before current can flow.

In a capacitor, there is also a 90-degree shift between the voltage and the current, but in this case it's the voltage that lags behind the current. That's because the capacitor has to first build a charge.

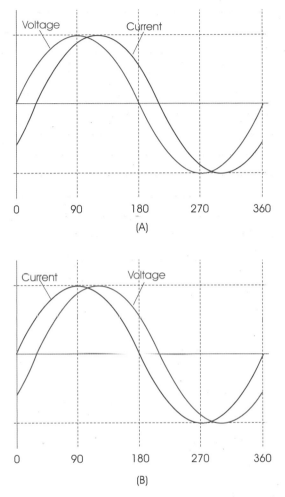

Figure 6-10 (A) The voltage leads the current by 45 degrees. (B) The current leads the voltage by 45 degrees.

In each case, the time lag between the voltage and current is referred to as a phase angle because it can be measured by the number of degrees relative to a complete cycle (360 degrees). For example, if, in a partially inductive load, the applied voltage leads the current by an eighth of a cycle, then the phase angle is 45 degrees (Figure 6-10).

The phase relationships between the voltage and the current in an inductor and a capacitor can more easily be remembered by memorizing the phrase "ELI the ICEman." ELI is a mnemonic for the voltage (E) leading the current (I) in an inductor (L). ICE is a mnemonic for the current (I) leading the voltage (E) in a capacitor (C).

Impedance

In real life, there is no such thing as a purely resistive load. Every load has some element of resistance and some element of inductance or capacitance. For example, loads with windings, like motors and transformers, are highly inductive. In addition, the resistance of the wire adds a resistive element, however small.

The combination of resistance, capacitive reactance, and inductive reactance make up the total impedance of a load. The letter Z is often used to represent impedance, which is a complex number in the mathematical sense; it has a real component, the resistance, and an imaginary component, the reactance. It can be represented as a vector in which the x-axis represents the resistance, or real part of the vector, and the y-axis represents the reactance, or imaginary part of the vector. If the reactance is positive then the impedance is an inductive load, and if the reactance is negative then it is a capacitive load (Figure 6-11).

The magnitude of the impedance (the length of the vector) can be found by using the following equation:

Impedance^2 (ohms) = resistance^2 (ohms) + reactance^2 (ohms),

where reactance = $X_L - X_C$, or

$$Z^2 = R^2 + (X_L - X_C)^2$$

Remember, the complete value of impedance includes both a magnitude and a phase. If a load is more inductive than capacitive, then the current will lag behind the voltage in that load. If the load is more capacitive than inductive, then the voltage will lag behind the current.

Example: In the 60-Hz circuit shown in Figure 6-12, the load has a resistance of 75 ohms, an inductance of 75 millihenries, and a capacitance of 25 microfarads. What is the magnitude of the impedance?

Step 1: First calculate the inductive reactance and the capacitive reactance:

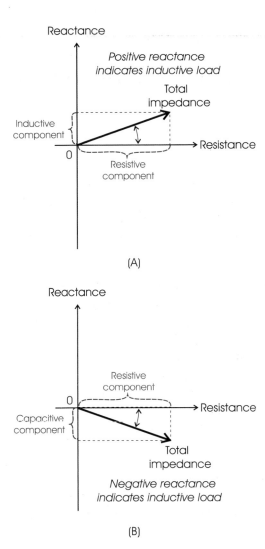

(A)

(B)

Figure 6-11 The total impedance is a complex number made up of the resistance (a real number) and the reactance (an imaginary number). (A) If the reactance is positive, then the impedance is inductive. (B) If the reactance is negative, then the impedance is capacitive.

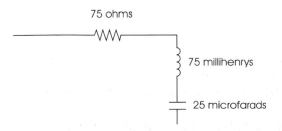

Figure 6-12

$$X_L = 2\pi f L$$

$$X_L = 2 \times \pi \times 60 \times 0.075 = 28.26 \text{ ohms}$$

$$X_C = \frac{1}{2\pi f C}$$

$$X_C = \frac{1}{2 \times \pi \times 60 \times 0.000025}$$

$$X_C = \frac{1}{0.00942} = 106.12 \text{ ohms}$$

Step 2: Calculate the impedance:

$$Z^2 = R^2 + (X_L - X_C)^2$$

$$Z^2 = 75^2 + (28.26 - 106.12)^2$$

$$Z^2 = 5.625 \times 10^3 + (-77.86)^2$$

$$Z^2 = 5.625 \times 10^3 + 6062.18$$

$$Z = \sqrt{11687.18} = 108.11 \text{ ohms}$$

Note: The value we calculated for Z, 108.13 ohms, is the magnitude of the impedance. Calculating the phase angle would require the use of vectors, which is beyond the scope of this book.

The Transformer

A transformer converts electric power from low voltage to high voltage or vice versa, which, as we will soon see, provides many benefits. In the process, energy is conserved, which means that, with the exception of inefficiency due to $I^2 R$ losses (heat losses), the power output is the same as the power input. The voltage and current change inversely, but the power remains the same.

Transformers play a very important role in the distribution of electricity. They were instrumental in the widespread acceptance of AC power distribution at the turn of the twentieth century. At the time there was much debate over the best way to transport and distribute energy. Thomas Edison was a proponent of DC power distribution, while Nikola Tesla and George Westinghouse believed that it was much safer and more economical to use

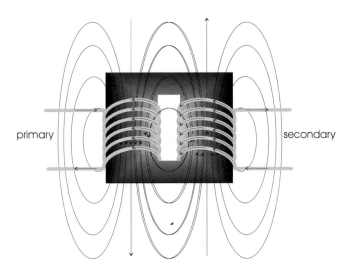

Figure 6-13 A transformer changes the voltage between the primary and the secondary windings.

AC power distribution. One of Edison's arguments against alternating current was that it was used for the electric chair; therefore, it *must* be more dangerous! Ultimately, the AC distribution model won out, and transformers enabled it to do so.

A transformer is merely a pair of windings wrapped around a common core (Figure 6-13). The windings are in close enough proximity to each other that they become inductively coupled or linked through the magnetic field generated when one winding is energized. The winding that is connected to the voltage source is the primary winding, and the side that is connected to the load is the secondary. When AC current is passed through the primary winding, the magnetic field increases as the current in the sine wave rises. As the magnetic field grows, the lines of flux cut the windings in the secondary, thus inducing a current in the secondary winding. Depending on the ratio between the number of turns in the primary winding and the number of turns in the secondary winding, the voltage is either increased or decreased. If the voltage is increased, the transformer is called a step-up transformer, and if the voltage is decreased, it's a step-down transformer.

The ratio of the number of turns in the primary winding to the number of turns in the secondary winding is called the turns ratio. The output voltage is the product of the input voltage and the turns ratio.

$$V_{out} = V_{in} \frac{turns-secondary}{turns-primary}$$

Example: A 120/240 V transformer has 50 turns in the primary. How many turns does the secondary winding have? A: 100.

Example: A transformer has a turns ratio of 8:115. What should the input voltage be in order to generate 6900 volts at the output?

$$V_{sec} = V_{pri} \times \frac{turns-secondary}{turns-primary}$$

$$6900 = V_{pri} \times \frac{115}{8}$$

$$V_{pri} = 6900 \times 8 \div 115 = 480 \text{ volts}$$

Transformers are rated according to the amount of power in watts, volt-amps (VA), or kilovolt-amps (kVA) that they can safely handle. They come in a wide range of sizes and styles, but they usually have at least four wires, two for the primary and two for the secondary, unless it is an autotrans-former, in which case the primary and secondary windings share a lead. This is usually the case in 120 V/240 V step-up transformers commonly used in automated luminaires. Some automated lights with 24-volt lamps have small transformers to step down the voltage from 120 or 240 volts. At the other extreme, some performance facilities have their own feeder trans-formers that distribute power at 480 volts or more and are rated for several thousand kVA.

A multi-tap transformer is one that has several connections, or "taps," along the secondary, allowing for multiple outputs with different voltages. For example, many automated luminaires have a multi-tap transformer that supplies 5 volts for the digital logic components and 24 volts for the motor drive circuits. (See Figure 6-14.)

AC Power

If the phase angle between the voltage and current is zero, the power is simply the product of the voltage and the current.

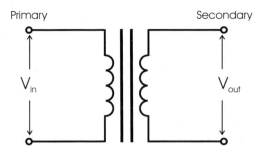

Figure 6-14 Transformer symbol showing the input voltage and the output voltage.

$$\text{Power (watts)} = \text{voltage (volts)} \times \text{current (amps)}$$

The product of the voltage and current in an AC circuit is also known as the apparent power. You will often see transformers and motors rated in volt-amps or kilovolt-amps.

If the phase angle is anything other than zero, then there is a reactive component of the power as well as a real component. Reactive power is the product of the voltage and the portion of the current that is due to the reactance of the load. In practical terms, it is the power that is used to maintain the charge in a capacitor or the magnetic field in an inductor. Other than the losses due to inefficiencies, reactive power is not used, and it is eventually returned to the system. Capacitive and inductive loads sometimes have a reactive power rating in units of VARs (volt-amps reactive) or kVARs.

When the voltage and current are out of phase, the power consumption in the load is reduced by a factor of the cosine of the phase angle (θ). The actual power consumed is the product of the cosine of the phase angle, the voltage, and the current.

$$\text{Power (watts)} = \cos\theta \times \text{voltage (volts)} \times \text{current (amps)}$$

You can see that if the voltage and current are in phase, then the phase angle is zero and the cosine is 1. Then the power is simply the product of the voltage and current. If the voltage and current are, for example, 45 degrees out of phase, then the power is 0.707 times the product of the voltage and current (cosine of 45 degrees is 0.707).

Example: If the voltage and current are in phase, the phase angle is zero. What is the cosine of zero? A: 1.

Example: How much power is consumed in a 24 VDC circuit if the current is 10.4167 amps? A: 250 watts.

Example: How much power is consumed if the above circuit is an AC circuit and the voltage and current are 45 degrees out of phase?

$$\text{Power (watts)} = \text{cosine (45)} \times 24 \text{ volts} \times 10.4167 \text{ amps}$$

$$\text{Power (watts)} = 0.707 \times 24 \times 10.4167 = 176.75 \text{ watts}$$

Power Factor

In the preceding power formula, the value of the cosine of the phase angle is known as the power factor. Power factor is a very important concept relating to power distribution. If the power factor is a very small number, then little power is being consumed even though the current flowing through the system is very large (Figure 6-15). That's because the voltage and current are so far out of phase that the actual power consumption is very low. The magnitude of the current flow is high, but much of it is returned to the power source without being consumed. It's actually flowing to the load and then back the other way to the power source.

When the phase angle is very large and the power factor is very small, the result is a large increase in the current for the same power consumption. Distributing power to a highly reactive load requires much more current-handling capability than is really necessary. Everything in the system has to be oversized to deliver the same amount of power—the generator, the power distribution cables, the switches, the transformers, the breakers, the connectors, and the transmission towers all have to be oversized to handle the increase in current. In addition, the manpower needed to install the larger system, including hundreds of miles of cables and distribution gear, adds to the inflated cost.

On the component level, an automated lighting fixture, for example, with a low power factor requires more current to produce the same amount of

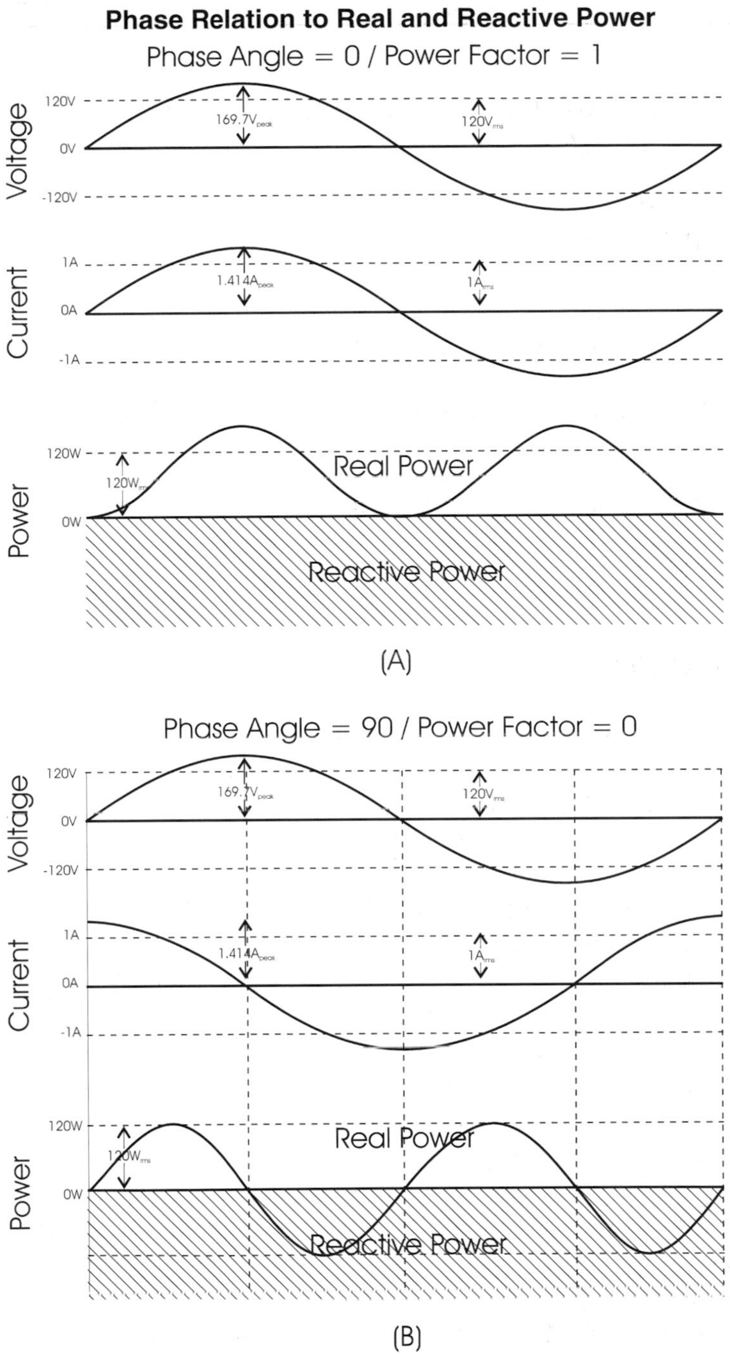

Figure 6-15 (A) When the voltage and current are in phase, then the phase angle is zero and the power factor is 1. (B) When the voltage and current are 90 degrees out of phase (phase angle = 90), then the power factor is 0. When the graph of the power drops below zero, then it is reactive power, indicating that power is being returned to the source. In the case of a completely reactive load, then the sum of the real power and reactive power over time is zero and the net consumed power is zero.

light. It also requires bigger fuses, breakers, internal wiring, transformers, switches, and power supplies, which add to the size, weight, and cost of the fixture.

It's easy to see why power factor is very important and why it's desirable to keep it as high as possible. Since most loads like transformers, heating elements, filaments, motors, and ballasts are inductive, the solution to keeping the power factor as close to unity as possible is to add capacitors to the circuit. For that reason, many automated lighting fixtures have a power factor correction capacitor. You may also see banks of large, oil-filled capacitors on transmission towers or in electrical substations, particularly in industrial areas like refineries that consume lots of power.

Because of the increased costs associated with reactive power, power companies normally build in a "demand" component in their billing to motivate consumers, particularly large consumers, of electricity to keep their overall power factor as high as possible. That helps them keep their costs lower by maximizing the amount of real power they can deliver over the same power distribution system.

Three-Phase Power

A generator has a stator with a bipolar magnet and a rotor with two windings rotating about an axis. If we added two more sets of magnets and rotor windings and placed them on the axis so that they were 120 degrees apart from each other, then we could generate three distinct voltage sine waves (Figure 6-16).

Such a generator produces three-phase power. Most modern power distribution systems are four-wire three-phase systems. The fourth and fifth wires (the fifth wire is the ground and is not considered a conductor) are for the neutral, which provides a return path for the current, and for the ground for safety.

The advantage of using a three-phase power distribution system is that it increases the current handling capability without increasing cable and wire sizes, and it provides more flexibility in wiring options, as we will soon see.

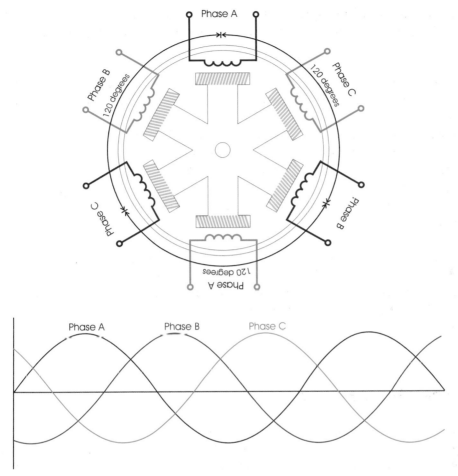

Figure 6-16 A three-phase generator uses three sets of windings spaced 120 degrees apart from each other to generate three voltage waveforms.

The Three-Phase Wye Configuration

The three-phase wye configuration is the most common power distribution scheme used in modern buildings and performance venues in North America. It uses five wires: three hot legs, a neutral, and a ground (Figure 6-17).

In a three-phase wye system, any one hot leg can be used for a 120 VAC supply to neutral. Any two hot legs can be used for 208 VAC from phase

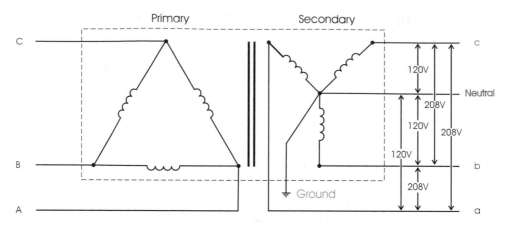

Figure 6-17 A three-phase wye hookup showing three hots (A, B, and C on the primary side and a, b, and c on the secondary side), a neutral wire, and a ground wire.

to phase. Despite the fact that it uses more than one phase of the three-phase system, it is still referred to as single-phase 208.

Three-Phase Wye Connections

In North America, a 208 Y/120 VAC four-wire system (Figure 6-18) is color coded as shown in Table 6-1.

Each of the three phases can be used to supply 120 VAC branch circuits. But it is important to note that special care should be taken to balance the loads equally between the three phases because an unbalanced load can overload the neutral and cause it to burn up. This presents a special problem for a theatrical lighting system that uses dimmers because the load varies from cue to cue. Therefore, many theatrical electrical distribution systems are engineered with an oversized neutral to accommodate a larger than normal current. For example, if the feeder cable is 0, then the neutral might be 00.

The Three-Phase Delta Configuration

Some older buildings have a different power distribution system with three wires plus a ground. This is called a delta system (Figure 6-19) and is more commonly used for high-voltage long-distance power transmis-

Table 6-1 Color coding of a North American three-phase, four-wire system.

Purpose	Color
Phase A	Black
Phase B	Red
Phase C	Blue
Neutral	White
Ground	Green

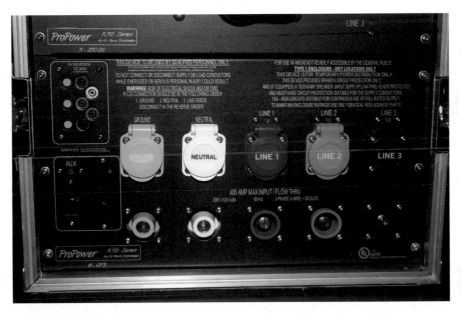

Figure 6-18 120/208 VAC four-wire plus ground electrical distribution panel.

sion. Because a delta system has no neutral, power companies can save millions of dollars in copper wires, smaller transmission towers, and labor in cross-country power distribution systems.

Electrical Safety

The two biggest hazards in lighting production are gravity and electricity. To protect yourself against the hazards of electricity is it important to arm yourself with knowledge and take steps to guard your safety.

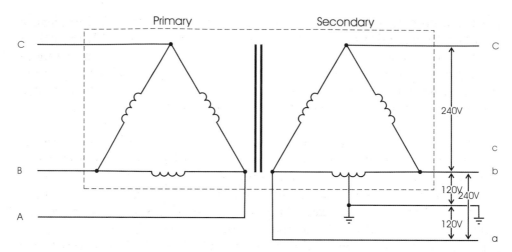

Figure 6-19 A three-phase delta system with three hot legs (A, B, and C on the primary side and a, b, and c on the secondary side) and a ground.

Current can kill. As little as 10 milliamps (0.01 amps) of current passing through a human heart can cause it to stop. Fortunately, human skin has a relatively high impedance value. That's not to say that we are immune from disaster, but our skin is the first line of defense against fatal accidents involving electricity.

We can further protect ourselves from the hazards of electricity by artificially increasing our resistance with the use of protective clothing. Wearing gloves adds a layer of insulation between your hands and a live wire. Rubber-soled boots help insulate your body from the ground, making it more difficult for electricity to find a path through you to ground. Long sleeves help insulate bare skin in the event that your arms accidentally come into contact with a live wire.

When a person comes in contact with electricity, it tends to make muscles contract. Therefore, it is a good practice to avoid grasping an exposed conductor with your hand, which could cause you to clench it tightly in the event that it is hot, making it very difficult to break free. Instead, use the back of your hand should you ever have the need to come in contact with a wire, only after cutting power to it.

Electricity is most likely to kill when it passes through the heart; therefore, it is always a good idea to practice habits that minimize the risk of completing a path to ground through your heart. For example, never grasp a grounded truss with one hand and probe near hot wires with the other. Instead, try to make sure that your shoulder on your probing arm is touching a grounded truss or structure. That way, if you do accidentally come in contact with a hot wire, it will hurt but it might not kill you. Just be sure that if you're in the air you're protected against falling.

Ohm's law tells us that, for a fixed resistance like your body, the current is directly proportional to the voltage. Therefore, higher voltage is potentially more dangerous than lower voltage because it can potentially cause more current to flow through your body. In addition, very high voltage is more dangerous because it can potentially ionize the air and cause a "flash," or a big ball of fire that can fill a small room in a fraction of a second. This sometimes occurs in electrical substations where equipment is operating at thousands of volts. Avoid high voltage whenever possible.

Drugs and Alcohol

Safely working around electrical and electronic gear is a matter of knowledge and good judgment. It requires a sharp mind and quick reflexes. The production environment is a dangerous place in which to bring drugs and alcohol, not only for the user, but also for everyone involved in the show, including the audience. For the sake of the safety of everyone involved, keep all drugs and alcohol away from the production crew. Even some prescription and over-the-counter drugs that cause drowsiness should be avoided. Every production and event is a potential safety hazard and deserves to be treated with care and the utmost attentiveness.

CHAPTER 7

Power Supplies

Electricity can be dangerous. My nephew tried to stick a penny into a plug. Whoever said a penny doesn't go far didn't see him shoot across that floor. I told him he was grounded.—Tim Allen

A power supply can be thought of as a power converter; its job is to convert the line level AC power to another form that is more useable for the load with as little loss as possible. Albert Einstein taught us that energy can be neither created nor destroyed; it can only change forms. A power supply's main function is to convert electrical energy from a certain voltage, current, and frequency to electrical energy with a different voltage, current, and frequency. Except for the losses due to the inefficiencies of the components, energy is conserved in the process of conversion.

In an automated luminaire, at least two power supplies are needed to reliably supply enough current at the proper voltage (and frequency in the case of an AC power supply) to drive the lamp, electronics, motors, and fans. The power supplies for the electronics, motors, and fans usually share a common multi-tap transformer and then separate into a low-voltage supply for the logic (CPU, memory, etc., usually either 3.3 VDC or 5 VDC) and a 24 VDC supply for the motors and fans. One of the keys to understanding how a DC power supply works is to understand rectification.

The Diode

A diode, or rectifier, is a component that allows current to pass in one direction and not the other. It acts as a sort of turnstile for electrons, letting them through as long as they are traveling in the right direction.

Like most electronics components, a diode can be a discrete component or it can be etched into an integrated circuit. Either way, it is made of a junction between two types of semiconductor material: an N type and a P type. These materials are made by "doping," or adding impurities such as silicon, germanium, or selenium to a semiconductor material. An N-type semiconductor has an excess of electrons, and a P-type has a shortage of electrons or an excess of "holes." When a junction is formed between an N-type and a P-type material, it makes a diode. The lead connected to the N-type side is called the cathode and the other lead is called the anode. When a positive voltage is applied to the anode and a negative voltage is applied to the cathode, then the diode is forward biased. The electrons in the N-type side are attracted to the positive voltage on the opposite side of the junction, while the holes in the P-type are attracted to the negative voltage on the opposite side of the junction. The electrons cross the junction and fill the holes.

Alternatively, if the diode is reverse biased (positive voltage applied to the cathode and negative voltage applied to the anode), then the electrons are pulled away from the junction and no current flows (Figure 7-1).

In real life, there is a forward-biased threshold voltage below which no current will flow. This is called the forward breakover voltage, which is 0.3 V for germanium diodes, 0.7 V for silicon diodes, and about 1 V for selenium diodes (Figure 7-2). The vast majority of discrete diodes in most electronics applications are silicon diodes.

Diodes (Figure 7-3) are used for a variety of functions, one of which is voltage rectification in a power supply. Voltage rectification is the conversion of AC to DC voltage or current.

Half-Wave Rectification

In an AC circuit, a diode will conduct only during the positive half cycle of the waveform. During the negative half of the cycle, the diode is reverse biased and does not conduct. The result is a half-wave rectified waveform that is a type of pulsing DC (Figure 7-4).

Full-Wave Rectification

A half-wave rectified DC waveform is not ideal for a DC supply because the pulses are too far apart. A better way of converting AC to DC is to use full-wave rectification.

Forward-Biased Diode

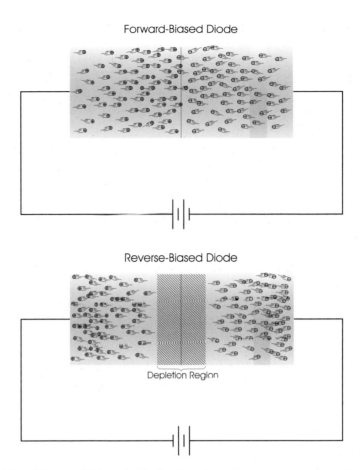

Reverse-Biased Diode

Depletion Region

Figure 7-1 Top: Forward-biased diode showing electrons crossing the P-N junction and filling the holes in the P-type semiconductor material. Bottom: Reversed-biased diode showing depletion zone. No charges cross the P-N junction, and therefore no current flows.

Full-wave rectification converts the entire AC waveform to DC by reversing the direction of the negative half of the sine wave. This is accomplished by using four diodes arranged in a certain configuration called a full-wave bridge rectifier (Figure 7-5). The diodes in a full-wave bridge rectifier conduct in alternating pairs depending on whether the AC voltage is in the positive half cycle or the negative half cycle.

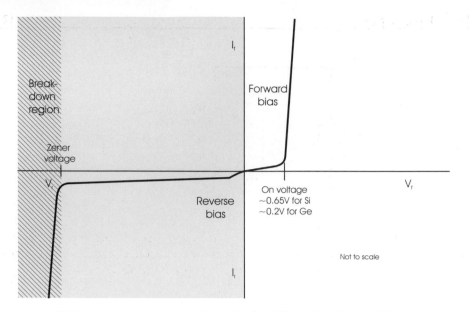

Figure 7-2 Voltage versus current in a diode. When the forward-biased voltage exceeds the turn-on voltage, then current starts to flow. A reverse-biased diode will not conduct current (except for the leakage current caused by the voltage drop across the junction) unless the breakdown voltage is exceeded.

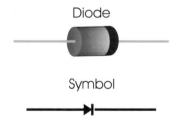

Figure 7-3 Symbol for a diode.

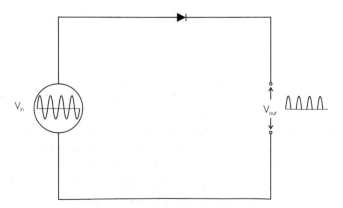

Figure 7-4 A single diode in series with an AC generator produces a half-wave rectified waveform.

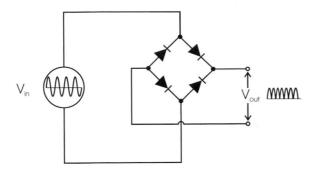

Figure 7-5 When an AC input is fed to a full-wave bridge rectifier, one pair of diodes conducts during the positive half cycle and the other pair conducts during the negative half cycle. The result is a full-wave rectified DC waveform.

The DC Power Supply

With an understanding of diodes and full-wave rectification, building a regulated DC power supply is simply a matter of adding a few components. Figure 7-6 shows a schematic diagram of the power supply for a Lightwave Research Trackspot fixture.

The first step in the DC power supply is to convert the power from the line level voltage to the maximum voltage required by the fixture. In this case both the fans and the motors need 24 volts. A multi-tap transformer steps down the voltage from the line voltage to 24 VAC (Figure 7-7).

The next step is to rectify the AC voltage and convert it to a pulsing DC voltage. The bridge rectifier is represented in the schematic in Figure 7-8 as a square block (Br1) with four leads. The input is 24 VAC and the output is a fully rectified DC pulsing waveform.

After the bridge rectifier, the voltage is split into two separate rails: one for the motors and one for the fan (Figure 7-9). The motor power supply rail is fused (F1) to protect it from current overload. From there, a pair of 2200 microfarad smoothing capacitors (C41 and C42) filter out the pulses in the waveform to convert it to a nonpulsing steady DC waveform. The capacitors filter out the ripples by holding a charge at the peak voltage. When the voltage tries to drop below the peak, they provide the energy to keep the circuit at steady-state DC voltage. When the voltage peaks, the capacitors recharge.

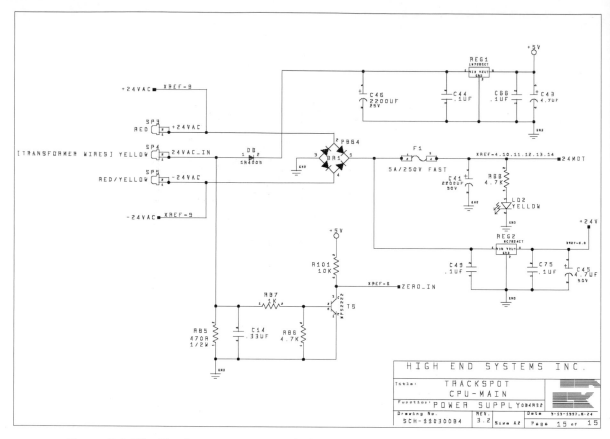

Figure 7-6 The Trackspot power supply has a 5 VDC rail for the logic section, a 24 VDC rail for motors, and another 24 VDC rail for the fan.

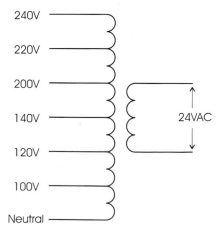

Figure 7-7 A multi-tap transformer accepts a line level voltage input and outputs 24 VAC.

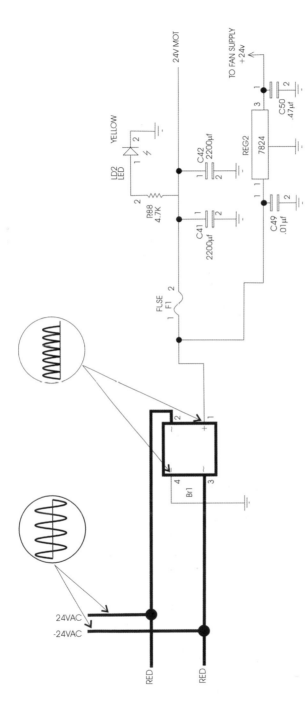

Figure 7-8 The bridge rectifier converts 24 VAC to DC with a pulsed output.

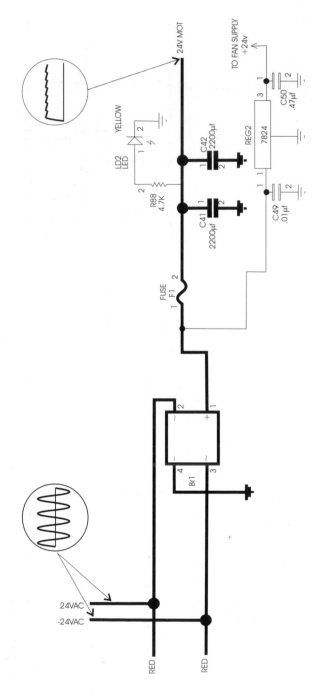

Figure 7-9 The capacitor filters the power supply ripple and smoothes the voltage.

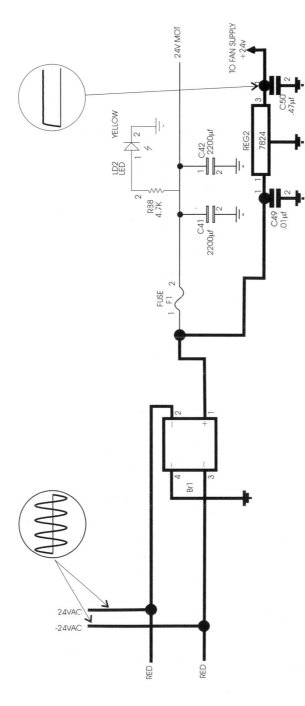

Figure 7-10 The voltage regulator holds the voltage at the prescribed level as long as the input is within the required limits.

There is also a 4.7k-ohm resistor (R88) and a yellow LED tied to the 24 VDC rail. The purpose of the resistor is to drop the voltage to the proper level for the LED. The purpose of the LED is to indicate when the motor circuit is energized. If the power to the fixture is not on or the fuse is blown, the LED indicator will be dark.

The fan circuit is regulated by a 7824 voltage regulator (Figure 7-10). A voltage regulator holds the output voltage at 24 VDC provided that the input is within the prescribed limits of voltage and current. The 7824 is rated for a maximum of 1 amp.

Switched-Mode Power Supplies

Linear power supplies, like the one detailed previously, are becoming a rarity as new, more efficient electronic switching power supplies are gradually taking over. A switched-mode power supply (SMPS) is an electronic power supply that uses a very fast switch that turns on and off to control the voltage and current to the load. They are often used to supply low-voltage DC for the logic and communications in automated luminaires. They are smaller, lighter, and more efficient than linear power supplies, but they are also more expensive and, in some instances, not as reliable.

Switched-mode power supplies are often auto voltage ranging, accepting an AC input anywhere from 100 to 240 volts at 50 or 60 Hz. The first stage of an SMPS is usually a full-wave rectifier with smoothing capacitors. The next stage, the inverter stage, switches on and off at a frequency in the range of ten to several hundred kilohertz using a high-current metal oxide semiconductor field-effect transistor (MOSFET) transistor or an insulated gate bipolar transistor (IGBT) (Figure 7-11). The duration of the on and off cycles is controlled by a controller in the feedback loop that monitors the output voltage and current. Depending on the application, the output of the switching device may be fed to another rectifying and smoothing circuit or components.

Switched-mode power supplies are tricky to design, have many components, and can be difficult to troubleshoot. Most field technicians opt to carry spare power supplies to swap with suspected failures and send them to the factory for repair.

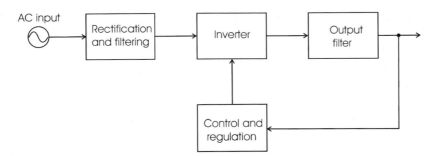

Figure 7-11 At the heart of a switched-mode power supply is an inverter that switches on and off to control the output voltage and current. An IGBT is commonly used as a switching component in an inverter.

Power Supplies for Arc Lamps

An arc lamp is unique in that it has no filament like an incandescent lamp. Instead, a pair of electrodes produces light by sustaining an arc between the electrodes. The most common arc lamps used in automated luminaires are Philips (www.philipslighting.com) MSR and MSD lamps, and Osram (www.osramsylvania.com) HMI and HSR lamps. In order to start and maintain the arcing process, arc lamps have special power supply requirements. First, there is a gas fill in the inner envelope of the lamp that has to be ionized by the application of a very high voltage. Ionization drops the resistivity of the gas and facilitates the start of an arc from one electrode to the other. Once the arc has started, the power supply must then detect the flow of current and drop the voltage to the normal operating level.

There are two distinct types of power supplies for discharge lamps: a magnetic ballast power supply and an electronic switching power supply. Each has its advantages and disadvantages in cost, performance, and packaging.

The Magnetic Ballast Power Supply

A magnetic ballast power supply (Figure 7-12) is the simpler of the two types of power supplies for arc lamps. It primarily consists of a few basic parts: a power input, a ballast (sometimes referred to as a choke), an ignitor, and a lamp.

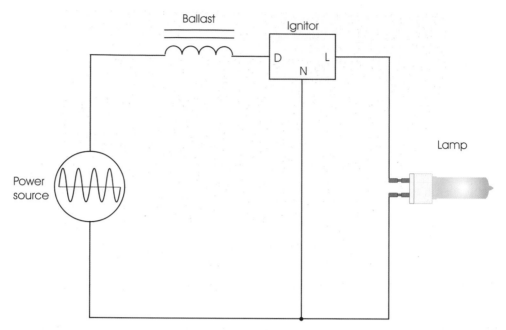

Figure 7-12 A magnetic ballast power supply is a simple circuit with a power source, a ballast, an ignitor, and a lamp. The ballast limits the flow of current by creating a magnetic field that impedes alternating current. The function of the lamp ignitor is to create a high starting voltage and then drop out of the circuit once the lamp ignites.

The lamp ignitor is a small self-contained unit whose job is to initiate the arcing process (Figure 7-13). When the circuit is first turned on, the lamp ignitor applies several thousand volts across the lamp terminals to ionize the gas in the lamp envelope. The rarified gas is a good pathway for the flow of current, and it makes it easy for the high voltage to jump the gap between the electrodes. As the arc jumps across the electrodes it produces a plasma ball made of hot gas that helps sustain the arc. As current starts to flow in the lamp circuit, the lamp ignitor senses it and drops out of the circuit. With the lamp ignitor out of the circuit, the current is regulated only by the ballast.

Lamp starters are typically sealed units and are not serviceable. They cannot be field tested with a continuity tester, nor can they be tested for impedance. The only way to test a lamp starter is to place it in a known good lamp circuit to see if it starts a lamp. They are prone to failure; if a fixture with an arc lamp does not strike after re-lamping it with a new or

Figure 7-13 A typical lamp ignitor for a magnetic ballast power supply.

a known good lamp, the starter should be among the first components to suspect of failure.

With the lamp starter out of the circuit, the ballast and lamp are in series. A ballast is simply a large inductor wound around an iron core (Figure 7-14). It provides enough impedance in an AC circuit to limit the current to the lamp so that it operates at the rated power.

Because a ballast is just a coil of wire, there are few things that can go wrong with it. However, it can fail in one of two manners: the varnish that is used to insulate the windings can break down, resulting in a short circuit, or the terminals can break, causing an open circuit. A continuity test can determine whether a ballast has an open circuit. However, it is very difficult to determine with common field testers whether a short circuit has occurred because the normal impedance is very low.

Electronic Switching Power Supply for Gas Discharge Lamps

An electronic switching power supply is a solid-state power supply that performs the same function as a magnetic ballast power supply but is much more efficient.

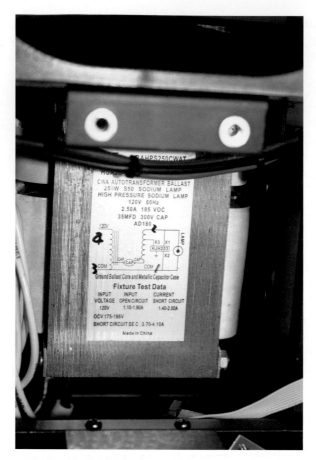

Figure 7-14 A magnetic ballast (sometimes called a choke) is a large inductor.

All power supplies are not created equal. While there are obvious advantages and disadvantages to each type of power supply as they relate to an automated luminaire, the right fixture and power supply are a function of the application. The requirements for permanent installations are different from those for rental and hire applications. Some of the considerations are budget, size, weight, reliability, and flicker.

Advantages of Magnetic Ballast Power Supplies

1. *Fewer components make it more reliable than an electronic switching power supply.* A magnetic ballast power supply has very few components, most of which provide several years of trouble-free operation.

2. *Three main components (ballast, starter, and lamp) make it easy to trouble-shoot.* A good tech can troubleshoot and repair a magnetic ballast power supply problem in the field using common field test equipment and a couple of hand tools.
3. *Relatively inexpensive compared to an electronic switching power supply.* In a permanent installation, most of the advantages of an electronic switching power supply are probably not worth the extra cost involved.

Disadvantages of Magnetic Ballast Power Supplies

1. *Frequency is dependent on power source and at 50 or 60 Hz causes flicker with film cameras.* The alternating current supply causes the arc to flicker at twice the rate of the supply frequency because the arc follows the peaks and valleys of each half cycle. Although this flicker is faster than the human eye response, it can affect film and video, which operate at 24 and 30 frames per second, respectively. Prior to the intro-duction of electronic switching power supplies, cameras and lighting power supplies had to be locked in synch in order to prevent flicker.
2. *Ballast is big and heavy.* A ballast for a 575-watt fixture can add 8 pounds to a fixture, and it requires a bigger chassis to house it.
3. *Relatively inefficient due to I^2R losses.* The resistance of the ballast, though small, translates to relatively large heat losses in the lamp circuit. Increased heat production in each luminaire adds to the heating, ventilation, and air conditioning (HVAC) costs in new con-struction. A typical system has multiple luminaires, each of which contributes to the energy consumption and heat generation, adding up to significant ongoing costs. The rate at which heat is generated in a luminaire can be calculated by multiplying the wattage of the fixture by the conversion rate for British thermal units per hour of operation (BTU/hour) to watts. That, in turn, determines how much air condi-tioning, in tons of AC, is needed to displace the equivalent amount of heat.

$$1 \, kWh = 3412 \, BTU = 0.284 \text{ tons of AC}$$

Advantages of Electronic Switching Power Supplies

1. *Better efficiency.* Because there is no ballast, the heat losses are much smaller in an electronic switching power supply. For permanent

installations, the long-term cost savings for electricity and HVAC can be significant.

2. *Smaller and more lightweight.* The lack of a ballast also significantly reduces the amount of copper in the unit, which translates to much less weight and a much smaller power supply.

3. *Flicker-free.* The output of an electronic switching power supply is a square wave rather than a sine wave; therefore, the voltage maintains the same level until it switches polarity, resulting in a constant intensity from the arc.

4. *Auto-voltage sensing.* Many automated luminaires with an electronic switching power supply have the ability to sense the input voltage and accommodate almost any voltage and frequency. The notable exception is fixtures with a 1200-watt source or higher, which draw too much current at voltages under 200 or 208 VAC. They are typically limited in voltage requirements.

Disadvantages of Electronic Switching Power Supplies

1. *More prone to failure.* There are many more parts that can fail in an electronic switching power supply, which makes them ultimately less reliable than their magnetic ballast counterparts.

2. *Higher cost.* The added cost of engineering and components makes them more expensive than a magnetic power supply. Often the difference can be hundreds of dollars per fixture.

3. *Harder to troubleshoot.* In the event of a failure, they can be almost impossible to troubleshoot on the component level in the field with common hand tools. Most failures are treated by replacing the entire power supply, and it can be expensive to carry a spare, particularly if you have several different types of fixtures.

CHAPTER 8

Overcurrent and Overvoltage Protection

Thus, the task is, not so much to see what no one has yet seen; but to think what nobody has yet thought, about that which everybody sees.—Erwin Schödinger, Nobel Prize-winning physicist

Murphy's Law states that anything that can go wrong will go wrong. In the design of electric power distribution and automated lighting systems, it is imperative to plan for the protection of personnel and equipment in the event of a fault (short circuit) or malfunction. One of the most important means of providing such protection is with the proper use of overcurrent and overvoltage protection.

Fuses

Electrical protection devices come in several varieties. The simplest is a fuse, which is a wire link that will predictably and reliably melt when a predetermined magnitude of current is reached for a designated duration. When the fuse element melts, the circuit is interrupted and the current will cease to flow.

Fuses are sized according to their rated current and voltage. If a fuse current is undersized then it is subject to nuisance tripping due to fluctuations and spikes in the line voltage. If it's oversized it can be a potential fire hazard or a hazard to personnel. When replacing a fuse it is critical to use the same fuse type, since UL and CSA ratings are different from IEC ratings. For a 250 V fuse, for example, a 1.4-amp UL/CSA fuse is approximately the same as a 1-amp IEC rated fuse. Therefore, if a fuse manufactured to UL standards is replaced with a fuse manufactured to IEC standards, then the circuit will no longer be protected properly. And it goes without saying that it's never a good idea, regardless of the circumstances, to bypass a fuse with a chewing gum wrapper or any other conductive material.

It is also very important that the fuse is rated at or higher than the circuit voltage; if not, there is a risk of arcing across the open fuse terminals, thus defeating the purpose of the overcurrent protection. Furthermore, a fuse with the wrong voltage rating will work just fine until the fuse link blows and an arc is generated across the terminals. Therefore, it is extremely important to pay close attention to the current *and* voltage ratings of replacement fuses. A properly rated fuse is designed to withstand the open circuit voltage for 30 seconds after the fuse blows or to have an interrupt resistance of at least 1 k ohms.

When a lamp is cold, it behaves differently than when it is at its normal operating temperature. Depending on the type of lamp, the temperature rises from room temperature to the lamp operating temperature, and in the process the lamp current changes. In the case of a cold incandescent lamp (a filament lamp), the inrush current peaks at approximately ten times the steady-state operating current, but it lasts a relatively short duration, no more than a few cycles. A cold arc lamp with a magnetic ballast exhibits a high inrush current and a relatively long stabilization period before reaching its steady-state temperature and operating conditions. The peak inrush current is approximately 50% above the steady-state current for a minute or so before gradually dropping to its normal level after approximately 5 minutes. An Intellabeam, for example, draws an initial current of approximately 12 amps for a minute or two before dropping down to a steady-state operating current of 8.5 amps. The main fuse, therefore, needs to be able to withstand the higher inrush current for a relatively long duration. For that reason, it is fused with a T15 fuse, which is a 15-amp time-lag fuse.

If the luminaire has an electronic switching power supply then the current is under control of the power supply and it never exceeds its rated value. Also, automated lighting manufacturers recognize the potential problems associated with an entire system of arc lamps all powering up at the same time and the effect that it can have on an electrical system. For this reason they sometimes build in staggered ignition so that each lamp strike is separated in time by a fraction of a second in order to ease the demand requirements for instantaneous current. Some manufacturers go further and program the luminaires to sequence the lamp turn-on and the homing of the motors so that the power consumption on start-up is less demanding.

In addition to time-lag fuses, IEC standards provide for the manufacture and testing of quick-acting fuses. In the UL standard, there are fast acting normal blow fuses and time delay fuses.

Table 8-1 Miniature fuse time-current characteristics for UL/CSA and IEC standards.

% Rated Current	UL/CSA 248-14			IEC 60127-2				
	Current Range	Fast-Acting Normal Blow	Time Delay	Quick-Acting I	Quick-Acting II	Time-Lag III	Time-Lag V	Time-Lag VI
100	0–10 A	*	*					
135	0–10 A	<1 hr	<1 hr					
150	50 mA–6.3 A			>1 hr	>1 hr	>1 hr	>1 hr	>1 hr
	32 mA–6.3 A							
	1 A–6.3 A							
200	0–10 A	<2 min						
	0–3 A		>5 s					
210	50 mA–6.3 A			<30 min	<30 min	<2 min	<30 min	<2 min
	32 mA–6.3 A							
	1 A–6.3 A							
275	50 mA–3.15 A			10 ms–2 s				
	4 A–6.3 A			10 ms–3 s				
	32 mA–100 mA				10 ms–500 ms	200 ms–10 s		200 ms–10 s
	125 mA–6.3 A				50 ms–2 s	600 ms–10 s		600 ms–10 s
400	1 A–6.3 A			3 ms–300 ms			1 s–80 s	
	50 mA–6.3 A							
	32 mA–100 mA				3 ms–100 ms	40 ms–3 s		40 ms–3 s
	125 mA–6.3 A				10 ms–300 ms	150 ms–5 s		150 ms–3 s
	1 A–3.15 A						95 ms–5 s	
	4 A–6.3 A						150 ms–5 s	
1000	50 mA–6.3 A			<20 ms				
	32 mA–6.3 A				<20 ms			
	32 mA–100 mA					10 ms–300 ms		10 ms–300 ms
	125 mA–6.3 A					20 ms–300 ms		20 ms–300 ms
	1 A–3.15 A						10 ms–100 ms	
	4 A–6.3 A						20 ms–100 ms	

Courtesy of Wickmann, www.wickmann.com.

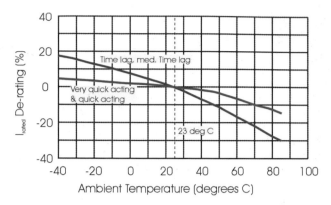

Figure 8-1 Ambient temperature at fuse versus de-rating. (Courtesy of Wickmann, www.wickmann.com.)

In high ambient temperature conditions it may be necessary to de-rate a fuse according to the graph in Figure 8-1. For example, if a MAC 2000 Profile is mounted inside of an enclosure in the Arizona desert, then the ambient temperature at the fuse may reach as high as 70°C. If the main fuse begins to nuisance trip during the day, then it may be de-rated 22% and replaced with a fuse of a higher value, with the caveat that the fixture will not be properly protected at night when the temperature drops.

Circuit Breakers

A circuit breaker is a resettable circuit protection device that senses current and automatically trips, opening a set of contacts, in the event of an overcurrent situation. Circuit breakers are necessitated by law and common sense in each and every power distribution system and are sometimes integrated into automated luminaires. Circuit breakers rated for up to 30 amps come in two main types: the thermal breaker and the magnetic breaker.

The typical household circuit breaker and the type most often found in North America is a thermal type. The mechanism by which they sense current is a bimetallic strip through which the current flows (Figure 8-2). The resistance in the metal causes them to heat up due to the current flow and to expand as they heat up. Because each of the two metal strips has a different coefficient of expansion, they expand at different rates. When the current reaches a predetermined magnitude there is enough of a difference in the amount of thermal expansion between the two that the bimetallic

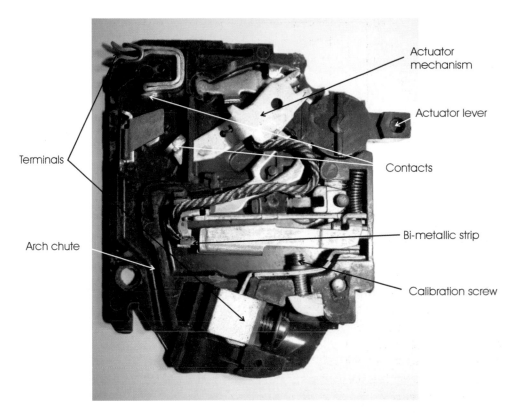

Figure 8-2 A thermal circuit breaker uses a bimetallic strip to sense current and trip the switch in the event of an overcurrent situation. The two metal strips have a different coefficient of expansion and expand at different rates current flows through them and resistance causes them to heat up.

strip will bend enough to trigger a spring-loaded switch. The switch then opens the contacts and breaks the circuit.

Thermal circuit breakers are somewhat forgiving of voltage spikes and surges because of the time it takes for the current to heat up the bimetallic strip. A spike or surge of a few cycles will have no obvious effects on a thermal breaker. A thermal breaker is temperature dependent; thus, they are less reliable in extreme ambient weather conditions. In hot environments they can nuisance trip and in extremely cold environments they may be slow to react. Thermal circuit breakers also tend to fatigue with each trip and eventually might have to be replaced.

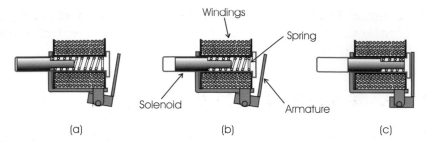

Figure 8-3 A magnetic circuit breaker senses current with a solenoid. The magnetic field of the inductor pushes a moveable core, which trips a spring-loaded switch at a predetermined current level. (A) Normal operating position. (B) As the current exceeds the allowable limit, the solenoid begins to trip the armature. (C) When the armature trips all the way, the circuit is interrupted.

Figure 8-4 An MOV is a type of diode with certain characteristics that make it ideal for overvoltage protection.

Magnetic circuit breakers (Figure 8-3) are more common in Europe and are found to a lesser degree in North America. Rather than using a bimetallic strip, magnetic circuit breakers use a solenoid, which is nothing more than an inductor with a moveable iron core. When the inductor is energized by the flow of current, it produces a magnetic field that pushes the core in a certain direction. When the current is strong enough, the core moves far enough to trip a spring-loaded switch.

Magnetic circuit breakers are much more accurate and fast acting than thermal breakers. They are unaffected by fluctuations in ambient temperature and they do not suffer from trip fatigue.

Metal Oxide Varistors (MOVs)

A metal oxide varistor (MOV) (Figure 8-4) is a type of overvoltage protection device. It is often used to protect a circuit from a high voltage spike caused by a lighting strike or the accidental application of the wrong voltage, such as when a 120 V fixture is connected to a 208 V supply.

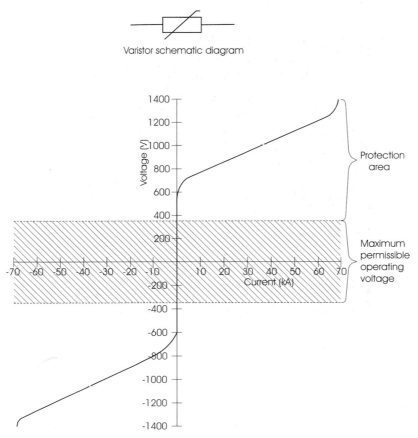

Figure 8-5 An MOV conducts no current under normal operating conditions. But if the threshold voltage is exceeded, it becomes a linear resistor and conducts current in direct proportion to the voltage. It can protect a circuit by shorting it at the input and blowing a fuse or tripping a circuit breaker.

An MOV is a type of diode called a tunnel diode. When low to moderate voltage is applied to it with the proper polarity (reverse biased), then it conducts only a small amount of current due to the leakage across the diode junction. But when the threshold voltage is exceeded, the diode breaks down because of something known as the avalanche effect, and it passes a very large current. It acts as a very nonlinear resistor exhibiting very high resistance below the threshold voltage and low resistance above the threshold voltage. In a power supply circuit, if it is placed in parallel across the input of the circuit (hot to neutral), then if the threshold voltage is exceeded it will short the conductors and blow a fuse or trip a breaker, thereby sparing all the components downstream of the MOV (Figure 8-5).

When an MOV experiences a high voltage spike, it is often destroyed in the process of protecting the circuit. If it is not destroyed, it should be replaced after it experiences high voltage because it will become stressed. Because it is usually in parallel with the circuit, an open circuit diode has no effect on the normal operation of the rest of the circuit, so it may not be apparent that anything out of the ordinary has occurred other than the possible exception of a blown fuse or a tripped breaker. If there is reason to believe that the threshold voltage has been exceeded, an MOV can be tested out of the circuit with a continuity tester. But very often a damaged MOV can be detected by visual inspection, and it will be very apparent by the bits and pieces found spread around the inside of the enclosure.

CHAPTER 9

Digital Electronics

The whole of the developments and operations of analysis are now capable of being executed by machinery. . . . As soon as an Analytical Engine exists, it will necessarily guide the future course of science.—Charles Babbage, from *Life of a Philosopher*, 1864

There is nothing magical about the decimal (base 10) numbering system; it is one of many different numbering schemes that just so happens to be the most common human numbering system. Is it just a coincidence that there are 10 unique numbers in the decimal system and that we have 10 fingers? Perhaps. But you can imagine that there exists some connection between the convenience of finger counting and the management of large numbers.

By the same token, a computer has two "fingers" to count on, so to speak, or two states by which to keep track of numbers—"on" and "off." At the heart of every computer is a complex arrangement of microscopic switches that do everything from carrying out instructions to keeping track of numerical and graphical data. Each of these switches can be turned on or off individually. By arranging them in groups called bytes, each group can represent a piece of data that, taken collectively, paints an entire picture.

The key to interpreting 0s and 1s as data lies in the processor's ability to encode and decode each switch, or "bit," of data. Because a switch has two states, on and off, the binary numbering system is a natural numbering system for a computer.

Binary Numbering

The binary numbering system has only two digits: 0 and 1. It works the same way the decimal system does in terms of place values—each number occupies a specific place and is assigned a value—except in binary the places are factors of two, not 10. Just as in the decimal system, the first place value in the binary system is the ones. In the decimal system, each subsequent place value is equal to 10 times the place value to its right, but in the binary system, each subsequent place value is equal to two times the place value to its right.

Counting in binary is very similar to counting in decimal, except that in binary, the number 1 is the highest single digit. To increment a binary number, add 1 to the ones place. If the result is higher than 1, then put a 0 in the ones place and carry 1 to the next place. If the carry results in a number higher than 1, put a 0 in that place and carry 1 to the next place, and so on.

Table 9-1 shows decimal numbers from 0 to 49 and their binary equivalents.

To convert a binary number to decimal, add the value of each place to find the sum. Table 9-2 shows the first 20 place values for binary numbers.

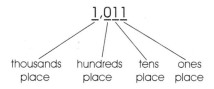

(A) Decimal numbering

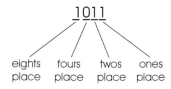

(B) Binary numbering

Figure 9-1 (A) Decimal numbering; (B) binary numbering. In both numbering systems, each place represents a multiplier.

Table 9-1 Decimal numbers and binary equivalents.

Decimal	Binary	Decimal	Binary	Decimal	Binary	Decimal	Binary	Decimal	Binary
0	0	10	1010	20	10100	30	11110	40	101000
1	1	11	1011	21	10101	31	11111	41	101001
2	10	12	1100	22	10110	32	100000	42	101010
3	11	13	1101	23	10111	33	100001	43	101011
4	100	14	1110	24	11000	34	100010	44	101100
5	101	15	1111	25	11001	35	100011	45	101101
6	110	16	10000	26	11010	36	100100	46	101110
7	111	17	10001	27	11011	37	100101	47	101111
8	1000	18	10010	28	11100	38	100110	48	110000
9	1001	19	10011	29	11101	39	100111	49	110001

Table 9-2 The first 20 place values for binary numbers.

Place	Value	Place	Value
1	1	11	1,024
2	2	12	2,048
3	4	13	4,096
4	8	14	8,192
5	16	15	16,384
6	32	16	32,768
7	64	17	65,536
8	128	18	131,072
9	264	19	262,144
10	512	20	524,288

Practice Problems

Convert the following numbers from binary to decimal:

1. 10
2. 100
3. 11101
4. 10011001
5. 111111
6. 1111111
7. 11111111

Convert the following number from decimal to binary:

1. 10
2. 100
3. 255
4. 1024
5. 50
6. 75
7. 99

Binary numbers are important in automated lighting for several reasons. First of all, some of the older automated luminaires use a series of DIP (dual inline package) switches for DMX512 addressing. Though there is sometimes a configuration chart next to the DIP switches telling you how to set the switches for a particular DMX512 address, it's important to understand how to calculate the settings in case a chart is not available. Second, understanding binary numbers helps to understand the encoding scheme for DMX512 data and the structure of computer data. It's quite possible that you could spend an entire career in lighting and never have to decode an electronic signal, but it's virtually impossible to have a thorough understanding of how DMX512 is generated, transmitted, and decoded without understanding binary numbers. Third, if you ever want to write computer code you should know binary. Writing code for lighting applications is a very specialized field, but if you understand lighting and you can write computer code, then you could be a valuable asset to a lighting or controller manufacturer.

Binary Offset

Some automated fixtures, like the Intellabeam, have eight DIP switches for DMX addressing. A switch in the off position is considered a binary 0 and a switch in the on position is considered a binary 1. However, when all the switches are off (00000000), the DMX address is 1. Even though the DMX512 addressing scheme is binary encoded, it has an offset of 1—we don't have an address 0.

Practice Problems

Write down the DIP switch configuration for the following DMX addresses if the least significant bit on the switches is at the left.

1. 32
2. 55
3. 256
4. 25
5. 15
6. 100
7. 125
8. 21

Hexadecimal Numbering

Computer data is arranged in groups of eight bits, which is called a byte. Whereas eight-bit binary numbers are somewhat large and unwieldy for human beings to manipulate, they can be broken into two four-bit numbers, which can then be easily converted to two hexadecimal numbers. The advantage of working in hex is that it is much more user-friendly for humans to work with.

There are 16 four-bit binary numbers ranging from 0000 to 1111. Each of these 16 unique binary numbers may be represented by a unique number in base 16. The 16 hexadecimal symbols are the following:

0 1 2 3 4 5 6 7 8 9 A B C D E F

So a computer programmer working in machine language would write the hexadecimal equivalent of 11 11, which is B B, instead of writing it in binary.

Table 9-3 shows decimal numbers 0 through 29 and their equivalent binary and hexadecimal numbers.

Hexadecimal is easier for people to deal with than binary, but remember, a computer understands only 0 and 1, so we use hex only as a shorthand method of writing code. A compiler is a software package that converts higher level computer languages like C or C++ to machine code, which the

Table 9-3 Decimal numbers and binary and hexadecimal equivalents.

Decimal	Binary	Hex	Decimal	Binary	Hex	Decimal	Binary	Hex
0	0	0	10	1010	A	20	10100	14
1	1	1	11	1011	B	21	10101	15
2	10	2	12	1100	C	22	10110	16
3	11	3	13	1101	D	23	10111	17
4	100	4	14	1110	E	24	11000	18
5	101	5	15	1111	F	25	11001	19
6	110	6	16	10000	10	26	11010	1A
7	111	7	17	10001	11	27	11011	1B
8	1000	8	18	10010	12	28	11100	1C
9	1001	9	19	10011	13	29	11101	1D

computer then works on. The lower level languages are closer to binary numbers and run faster than uncompiled code, but they are harder to deal with than higher level languages that use mnemonic codes to represent commands.

Practice Problems

Convert the following numbers from hexadecimal to decimal:

1. 100
2. 10
3. 2A
4. 21
5. 3F
6. FF
7. AF

Convert the following numbers from binary to hex:

1. 11110000
2. 11010010
3. 110111
4. 100110
5. 101111
6. 110110
7. 10101111

Digital Electronics

The key to digital electronics lies in the ability to turn a switch on and off electronically. That allows a digital circuit to process data in the form of a logical 1 or a logical 0. A logical 1 corresponds to a high voltage, typically +5VDC, and a logical 0 corresponds to a low voltage, which is 0V or ground.

Some of the earliest electronic computers, like the ENIAC (Electronic Numerical Integrator and Computer, circa 1943), used electromechanical relays or a combination of relays and vacuum tubes to process data and store numbers. An electromechanical relay is a dry contact closure switch that is activated by an electromagnet. When the coil in the electromagnet is energized, it closes the contacts and completes the circuit. These relays were simply a means of tracking and processing data by holding a switch open or closed.

The same principles apply to modern computers, except the switches are completely electronic and very much smaller and faster. As developments in electronics advanced computer technology, the electromechanical relay gave way to the vacuum tube, then the solid-state transistor, and finally the integrated circuit. A typical microprocessor chip contains hundreds of millions of transistors and electronic components.

Electronic Switching

A transistor can be used in a digital circuit as an electronic switch. It functions the same as a switch, with the action being controlled by a low-voltage signal. One side of the switch is tied to the voltage rail, or VCC, and the gate controls the switch. When the gate sees a logical 1 it closes the switch (or opens it, depending on whether it's a positive or negative logic circuit), and the output of the transistor goes to a logical 1. A simplified representation of a transistor is a low-voltage operated switch (Figure 9-2).

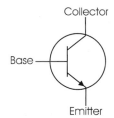

NPN transistor circuit diagram

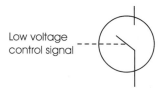

Schematic equivalent of transistor in digital circuit

Figure 9-2 A transistor in a digital circuit is similar to a switch that is controlled by a low-voltage control signal.

Electronic switching plays a vital role in automated lighting systems. The three areas in which digital circuits handle data are transmission, storage, and processing.

Example: For each of the four-bit switch banks shown in Figure 9-3, write down the equivalent binary number and convert it to decimal. A: (1) 1010; 10. (2) 1100; 12. (3) 0100; 4. (4) 1111; 15.

Data Transmission

In the preceding example, we discussed static data states, in which a set of data is temporarily stored in a known location. However, a data set is only useful if we can get it to the right place at the right time. One of the ways in which we accomplish this is by transmitting it across copper wires or through the air in the case of wireless data transmission.

If we want to transmit a series of logical 1s and 0s, then we have to agree to a certain set of rules by which we can transmit and receive data in order for it to make any sense. For example, if you were to transmit a series of

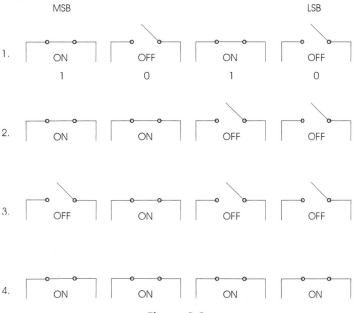

Figure 9-3

logical 0s, it might appear on the receiving end that you are not transmitting anything at all, since a logical 0 is the same as 0V or ground. To prevent that from happening, we have to establish a protocol or a set of rules by which we all agree to abide. Some of the issues we have to concern ourselves with are the following:

- Starting point: when does the transmission start?

- Duration of each bit of data: if we receive a series of logical 1s, how do we know how many there are? If we know the duration of each bit of data, then we can slice the data into a set number of bits.

- Transmission rate or baud rate: how many bits per second will we transmit and receive?

- Packet size: how many bits of data represent a single number? Does 1011 mean binary 10 and binary 11, or is it just binary 1011?

- Ending point: how does the receiver know when we are finished transmitting data for the time being?

These are some of the issues with which we have to be concerned in order to transmit digital data. We will cover these topics in more detail when we discuss DMX512 and Architecture for Control Networks (ACN).

CHAPTER 10

Computer Architecture

We have modified the bugs in the program.—Japanese user manual

It's no accident that the advent of automated lighting coincided with the proliferation of cheap, easy-to-use microprocessors. Some of the earliest automated lights, like the Coemar Robot, used an eight-bit Zilog Z-80 microprocessor with a clock speed of no more than 1 or 2 MHz (1000 to 4000 times slower than today's microprocessors). The processors that are used in today's automated lighting are usually not the fastest or most powerful available, though they sometimes come from the same product families as high-end processors. The demands of a moving light—receiving data, repositioning stepper motors, storing data, etc.—are easily met by processors of moderate speed and power. The overriding factor in engineering most automated lighting computer systems is having enough power and speed for the minimum cost. But the trend toward the convergence of lighting and video will place increasing demands on the processing power and speed of the new hybrid luminaires.

Computer manufacturers and component manufacturers have always developed the enabling technology for automated lighting manufacturers. Virtually all automated lighting uses computer technology to some degree. Although most automated lighting uses modular components and requires very little component-level troubleshooting, it is imperative to at least understand the basics of computer architecture in order to fully understand automated lighting.

The three major parts of a computer system are the central processing unit (CPU) or microprocessor (μP), the input/output (I/O) ports, and the memory (Figure 10-1). We will discuss each of these areas as they relate to automated lighting.

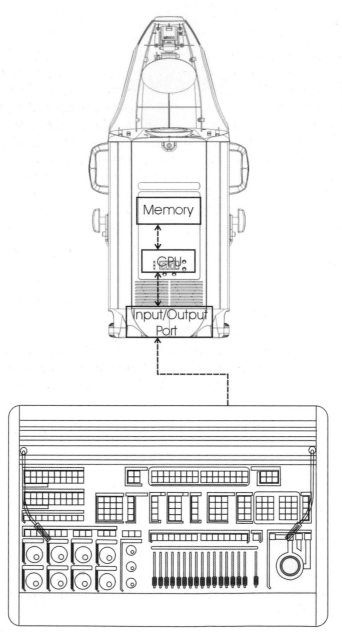

Figure 10-1 The three main parts of a computer are the CPU, memory, and I/O ports.

The CPU

The CPU is the brains of an automated light fixture. It is responsible for processing data, performing arithmetic operations, executing instructions, and outputting data. There are several different types of CPUs. For general applications the most common is a μP. Every desktop and laptop PC and server has at least one μP residing on the motherboard. Many automated luminaires also have a μP, but some use a microcontroller, which is essentially a computer on a chip, or an application-specific processor called an ASIC, or application-specific integrated circuit. A microcontroller is a lower-cost alternative to a μP that combines a CPU with onboard memory (both static and volatile) and all the I/O interfaces required. One variation of a microcontroller that has been used in automated lighting is the DSP, or digital signal processor, which is designed for specific applications in the digital domain.

For example, the Martin MAC 500 and 600 use an Infineon Technologies (formerly Siemens) SAB 80C165 microcontroller (μC). It is a 16-bit single-chip μC that operates at 25 MHz. It has 2 K bytes of internal RAM and up to 77 general purpose I/O data lines. The fact that it is a 16-bit chip means that it can handle two bytes of data or instructions at a time and the "word" size is 16 bits. There are 24 address lines, meaning it can address 16 MB of data.

Regardless of the type, the function of the processor is the same. Some of the main functions include the following:

- Receive (and sometimes transmit) serial data through the data link (DMX512, RDM, or ACN)

- Interpret incoming data (e.g., intensity level, color wheel position, gobo wheel position, focus position)

- Translate data into action (e.g., change intensity level, change color wheel position)

- Execute command (e.g., send new attribute information such as intensity level, color wheel position)

- Output information about the current status of the luminaire (e.g., menu display output or bidirectional communications with controller,

LED status information about lamp status, DMX512 activity, power status)

All of this activity, and more, is coordinated and executed by the CPU (Figure 10-2).

Memory

Memory is the part of the computer that stores information, such as data and instructions. There are several different types of memory devices, but they each function in a similar manner. Every memory device is made up of groups of storage cells, and each cell can store one bit of information in the form of a binary 0 or a binary 1. The storage cells are organized in groups of eight cells, which is one byte of memory. A 1-MB memory chip has 1,048,576 such groups (2^{20} = 1,048,576).

Figure 10-2 Left: A Motorola MC68332 microcontroller, which is used in the High End Systems Color Command, among others. Right: A Microchip PIC17C43 microcontroller as found in a Chinese manufactured automated color wash luminaire.

For example, if we store an intensity level of 50% in a cue, the console puts the binary equivalent of 128 (50% of 256) in memory.

1	0	0	0	0	0	0	0

Each of the memory cells above stores one bit of the eight-bit binary number corresponding to the intensity level of 50% (10000000 binary or 80 hex).

In order to retrieve data that has been stored, each byte of memory must also point to an address. In our previous example, if the first intensity level was stored at address 10 hex (00001010 binary), then the intensity level for the next cue, say 100%, might be stored at address 11 hex (00001011 binary) (Table 10-1).

A memory device has both data lines and address lines. The number of data and address lines depends on the size of the memory. For example, a 16-MB memory chip uses a 24-bit address (Figure 10-3). But rather than dedicating 24 pins on a RAM chip to addressing, a chip will often use a multiplex control scheme to switch the same set of address lines between rows and columns; when the row address select pin is asserted, then the values on the address lines are applied to the address row. When the column address select pin is asserted, then the values on the address lines are applied to the column. These are the same pins on the RAM chip; they're just switched internally. In this example, there are 12 row address lines ($2^{12} = 4\,K$ unique addresses) and 10 column address lines ($2^{10} = 1\,K$), for a total of 22 lines that can address 4MB of storage ($4\,K \times 1\,K = 4\,MB$). In addition, there are two bank address lines that can address four separate banks, yielding a total of 16 MB ($4\,MB \times 4$ banks $= 16\,MB$).

Memory comes in many forms, all of which can be classified as one of two basics types: volatile and nonvolatile. Volatile memory is temporary

Table 10-1 Two memory cells showing the location (Address) and content (Data).

Address								Data							
0	0	0	0	1	0	1	0	0	1	0	0	0	0	0	0
0	0	0	0	1	0	1	1	1	1	1	1	1	1	1	1

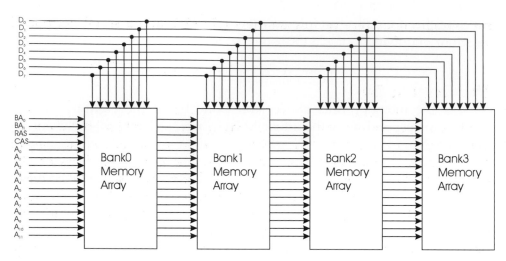

Figure 10-3 A 16-MB memory chip with 16 multiplexed address and control lines arranged in four banks of 4MB each. The eight data I/O lines are labeled D_0–D_7; the address lines are labeled A_0–A_{11}. The control lines include a column address line (CAS), row address line (RAS), and two bank address lines (BA$_0$, BA$_1$).

memory that loses its data when it is powered down. Nonvolatile memory keeps data indefinitely regardless of the state of the power supply. Examples of nonvolatile memory include ROM (read only memory), PROM (programmable read only memory), EPROM (erasable programmable read only memory), and EEPROM (electrical erasable read only memory, also known as flash memory). Random access memory, or RAM, is volatile memory that loses its data when it loses power.

Input/Output Ports

An automated luminaire needs a way of communicating with the outside world in order to accept control information from the user or from a controller and to transmit data or information about the fixture. The most common way of communicating is by way of a data line, which is connected directly to the processor by way of the I/O ports. In some computers the I/O port is a discrete chip called a peripheral interface adaptor (PIA) or a programmable peripheral interface (PPI). The job of the PIA or PPI is to act as a buffer between the I/O signals and the processor, affording protection to the CPU and ensuring that the proper voltage levels operate reliably. On the other hand, a typical microcontroller might have a variety of built-in I/O devices such as digital-to-analog converters (DACs), universal asynchronous receiver transmitters (UARTs), and a serial peripheral interface.

The System Bus

A bus is a set of wires or copper traces on a printed circuit board (PC board) that interconnect the major parts of a computer. It normally comprises an address bus, a data bus, and a control bus. The number of lines on the address bus corresponds to the amount of memory the system can address. For example, an address bus with 20 lines can address 1 MB of memory. By setting each line high or low, the proper address is placed on the address bus allowing the memory or I/O port to decode it and route it properly. The data bus transmits data or instructions between the CPU, memory, and the I/O port. The control bus is used to transmit special instructions between the CPU and other devices in the system.

Microprocessor Architecture

In a μP there are four fundamental parts: the registers, the arithmetic and logic unit (ALU), timing and control, and decoding circuitry. These parts are integral to the programming and function of the computer system.

A register is a temporary storage location with a very specific purpose. For example, to operate on two numbers, the input device places each of the binary numbers in a register, and the result of the operation, such as a multiplication or division, appears in another register. Typically, there are at least three registers in a μP. The accumulator stores the results of arithmetic and logical operations. The program counter stores the address of the next instruction in line for operation. And the instruction register stores the binary coded instruction, such as an add, subtract, multiply, or divide instruction, on which the μP is currently working.

The ALU is the part of the CPU that performs arithmetic and logic operations on the data. It can add, subtract, multiply, and divide as well as perform the logical operations AND, OR, exclusive OR, and complement, plus much more.

The timing and control sections may or may not include an internal clock that outputs clock signals for timing purposes. The decoding circuitry decodes the binary coded instructions in the programmed code. For example, if the binary code for add is 10000110, the decoding circuitry interprets it and sets up the microcode to perform that operation.

Execution of a Cue

All of the parts of the computer system come into play during the execution of a cue. When the operator presses the "go" button on the console, it sets in motion a chain of events. The exact procedure depends on the type of processor and the firmware, but a typical chain of events might be as follows:

1. The console outputs a serial digital signal with binary encoded information about the execution of the cue including the data (in binary) and, implicitly, the DMX512 address for which it is intended. The address is actually determined by its place in the data packet.
2. The data is brought in through the I/O port and loaded into a register in the CPU.
3. The incoming DMX512 signal makes one of the control lines, the interrupt line, go high, signaling to the processor that an interrupt has occurred.
4. The decoding circuitry analyzes the data and decides if any further action is warranted.
5. If the fixture determines that it is the intended target of the data, then it goes to work. The memory address of the first instruction, which is stored in an EPROM, is loaded into the program counter.
6. The program counter puts the memory address onto the address bus lines.
7. The EPROM sends the instruction to the µP by way of the data bus lines.
8. The instruction is placed in the instruction register in the µP.
9. The µP decodes the instruction.
10. If the µP decides it needs to update the data, it sends the new binary encoded data to a buffer before it is passed on.

All of this happens in a tiny fraction of a second. The performance of a µP is measured in millions of instructions per second, or MIPS. Given the speed and efficiency of µPs, it's easy to see why an automated lighting luminaire uses but a fraction of the available computing power. Therefore, some manufacturers seek to minimize their costs by using more economical microcontrollers.

SECTION 3

Electromechanical and Mechanical Systems

CHAPTER 11

Electromechanical Systems

I do not feel obliged to believe that the same God who has endowed us with sense, reason, and intellect has intended us to forgo their use.—Galileo Galilei

June 6, 1986 is the day I started working in the entertainment industry. As an electronics technician, I was hired by my new employer, Blackstone Audio Visual, to help keep the lighting, audio, and video gear working that was installed in various nightclubs around the country. Late that summer I got my first hands-on experience with an automated moving fixture. It was a 350-watt moving mirror fixture manufactured by an Italian lighting company called Coemar. It had exactly five control channels: pan, tilt, color, gobo, and shutter.

At about $2500 each, these fixtures were popular sellers in nightclubs with a moderate or large budget. We had no problem selling and installing all that we could import. The problem was keeping them running. After the initial batch of installations, we soon learned that the plastic Airtronics servo motors driving all the motorized functions were reliable only to a point, and that point was usually surpassed shortly after the fixtures were turned over to the club operators. The robotic movement was such a novelty, it seems, that the club operators loved to program lots of very fast movements. The result was that the motors were getting thrashed to death. They were failing as fast as we could replace them.

Our failed attempts to find more robust servo motors led to much hand wringing and head scratching. Autopsies of the dead servos revealed two problems: the plastic gears in the gear box were breaking and the carbon contacts on the feedback potentiometers were deteriorating and turning into black powder, which caused the contacts in the wiper arm to conduct erratically.

A few months later, another Italian lighting manufacturer, Clay Paky, started manufacturing moving lights called the Golden Scan. Since Blackstone A/V was also a Clay Paky distributor, we wasted no time bringing in stock of those fixtures as well. As was customary in the shop, the first order of business when we got a new shipment was to dissect the new gear and examine it closely. What we found in the new Golden Scan fixtures were stepper motors instead of servo motors. Within a very short time we learned that stepper motors were far more reliable than typical servo motors, and over time we learned why. Stepper motors are inductively coupled, which means they have no commutators or brushes to wear out, nor do they have positional feedback so there are no potentiometers to fail.

Much of what was learned about motor technology was later put to very good use when Blackstone Audio Visual later changed names and became an automated moving light manufacturer. The new name? High End Systems.

Stepper Motors

The single biggest characteristic that distinguishes automated lighting from conventional lighting is its ability to receive data and translate it to mechanical motion, whether it's moving the fixture or changing an effect like a color or gobo wheel. The most common way of producing movement is with stepper motors.

A stepper motor is a type of motor with a unique ability to rotate its shaft a number of steps with a measurable distance and stop at a known angle of rotation. It also has a holding torque that provides a certain amount of holding power in a static position when its coils are energized.

There are three types of stepper motors: variable reluctance motors, permanent magnet motors, and hybrid motors. The vast majority of stepper motors used in automated lighting are hybrid motors, although some moving yoke fixtures use permanent magnet motors in multiphase configurations because they provide more torque at low speeds. We will limit most of our discussion to hybrid motors.

Hybrid Stepper Motors

Just like any other motor, a stepper has a stator and a rotor (Figure 11-1). The stator, or stationary chassis, has a number of coils, called windings, in an angular array about the chassis that function as electromagnets. The rotor rotates about the axis on bearings or bushings inside the stator.

In a hybrid motor, the rotor is made of a cylindrical permanent magnet with its poles oriented along the length of the axis; one end of the axis is magnetic north and the other is magnetic south. Each half of the magnet, or "cup," has a number of grooves cut into it, and the ungrooved portions form teeth. One of the most common hybrid motors, a two-phase bipolar stepper motor (Figure 11-2), has 50 teeth cut into each cup, yielding a pitch of 7.2 degrees per tooth. The second cup is offset 3.6 degrees, and as we will see shortly, each step is half that distance, or 1.8 degrees.

The stator has two sets of coils, or two phases, each of which has four windings spaced 90 degrees apart from one another. They are oriented so that if the windings of phase A are at 0, 90, 180, and 270 degrees, then the B phase windings are at 45, 135, 125, and 315 degrees. Further, every other winding in a phase is wound in the opposite direction. So when the phase is energized, the windings at 0 and 180 become magnetized in one direction while the windings at 90 and 270 are magnetized in the opposite direction.

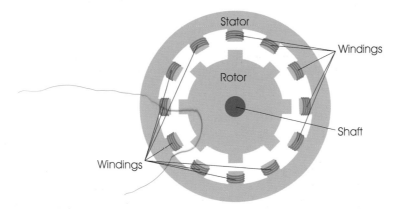

Figure 11-1 Cross-sectional view of a stepper motor. A series of electromagnets arranged around the circumference of the stator can be turned on and off to align the rotor in a precise orientation.

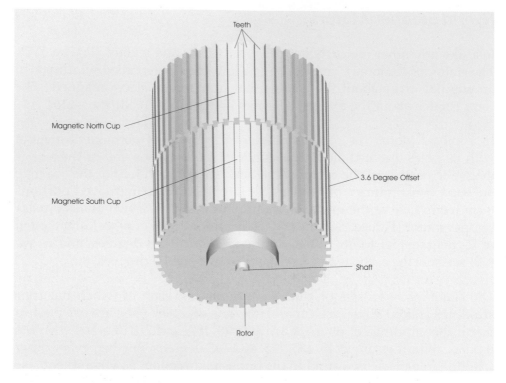

Figure 11-2 Illustration of a rotor from a two-phase bipolar stepper motor showing two cups offset by 3.6 degrees, each with 50 teeth.

If phase A is energized and phase B is off, then the 0- and 180-degree windings are a magnetic north and attract the teeth of the magnetic south rotor cup, while the 90- and 270-degree windings are a magnetic south and attract the teeth of the magnetic north rotor cup (Figure 11-3). As long as the windings are energized, the motor will have a holding torque.

When a phase is energized and the rotor is locked in position, some of the rotor teeth are aligned with the stator teeth, but some are out of alignment by three-quarters, one-half, and one-quarter of a tooth pitch. As the currently energized phase is de-energized and the next phase is energized (Figure 11-4), the rotor will rotate so that the most closely aligned teeth, the ones one-quarter of a tooth pitch out, will line up with the stator teeth. Consequently, each full step movement is one-quarter of a tooth pitch, or 1.8 degrees.

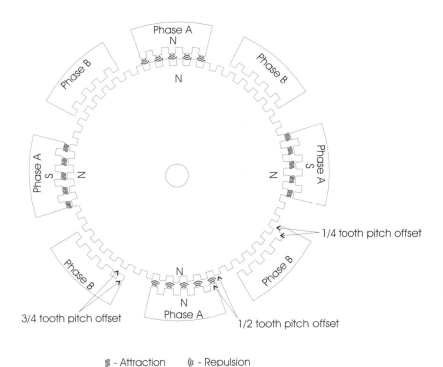

⍥ - Attraction   ⍦ - Repulsion

Figure 11-3 In this illustration, phase A is energized and phase B is de-energized. Because the windings at 90 and 270 degrees are wound in the opposite direction as the windings at 0 and 180 degrees, they become a magnetic south when the other two become a magnetic north. When they are energized they attract the teeth of the magnetic north rotor cup, while the windings at 0 and 180 degrees attract the teeth of the magnetic south rotor cup (not shown).

Single-Phase Excitation Mode

By energizing the windings in alternating phases (A/B/A/B, etc.) and by reversing the polarity of the winding every other time it's energized (+A/+B/−A/−B, etc.), the rotor will spin. Each time the phase sequence is advanced, the rotor will move a full step (1.8 degrees), and after 200 steps it will complete one revolution. This is known as single-phase or "one phase on, full step" excitation mode (Figure 11-5). This mode requires less power than other excitation modes but provides the least amount of torque.

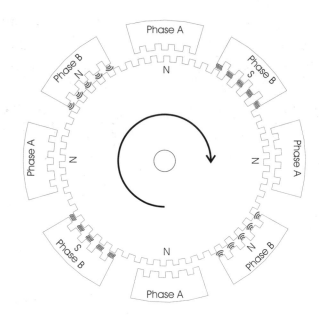

Figure 11-4 When phase B is energized and phase A is de-energized, the windings at 45 and 225 degrees become a magnetic south and attract the teeth of the magnetic north rotor cup. The windings at 135 and 315 degrees become a magnetic north and attract the teeth of the magnetic south rotor cup (not shown).

Figure 11-5 In single-phase excitation mode, the windings are turned on in sequence, but the polarity alternates between positive and negative on the same phase. This mode requires less power but delivers less torque than other excitation modes. (A) Phase A is energized, causing the north cup to align with the south pole pieces of phase A. (B) Phase B is energized, causing the north cup to align with the south pole pieces of phase B. This moves the shaft 1.8 degrees clockwise. (C) Phase A is energized in reverse polarity compared to step (A), causing the north cup to align with the south pole pieces of phase A [different pole pieces than in step (A)]. This moves the shaft an additional 1.8 degrees clockwise. The shaft is now 3.6 degrees away from its starting position. (D) Phase B is energized in reverse polarity compared to step (B), causing the north cup to align with the south pole pieces of phase B [different pole pieces than in step (B)]. This results in a shaft movement of 1.8 degrees clockwise. The shaft is now 5.4 degrees away from its starting position.

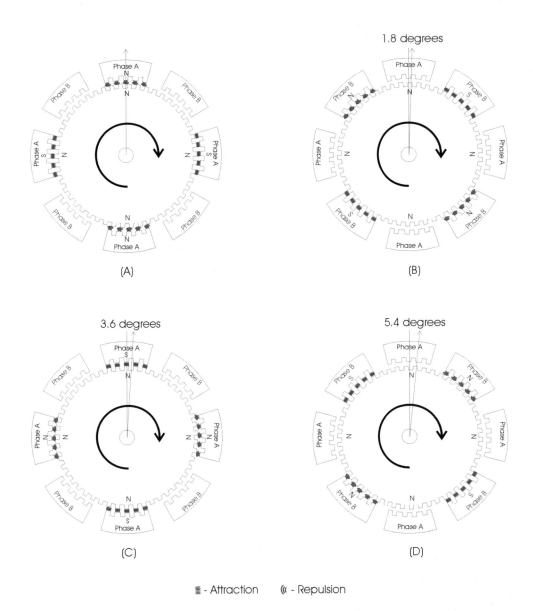

(A)   (B)

(C)   (D)

≣ - Attraction   《 - Repulsion

Dual-Phase Excitation Mode

By energizing both phases at one time and alternating their polarity in sequence, we can achieve the same full step motion as with the one-phase, full-step mode. This mode of excitation is known as dual-phase or "two phase on, full step" excitation. It requires twice as much input power but delivers 30–40% more torque.

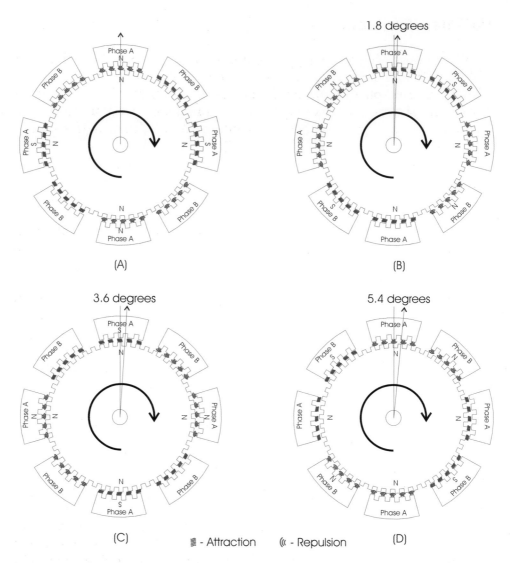

Figure 11-6 In dual-phase mode, both phases are turned on at once and the teeth of the rotor are locked between the two. Each time the polarity is changed the rotor moves a full step. This mode requires double the power input compared to single-phase mode, but it delivers 30–40% more torque.

Half-Step Excitation

By alternating between single-phase and dual-phase excitation, the rotor will move in half steps, resulting in twice the resolution but about 15% less torque than dual-phase stepping. By increasing the current in the windings during the single-phase step, the torque remains comparable to that of dual-phase stepping. This method is known as modified half stepping (Figure 11-7).

Microstepping

Microstepping is a technique that is often touted in automated lighting literature as a special feature. But, as we will see, it is fundamental to the smooth, natural movement of an automated luminaire.

Until now we have been discussing a hybrid stepper motor with 1.8 degree steps. With that degree of resolution, a 100-foot (30.5-m) throw yields a movement of 3 feet 2 inches (0.97 m), which is altogether unacceptable for fluid movement and accurate positioning of a luminaire. By microstepping a hybrid motor, we can increase the step resolution considerably. Suppose, for example, that you configure the control of a stepper motor so that you increase the resolution 256 times higher than a full step. Now, instead of moving 3 feet 2 inches (0.97 m) for every step at a 100-foot (30.5-m) throw, each step results in a movement of only 0.15 inches (3.81 mm).

Instead of simply energizing the windings fully on or fully off as in single-phase and dual-phase excitation, a sinusoidal input on phase A and a simultaneous cosine input on phase B produces, in theory, less than full steps and smoother rotation. In practice, the control signal is not a true sine or cosine, but it is typically modified by adding third-order harmonics in order to compensate for the geometry of the motor and how the shape of the teeth affects the torque at specific angles. Alternatively, a pulse-width modulated (PWM) control signal with a fixed voltage and variable current is often used to control a microstepping system (Figure 11-8). A PWM signal looks like a square wave with a variable duty cycle. The width of the pulse corresponds to the amount of energy that is sent to the motor. Although microstepping produces about 30% less torque than dual-phase stepping, it vastly improves smoothness of movement and positional accuracy.

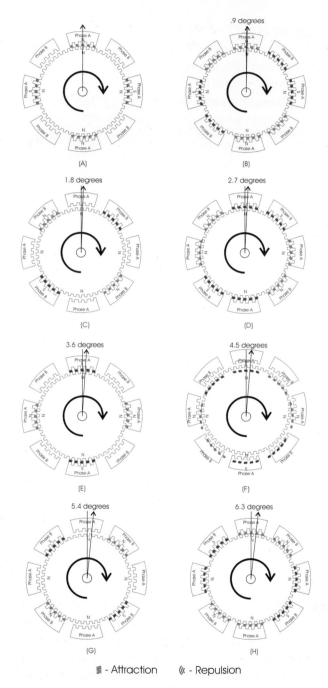

Figure 11-7 Alternating between single-phase and dual-phase excitation for each step results in half-step rotation. This mode provides about 15% less torque than dual-phase stepping, but by increasing the current in the winding during the single-phase step, the loss of torque can be eliminated.

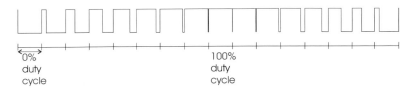

Figure 11-8 A pulse-width modulated (PWM) signal is often used to control stepper motors. The duty cycle varies according to the speed and torque required of the stepper.

Resonance

When a stepper motor moves from step to step, it tends to overshoot its destination and then overcorrect, moving back and forth a few times before finally stopping. This phenomenon is known as ringing, and it occurs each time a stepper motor takes a step.

The frequency at which ringing occurs is the natural resonant frequency of the system in which that stepper motor belongs. When the control frequency matches the natural resonant frequency of the system, the two frequencies reinforce each other, and it results in a very strong vibration known as resonance. If the vibrations are strong enough it can cause the motor to lose steps and fall out of synch. This can be a problem for automated lighting design engineers who understand how critical it is to maintain proper positioning. Consequently, much attention is paid to the problem of resonance, and the control software is written to avoid resonant frequencies. The resulting control system either accelerates quickly through the resonant frequency or skips the resonant frequency altogether by writing acceleration and deceleration curves into the control systems.

Some automated luminaires use a spring-loaded plunger to dampen the vibrations and reduce the resonance problem (Figure 11-9). In addition, the dampening helps prevent overshooting and the subsequent "nodding bucket" effect, in which the head of a moving yoke fixture wobbles until it comes to a complete stop. Dampening has another side effect: it exacerbates hysteresis. Hysteresis is a property of a system whereby its state depends on its recent history. For example, an automated luminaire can exhibit hysteresis in its pan and tilt system by stopping at a slightly different focus position depending on the direction from which it arrives. It is caused by slack in the gearing and other parts of the system. Also, the greater the dampening, the greater the hysteresis

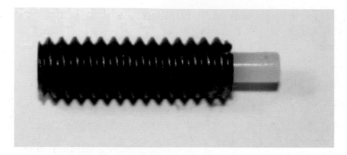

Figure 11-9 A spring plunger is sometimes used in pan and tilt systems to dampen vibrations and reduce resonance. They also increase hysteresis.

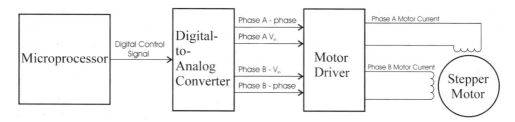

Figure 11-10 A stepper motor system consists of the motor, a controller, and a motor drive circuit. The motor drive circuit typically has a digital-to-analog converter (DAC) and a motor driver.

problem. Dampening is a trade-off between smooth movement and increased hysteresis.

If a stepper motor has gearing or a belt drive, as moving yoke fixtures do, then the gear ratio increases the resolution and decreases the resonance by a factor of the gear ratio. Gear ratios typically range from 1:4 to 1:8. For a gear ratio of 1:8, the resonance is decreased by a factor of eight and the resolution is increased by the same.

Stepper Motor Control Systems

In order for a stepper motor to move, it must have two additional system components: a controller and a motor drive circuit (Figure 11-10).

The control of a stepper motor in an automated luminaire originates at the console, which sends instructions to the luminaire via a DMX512 signal. The data are interpreted by an onboard processor, which then sends a digital control signal to the digital-to-analog converter (DAC). A typical converter is an eight-bit DAC, such as an Ericsson PBM 3960 eight-bit DAC. The DAC outputs two signals for each of the two phases in a two-phase bipolar stepper motor, one to control the speed and another to control the direction for each phase (four signals total). The analog outputs of the DAC are fed to a motor driver chip such as the Ericsson PBL 3771, which provides the current to drive the stepper motor. The final output of the motor driver is typically two constant current PWM control signals that are fed to each of the two windings in the stepper motor.

Some processors have a built-in DAC, in which case it is not necessary to use an external DAC and motor driver combination. Instead, a microcontroller with a built-in DAC outputs a PWM signal and an H-bridge is used to provide the current to drive the stepper motor. An H-bridge is a motor drive circuit with a power supply and four switches that can energize the stepper motor windings in either direction (Figure 11-11). The switches can be opened or closed by the PWM control signal in such a manner as to control the direction of current flow through the stepper motor windings and thus control the speed and direction of rotation.

Because motor driver chips are manufactured in relatively small quantities, they are relatively expensive to use with a microprocessor and DAC combination compared to a microcontroller with a built-in DAC and an H-bridge combination. When this type of control is used, then a sense resistor is used to detect the current flowing through the windings. That information is fed back to the microcontroller to create a closed loop between the stepper motor and the controller.

Position Sensing and Encoding

Steppers have no built-in position feedback to monitor the current angular position of the motor shaft. Yet it's imperative for an automated luminaire to keep track of the position of all of its functions at all times in order to operate accurately and reliably. Therefore, they always have secondary means of determining the starting position or home position of each stepper motor in the luminaire. In addition, most moving yoke fixtures have position encoders for their pan and tilt motors to count steps and monitor the

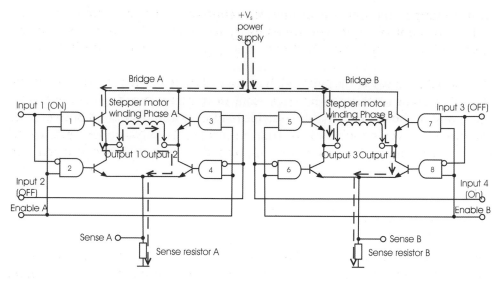

Figure 11-11 A simplified block diagram of a typical dual H-bridge. The four AND gates in each bridge act as a switch to turn the transistors ON and OFF. When both inputs are high (logic 1), then the AND gate turns on the transistor to which it is tied. In the bridge on the left, Input 1 is ON and Input 2 is OFF, and in the bridge on the right, Input 3 is OFF and Input 4 is ON. Note that the top input in AND gates 2, 4, 6, and 8 are NOT inputs (inverted inputs) so that when the input signal is high, the AND gate reads it as a low.

current position of the drives. They effectively make them stepper servo drives. Once the fixture is homed, the microprocessor keeps track of each step or fractional step taken by each stepper motor. That way, as long as the stepper does not lose synch, the fixture knows the current position of every stepper motor and, thus, each attribute of the fixture.

There are at least three methods of setting the home position of a stepper motor: a mechanical stop, a magnetic encoder, and an optical encoder.

The Mechanical Stop

The simplest means of setting the home position of a stepper motor is to physically restrain it from traveling beyond a predetermined point by use of a hard stop or a mechanical stop. A typical mechanical stop is simply a bolt or a standoff attached to the shaft of the motor that, at the far end of travel, hits another bolt or standoff, preventing it from traveling any farther.

Since stepper motors are inductively coupled, it simply stops the rotor while the control signal continues to try to rotate it. The result is a repetitive clicking sound associated with homing an automated luminaire.

In the early days of automated lighting, almost all attributes, including pan, tilt, color selection, and gobo selection, had a mechanical hard stop. As a result, the color and gobo wheels could not rotate beyond 360 degrees and had to reverse their direction at the end of travel. Now most automated luminaires have a hard stop for pan and tilt, though they can often pan 540 degrees.

Optical Sensing

In the case of effects wheels like color and gobo wheels, a mechanical stop prevents continuous rotation. In addition, it might have to rotate almost 360 degrees to change to an adjacent color or gobo if that color or gobo happens to be on the other side of the stop. A much better way of tracking position in a wheel is with the use of an optical sensor.

An optical sensor is an infrared (IR) transmitter and a photoelectric device, such as a photoresistor that senses the presence or absence of the IR beam (Figure 11-12). A photoresistor is a semiconductor, such as cadmium sulfide, that has a very high resistance in total darkness but decreases in resistance in proportion to the amount of light energy falling on it. In an optical sensor, when the IR beam path is interrupted it raises the resistance of the receptor and changes the output voltage of the photocell. When an opening allows the IR beam to pass uninterrupted, the resistance drops significantly, thus triggering an event in the feedback circuit.

In an automated light, a disc or wheel is positioned between the IR transmitter and optical receiver so that it either interrupts the path of the beam or is positioned close enough to the beam path that a protruding tab will interrupt the beam when it passes (Figure 11-13). In the first instance a notch cut in the disc allows the light to pass, and in the second instance the tab blocks the beam when it is in the home position. In each case, the interruption alerts the microprocessor that some event has occurred, with the event most likely being that the parameter in question is in the home position. From that point on, the microprocessor tracks the movement of the stepper motor and compares the results with the sensor each time the notch is detected.

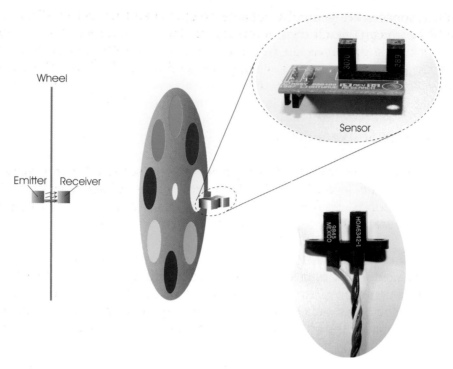

Figure 11-12 An optical sensor is used to signal the processor that a stepper motor is in its home position. It senses correct angular position of a wheel by detecting the presence or absence of an IR beam with the use of a photoreceptor. Left to right: Side view of wheel in optical path; isometric view of color wheel and optical sensor. Inset: PC board-mounted optical sensor and optical sensor with wire leads.

Figure 11-13 Left: Typical color wheel showing a notch that allows the IR beam to pass when the wheel is in the home position, signaling the processor to mark the stepper motor alignment. Right: Color wheel showing alternative homing tab, which blocks the IR beam when the color wheel is in the home position.

Optical sensors are generally reliable except when they get so dirty that the IR beam can't reach the photoreceptor. This often happens when dust collects in the gap between the transmitter and photoreceptor. Fog and haze exacerbate the problem when glycol and mineral oil coat the sensor and attract dust.

Hall Effect Sensors

In 1879, a physicist named Edwin Herbert Hall discovered that a current-carrying conductor in a magnetic field produced a voltage perpendicular to the direction of the flow of current and to the magnetic field. This phenomenon became known as the Hall effect (Figure 11-14).

A Hall effect sensor makes use of the Hall effect by generating a measurable voltage in the presence of a magnetic field (Figure 11-15). Automated luminaires sometimes employ Hall effect sensors in position-sensing circuits. By attaching a small magnet to a moving wheel, a Hall effect sensor sends a voltage signal to the processor indicating that the wheel is in the

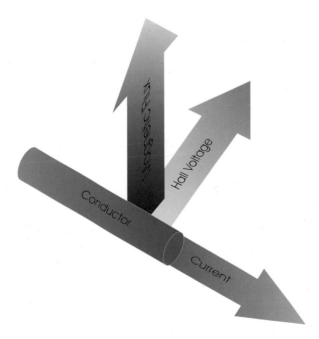

Figure 11-14 The voltage produced by a current-carrying conductor in the presence of a magnetic field is called the Hall voltage. This phenomenon is known as the Hall effect.

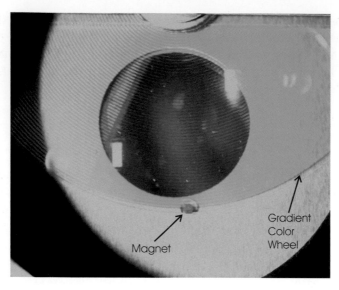

Figure 11-15 A small magnet attached to a moving wheel triggers a Hall effect sensor when the wheel is in the home position. The sensor then sends a voltage signal to the microprocessor.

home position. Once home is located, the microprocessor counts steps to keep track of the angular position of the stepper motor.

Hall effect sensors are normally very reliable as long as they remain positioned correctly. In some automated fixtures, they tend to move when they are handled roughly because the sensors have long leads holding them in place. If they move far enough then the magnetic field is too weak to trigger the sensor. The simple fix is to bend them back in place without breaking the leads.

Focus Correction

A feature unique to moving yoke fixtures found on some models is the ability to autocorrect the pan and tilt position in the event that it is bumped out of focus. This is an important feature in moving yoke fixtures because the yoke makes them more prone to being bumped, particularly if they are located on the floor or another accessible location.

Fixture manufacturers use different terminology for focus correction, including position encoding and automatic feedback, but functionally they are the same. They use optical sensors with an encoder wheel linked to the pan and tilt, or Hall effect sensors with a magnet linked to the pan and tilt. An encoder wheel is a small disc, approximately 3 to 4 inches (7.6 to 10.2 cm) in diameter with a series of small "windows" cut into the circumference of the disc that allow light to pass (Figure 11-16).

Fans

Cooling fans are another type of electromechanical device commonly used in automated lighting. Because of the intense heat generated by the lamp and power supply, air circulation is critical to the reliable operation of automated luminaires. If a fan fails and the lamp stays on, there is a strong possibility that the fixture will overheat and some components will be destroyed.

Cooling systems are becoming increasingly important in automated lighting for a few reasons. The ratio of power consumption to fixture size is increasing in automated lighting; automated lighting is increasingly finding applications in noise-critical environments like theatres and houses of worship; and cooling in the newer short arc technology lamps is very critical (they can't operate in open air without forced air cooling). As

Figure 11-16 This encoder wheel works with optical sensors to locate the angular position of a stepper motor. It feeds position information back to the microprocessor to automatically correct the position should it become misaligned. This feature is often used with pan and tilt in moving yoke fixtures.

manufacturers attempt to package high-powered automated lighting in ever-shrinking housings, heat management becomes a critical issue. At the same time, the demand for silent fixtures is driving the development of solutions with lower levels of audible noise. For this reason, some automated luminaires have DMX-controllable variable fan speed. However, those fans also have temperature control that overrides the user control to prevent overheating. Another approach to silencing fans is to use a noise-absorbing baffle.

The critical areas in an automated light that demand temperature control are along the optical path and near the electronic components. Consequently, fans are typically located in the head of moving yoke fixtures as well as in the base, where most of the sensitive electronics are located. In addition to selecting the proper fans based on air flow, size, power consumption, and noise ratings, the automated lighting engineer must be concerned with routing the air flow across the protected components and preventing, to the extent possible, light leakage.

Fan Types

There are at least two types of fans used in automated lighting: axial fans and radial fans. The most commonly used fans in automated lighting applications are axial fans, sometimes referred to as muffin fans (Figure 11-17).

Figure 11-17 Left to right: Axial fan; radial fan; squirrel cage fan.

Fan Cleaning and Maintenance

Since a fan circulates air through a luminaire, it is usually one of the central gathering spots for dust and filth. In order to maintain good airflow in the fixture, it's important to clean the fans regularly. Compressed air in a can is a convenient tool for blowing out all the dust and filth from the fan and fixture. However, it's important to prevent the fan from spinning from the force of the compressed air because it will generate back EMF (or voltage), and the resulting current flowing through the windings could overload and destroy the fan. Simply place your finger on a blade of the fan while blowing it out with compressed air.

CHAPTER 12

Mechanical Systems

If you want to achieve excellence, you can get there today. As of this second, quit doing less-than-excellent work.—Thomas John Watson, Jr., former CEO of IBM

The science and engineering of automated lighting systems have matured to the point at which reliability, in general, has greatly improved and the mean time between failures is surprisingly high. This wasn't always the case. Automated lighting used to be one part engineering and three parts reengineering.

Part of the reason for this improvement is the natural evolution and development of products, and part of it is due to the application of better materials, such as the introduction of high-tech plastics, and manufacturing techniques, such as surface mount technology. With smaller, more lightweight fixtures, the demands on the mechanical systems are not as great, but as manufacturers increasingly push the envelope of small size versus high output, the operating temperatures of the luminaires are going up, placing greater importance on heat management. At the same time, the demand for more and more light output is driving the production of larger fixtures. Even if they are more efficient, the 1200-watt and larger fixtures operate in an environment that demands careful engineering with a greater importance placed on materials and construction techniques. Also, the rigors of touring place great demands on the physical structure and strength of automated lighting.

If you have ever focused a PAR can or optimized the lamp in a Leko then you know how much heat a medium-sized fixture can generate. Lamp operating temperatures can reach 350°C (662°F) or higher, depending on the wattage. In order for a luminaire to operate reliably over its expected life, a variety of materials, including glass, optical coatings, metal and metal finishes, adhesives, lubricants, plastics, and rubber compounds, have to be able to withstand or be protected from immense heat. The components in the optical path—the reflector, IR glass, gobos, dichroic filters, and lenses—are perhaps most susceptible to heat damage. Even if the luminaire is designed with proper heat management, an improperly optimized lamp or a damaged IR filter could overload the heat-bearing capacity of those materials in the optical path. If a luminaire is not designed with good heat management, then the electronic components, which are designed to operate within specific temperature parameters, could be at risk for premature failure. If heat is not managed properly it could damage any or all of these components.

Perhaps more importantly, the components, particularly those in the optical path, need to interface in such a manner as to endure the constant cycle of expansion and contraction as they heat and cool. If their respective rates of expansion and contraction differ significantly, they could compress or expand beyond their capacity to withstand the pressure and cause mechanical damage. For these reasons, the mechanical systems in today's automated lighting are highly developed and well engineered.

Heat management is one of the major considerations in the design of automated lighting, but it's not the only consideration. Careful attention must be paid to protect against excessive shock and vibration, mechanical noise, electromagnetic radiation, and especially the hazards of electrical shock and fire. In addition, it is desirable, though not always necessary, to build lightweight luminaires that are small and easy to handle. This is particularly true when they will be used in temporary portable applications but is less of an issue in permanent installations. When fixtures will be temporarily set up and transported on a regular basis, the size and weight can dramatically influence the truck pack (the amount of space required to transport the lighting rig and thus the number of trucks and personnel and cost of transportation), the cost of fuel, and the ease and speed of load-in and load-out.

Materials

The choice of materials used in the fabrication and construction of automated lighting is a major influence on the durability, size, weight, aesthetic quality, and cost of the final product. There is a wide range of options from which to choose for almost every aspect of construction, and the methods and techniques are becoming more sophisticated and refined. Compared with the sheet metal construction of the early automated luminaires, today's fixtures are much more advanced. Some of the more common materials and fabrication techniques are discussed in the following sections.

Aluminum

Aluminum is by far the most common of the metals used in the fabrication of automated lighting. It is preferred over steel because it is one-third the weight, yet it has good strength and hardness and is relatively easy to work. It also is corrosion resistant, has very good thermal conductivity and electromagnetic interference (EMI) shielding properties, takes finishes well, and is recyclable. Aluminum is a commodity; its price fluctuates depending on the supply and demand. At roughly $1 per pound, it is relatively expensive compared to steel, yet its advantages more than outweigh the costs. Aluminum is used in everything from housings to stand-offs to gobos to reflectors to mechanical parts such as gears and lens tubes.

Rarely is pure aluminum used in the construction of automated lighting, with the sole exception of spun aluminum reflectors. Aluminum reflectors are electropolished by immersing them in an electrolyte bath and connecting them to the positive terminal of a DC power supply. The negative terminal attracts microscopic particles of aluminum from the reflector and results in a highly polished aluminum surface. It's the opposite of the process of electroplating. In the electropolishing process, the more pure the aluminum, the better the finish.

Aluminum parts in automated luminaires are more commonly alloyed with other elements to improve specific material properties. Copper, magnesium, manganese, zinc, silicon, iron, chromium, and nickel are commonly used in aluminum alloys. For example, 6061-T6 and 6082-T6 are alloys that are commonly used in North America and Europe, respectively, to fabricate truss and components. 6061-T6 contains 95.8–98.6% aluminum, 0.04–0.35% chromium, 0.15–0.4% copper, no more than 0.7% iron, 0.8–1.2% magnesium, no more than 0.15% manganese, 0.4–0.8% silicon, no more than 0.15% titanium, and no more than 0.25% zinc. This alloy combines the strength, workability (ease of welding), and corrosion resistance that make it ideal for certain applications. Aluminum extrusions and casting used in automated luminaires typically have higher aluminum content, but the alloys vary.

Aluminum can be rolled into sheets, extruded, or cast. Sheet aluminum can be cut, bent, punched, and drilled to form and fabricate parts such as gobo wheels and shutters. Computer numeric control (CNC) machines are often employed to fabricate hundreds or thousands of parts in a single day. CNC machines are computer driven using software models designed by engineers. This allows for precision, speed, accuracy, and repeatability in the manufacturing process.

Aluminum extrusions are commonly used for a variety of purposes in the structure of automated lighting. Aluminum is extruded by heating aluminum billets until they are malleable, then they are forced through a die to extrude the desired profile. The profile can then be cut to size, drilled, and tapped. Extruded aluminum housings used to be very popular and were used mainly with moving mirror fixtures such as Cyberlights, Roboscans, Intellabeams, and the Clay Paky scans. With the trend toward moving head fixtures, the popularity of plastics in fixture housings has overtaken that of aluminum, although aluminum extrusions and aluminum sheet metal are still used extensively to house the base of moving head fixtures.

Die cast aluminum parts are less common for large parts such as housings, but they are becoming more common for small precision parts. Aluminum parts are die cast by injecting high-pressure molten aluminum into a steel mold (called a tool). It is then cooled, solidified, and extracted. Casting aluminum is cost effective in high volumes, and it can achieve tight tolerances (high dimensional accuracy).

Stainless Steel

Stainless steel is an iron alloy with a minimum of 12% chromium, which helps prevent corrosion and oxidation. It is used primarily where high temperatures limit the use of aluminum, such as in the case of stainless steel gobos, and in highly corrosive atmospheres, such as onboard ships and in resorts that are in proximity to salt water. Stainless steel is relatively expensive compared to aluminum and steel, but its superior heat handling and corrosion resistance properties make it ideal for certain applications. There are several grades of stainless steel, but the two most commonly used in automated lighting are austenitic and ferritic grades. One of the most common of the austenitic grades of stainless steel is 18-8, which has 18% chromium and 8% nickel. 18-8 stainless steel is nonmagnetic, and the nickel component improves the corrosion resistance, especially at high temperatures. Ferritic stainless contains iron, which improves its strength at high temperatures. Both types are used for gobos when more detail and higher resolution are required than can be afforded with aluminum gobos. They are made by an etching process that affords relatively fine detail.

Plastics

A plastic is a chain of molecules called a polymer. Polymers are made by linking molecules of carbon, hydrogen, and sometimes other elements in a polymerization process. Plastics have become increasingly popular for use in automated lighting since the popularity of moving heads has overtaken that of moving mirrors. There are several reasons for this. Plastics are very lightweight, and when they are reinforced with fillers, such as aluminum powder, graphite, nylon, or fiberglass, they can exhibit much improved resistance to heat and chemicals, electrical insulation, and strength. They are also easier to stylize to add aesthetic appeal, which has become increasingly important in the marketplace. Also, plastic housings and parts are much cheaper to produce in large quantities, but in small quantities the cost of the tooling is relatively high and often prohibitive.

ABS (acrylonitrile butadiene styrene) is a polymer that is commonly used in the manufacture of automated luminaire housings. It is often mixed with flame retardants and UV inhibitors to protect against fire hazards and UV damage.

Glass

Glass is silica (sand) fused by heat with lime and an alkali, such as soda or potash. The alkalis help lower the melting point and thus make it easier to fuse, and the lime is a stabilizer. Additives are sometimes used to influence the properties of the final product. Boron, for example, increases the thermal and electrical resistance, while barium increases the refractive index.

There are several types of glass, but a few of them are more commonly used in automated lighting than others. Borosilicate glass, better known under the trade name Pyrex, is commonly used as a substrate for dichroic filters and glass gobos. A type of borosilicate glass called barium borosilicate glass made by Corning (7059 glass) and Borofloat made by Schott are used by several manufacturers for this purpose. They are made mostly of silica (SiO_2, 70–80%) and boric oxide (B_2O_3, 7–13%), plus small amounts of alkalis and aluminum oxide. The lower alkali content gives it good chemical durability and thermal shock resistance. It also has a low coefficient of expansion, which means that it doesn't expand and contract a great deal when it heats up and cools down. This property is very important because it prevents the optical thin-film coatings from separating from the substrate due to excessive expansion and contraction.

Fused Quartz

Pure SiO_2 glass, also known as fused quartz or fused silica, is manufactured by gassifying silicon and oxidating it to make silicon dioxide, then fusing the silicon dioxide dust to make glass. It has a remarkably low coefficient of thermal expansion, and it is transparent to UV and near IR wavelengths. For these reasons it is commonly used to make glass envelopes for halogen lamps and arc tubes for discharge lamps.

Optical Glass

Optical glass, which is used to make lenses and critical optical elements, is manufactured under very carefully controlled circumstances in order to accurately reproduce certain characteristics useful in the design of optical systems. Consequently, it can be very expensive. Optical glass is classified according to its index of refraction, coefficient of dispersion, coefficient of optical transmission, purity, hardness, and more. There are certain additives, such as calcium fluorite, phosphate, zinc, barium, lanthanum, and antimony, that can be introduced in the manufacturing process to shape the characteristics of the final product. The two principal types of optical glass are crown glass and flint glass, but there are many variations of each. Additives are used in their construction to tailor the product to the application.

Metal Finishes

Once the parts for an automated luminaire are fabricated, they are often finished to provide additional protection and aesthetic value and to control light reflections. One of the most common metal finishes is powder coating, an application of a resin-based paint that is durable enough to withstand the rigors of touring, resist wear, and provide electrical insulation. The powder coating process takes place in a paint booth whereby electrically charged powder coating material is sprayed on the parts to be painted, which are electrically grounded. The electrostatic attraction between the coating material and the metal ensures uniform coverage and holds the powder to the part until it is cured with heat. If the uncured powder is blemished for any reason, it can be blown off with compressed air and reapplied. Powder coating is an efficient process because most of the powder overspray can be reclaimed and used again.

Fasteners

The fasteners used in the manufacture of automated lights play the dual important roles of securing the integrity of the joined material and allowing for easy access for serviceability. There are many types of fasteners, including bolts, screws, rivets, welding, and adhesives. Most of the joints in automated lighting components are fastened with threaded fasteners.

A bolt is distinguished from a screw by the fact that a bolt always has a standard thread with a parallel shaft. It fits into a nontapered nut, threaded hole, or a nut insert. A screw, on the other hand, always cuts its own thread on the first insertion, and that thread is nonstandard and tapered (Figure 12-1). Consequently, a housing made of sheet metal should not be fastened with screws (it's been attempted before).

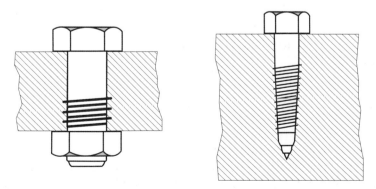

Figure 12-1 Hex cap bolt (left) and hex cap screw (right).

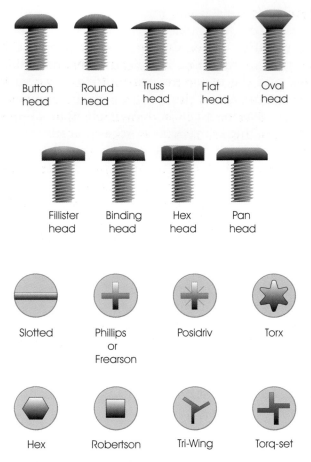

Figure 12-2 Various screw and bolt head shapes and drive types.

There are a variety of bolts and screws, as shown in Figure 12-2. Some of the most commonly used in our industry include socket head screws, hex bolts, and square head cup point set screws for c-clamps and sheet metal screws. Many of the fasteners used for components that require regular access, such as lamp access doors, use captive fasteners in order to prevent the hardware from getting lost or falling into the fixture. A variety of fasteners are also illustrated in Figure 12-2.

Thread Standards

The American standard for fastener threads is currently ANSI B1.1-2003/ ASME B1.1-2003:Unified Inch Screw Threads, UN and UNR Thread Form. Fasteners that are manufactured to conform to this standard are known as unified threads. The standard that covers metric threads is ANSI B1.13M-2001: Metric Screw Threads-M Profile. Fasteners that are manufactured to conform to this standard are known as M-series.

In the design of mechanical systems, inch series bolt and screw threads are designated by their nominal size or diameter, pitch (number of threads per inch), thread series (either course or fine), thread class (tolerance), and whether it's an internal thread or an external thread. For example, a typical inch series thread designation showing the nominal size, pitch, thread series, and class is

$$\text{½-20UNC-2A}$$

For metric series threads, the designation differs. A typical metric series thread designation showing nominal diameter, pitch (mm), and tolerance classification (lowercase = external thread) is

$$\text{4g6g(22) M6x1}$$

In addition to thread designations, fasteners are rated according to their tensile strength, which is extremely important for load-bearing structures like trussing and c-clamps. The grade of steel used in the fabrication of fasteners determines the tensile strength (Tables 12-1, 12-2, and 12-3).

It's important to use the proper sized tool and driver to remove and replace fasteners or they can be damaged. Also, remember the mnemonic for removing and replacing mechanical fasteners: "lefty loosey, righty tighty."

Preventing Vibrational Loosening

The main advantage of using a mechanical fastener over a permanent bond is that it allows for easy access for service and maintenance. The disadvantage is that it can become unfastened unintentionally due to vibrational

Table 12-1 Society for Automotive Engineers (SAE) bolt strengths. Reprinted with permission from SAE J429 ©1999 SAE International.

SAE Grade Number	Size (inches)	Minimum Proof Strength (kpsi)	Minimum Tensile Strength (kpsi)	Minimum Yield Strength (kpsi)	Material	Head Marking
1	$1/4$–$1\frac{1}{2}$	33	60	36	Low or medium carbon	
2	$1/4$–$3/4$	55	74	57	Low or medium carbon	
	$7/8$–$1\frac{1}{2}$	33	60	36		
4	$1/4$–$1\frac{1}{2}$	65	115	100	Medium carbon, cold drawn	
5	$1/4$–1	85	120	92	Medium carbon, quenched & tempered	
	$1\frac{1}{8}$–$1\frac{1}{2}$	74	105	81		
5.2		85	120	92	Low-carbon martensite, quenched & tempered	
7	$1/4$–$1\frac{1}{2}$	105	133	115	Medium-carbon alloy, quenched & tempered	
8	$1/4$–$1\frac{1}{2}$	120	150	130	Medium-carbon alloy, quenched & tempered	
8.2		120	150	130	Low-carbon martensite, quenched & tempered	

Table 12-2 ASTM bolt strengths.

ASTM Grade	Size (inches)	Minimum Proof Strength (kpsi)	Minimum Tensile Strength (kpsi)	Minimum Yield Strength (kpsi)	Material	Head Marking
A307	¼–1½	33	60	36	Low carbon	
A325, type 1	½–1 1⅛–1½	85 74	120 105	92 81	Medium carbon, quenched & tempered	
A325, type 2	½–1 1⅛–1½	85 74	120 105	92 81	Low-carbon martensite, Q&T	
A325, type 3	½–1 1⅛–1½	85 74	120 105	92 81	Weathering steel, quenched & tempered	
A354, grade BC					Alloy steel, quenched & tempered	
A354, grade BD	¼–4	120	150	130	Alloy steel, Q&T	
A449	¼–1 1⅛–1½ 1¾–3	85 74 55	120 105 90	92 81	Medium carbon, quenched & tempered 58	
A490, type 1	½–1½	120	150	130	Alloy steel, quenched & tempered	
A490, type 3					Weathering steel, quenched & tempered	

Table 12-3 Metric bolt strengths.

Property Class	Size (mm)	Minimum Proof Strength (MPa)	Minimum Tensile Strength (MPa)	Minimum Yield Strength (MPa)	Material	Head Marking
4.6	M5–M36	225	400	240	Low or medium carbon	
4.8	M1.6–M16	310	420	340	Low or medium carbon	
5.8	M5–M24	380	520	420	Low or medium carbon	
8.8	M16–M36	600	830	660	Medium carbon, quenched & tempered	
9.8	M1.6–M16	650	900	720	Medium carbon, quenched & tempered	
10.9	M5–M36	830	1040	940	Low-carbon martensite, quenched & tempered	
12.9	M1.6–M36	970	1220	1100	Alloy, quenched & tempered	

loosening. In automated luminaires there is abundant opportunity for such vibrational loosening, whether from rough handling from stage hands or from bouncing around in the back of a tractor-trailer rig traversing the outback of Australia. Extreme temperature changes can also contribute to the loosening of fasteners. When a lighting rig spends the night in the back of truck in the dead of winter in Toronto and is put up first thing in the morning, the internal temperature of a luminaire will change from freezing to extremely hot in a very short period of time. The cycle of contraction and expansion is very hard on fastened joints.

Fortunately, there are a number of options for securing fasteners to help prevent vibrational loosening. The American Standards Subcommittee B18:20 identified three categories of locking fasteners: free spinning, friction locking, and chemical locking. Free spinning fasteners have a row of ramped teeth under the head that allow the bolt to rotate in the tightening direction but not in the loosening direction. Friction locking fasteners, such as Nyloc nuts, have nylon inserts that prevent vibrational loosening. Chemical locking solutions, such as Loctite, are adhesives that bond the threads of the male and female parts. It is believed that conventional spring lock washers are not effective and may actually promote vibrational loosening rather than prevent it.

Gears

A gear is a means of transferring energy in the form of angular motion from one gear to another, changing the speed of rotation and the torque through mechanical advantage in the process. In automated luminaires, gears are sometimes used to trade speed for greater torque or greater accuracy or to translate the rotary motion of a motor into linear motion in order to reposition focus and zoom lenses.

In a gear train with a large gear and a small gear, the large gear is called a wheel and the small gear is called a pinion. The ratio of the number of gear teeth in each of the two gears is known as the gear ratio. For example, if the driving gear has 64 teeth and the driven gear has 32, then the gear ratio is 2:1. The first number in a gear ratio is the gear to which power is applied. The inverse of the gear ratio indicates how the speed and torque are transferred. In a 2:1 gear ratio, for example, the second gear rotates twice as fast as the first gear but has half the torque.

Figure 12-3 A spur gear is flat and its teeth are in the same plane as the rest of the gear. Left: Profile of a spur gear. Right: A spur gear mounted on a stepper motor shaft.

There are several different types of gears, the most common of which is a spur gear (Figure 12-3). A spur gear is flat and its teeth are in the same plane as the rest of the gear. All spur gears in a gear train have to be in the same plane in order to function, and all the gear axles have to be parallel to each other.

A rack and pinion is a type of gear train that has a spur gear that mates to a linear gear. It converts rotary motion to linear motion. The spur gear is called a pinion and the linear gear is the rack. This is one of two methods used to adjust focus and zoom lenses in an automated luminaire. The other method uses a worm gear, which is a type of helical gear with one tooth in the form of a screw thread (Figure 12-4). It has a large gear ratio, which helps move the greater distances required by the lenses.

Gears in automated luminaires can be made of aluminum, stainless steel, brass, or plastic. Brass gears wear well because of their hardness, but they are relatively heavy and more expensive than gears made of other materials. Plastic gears can be injection molded with unfilled or fiberglass-

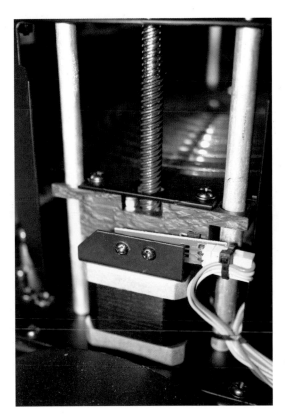

Figure 12-4 A worm gear shown in a Fresnel focus mechanism.

reinforced polymers. They are lightweight, relatively inexpensive in large quantities, quiet, and relatively durable. Plastic gears used to be reserved for low-torque applications because they weren't strong enough for more heavy-duty applications. But improved materials and molding processes are changing the way plastic gears are used. They can help reduce the weight of automated luminaires, reduce friction and noise, and reduce costs. Aluminum alloys are also used to make lightweight, relatively inexpensive gears.

Belts

A belt drive is functionally similar to a gear drive in that it transfers motion and changes the rate of rotation and the torque. The ratios of the speed reduction and torque amplification are both equal to the ratio of the radii

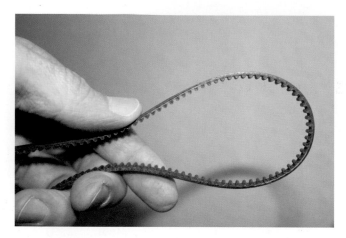

Figure 12-5 A toothed belt is functionally similar to a spur gear.

of the prime mover and the load, assuming no slipping. Toothless belts rely strictly on friction to prevent slipping, but belts with teeth are functionally similar to a spur gear (Figure 12-5). Such belts are known as synchronous belts. Belts are typically made with polyurethane and reinforced with fiber.

SECTION 4
Optical Systems

CHAPTER 13

Lamp Technology

The electric light has caused me the greatest amount of study and has required the most elaborate experiments.—Thomas A. Edison

Some of the biggest advances in automated lighting technology have been in the area of optical systems. Computer-aided design of reflectors, lithographic techniques, and optical thin-film coatings have helped to improve efficiency, color saturation, and the clarity of image projection. But perhaps the biggest advances have been in the area of lamp technology—the area with the most potential for advances. Years of research have led to the development of lamps with improved average life, color rendering, imaging, and efficiency. Still, our most efficient lamp sources waste more than half of the energy they are fed.

The Incandescent Lamp

Since the commercialization of automated lighting systems, the majority of them have used arc lamps. Over the years there have been a few fixtures using incandescent lamps, including the Vari-Lite VL5. But recently, some automated lighting manufacturers have recognized the demand for high-end automated lighting with an incandescent lamp source. Among them are the Vari-Lite VL1000 Tungsten ERS, the VL500, and the ETC Source Four Revolution.

There are several reasons for the market's interest in automated lighting with an incandescent lamp source. Incandescent lamps have a characteristic color temperature, spectral distribution, and color rendering that are difficult to match with discharge lamps. By using incandescent lamps, the automated lighting will more closely match the quality of light from conventional lighting. And incandescent lamps can be dimmed electronically, which is much smoother than a mechanically dimmed discharge lamp.

They are also generally less expensive to replace than discharge lamps, and because they draw no power when they are 100% dimmed (save for the inefficiency of the dimmer) they can potentially save energy and money.

The drawbacks are that they are less efficient than discharge lamps, they change color temperature as they dim, and they can lose lamp life due to physical shock, vibration (e.g., bass notes), and overvoltage. An incandescent lamp produces less than 30 lumens per watt, while a discharge lamp produces as much as 85 lumens per watt.

Incandescence

When an object is so hot that it begins to glow or emit light, it is said to be incandescing. Consequently, an incandescent lamp is any lamp that emits light by the process of incandescence. An incandescent lamp has a filament—a fine wire made of tungsten or an alloy of tungsten—through which a current is passed. Due to the resistance in the filament, the current causes it to heat to the point of incandescence (Figure 13-1).

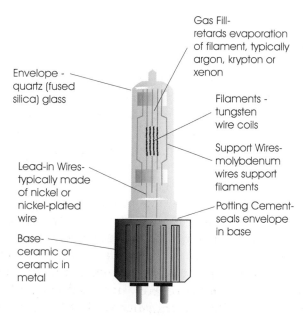

Figure 13-1 Incandescent lamp, filament, and quartz envelope.

Most stage and studio lamps are made with a quartz (fused silica) envelope. Quartz, with a softening point of 1600°C, can withstand the very high temperatures associated with higher powered lamps, it transmits visible light very well while blocking some UV, and it's very hard. Because of the extremely high operating temperature on the surface of a quartz envelope, precautions should be taken against touching it with bare hands, not only because it is a burn hazard, but also because the oil from your hands will deposit on the envelope and could cause the lamp to explode when it reaches operating temperature. Oil also forms a seed point for the quartz to divitrify. Always wear gloves or use a tissue when handling a quartz lamp. If you inadvertently touch the lamp with your bare hands, wipe it with alcohol to remove the oil and clean the surface.

Gas Fill

When a metal, like tungsten, is heated in the presence of oxygen it oxidizes and decomposes. To extend the life of the filament, incandescent lamps are either sealed in a vacuum or filled with an inert gas like argon, krypton, or xenon. These fill gasses do not react with metals and therefore do not promote oxidation or deterioration. The Philips HPL (ETC Source Four lamp), for example, has a krypton gas fill.

Halogen Lamps

Even with a gas fill, the extreme temperature of the filament causes it to slowly evaporate over time. When enough of the filament evaporates it becomes so thin that it eventually breaks, leading to the normal end of its life. By adding a halogen to the fill, the lamp life is extended and it can operate at higher temperatures, which produces a higher color temperature.

A halogen is an element that easily forms a salt compound by being combined with other elements. Halogens, like bromine or iodine, become a gas at the operating temperature of the lamp. They extend the life of a halogen lamp by a process known as the halogen cycle. As the filament incandesces, the intense heat boils off molecules of tungsten, and the tungsten vapor circulates in the envelope by convection. In a nonhalogen lamp, the tungsten molecules are deposited on the inner wall of the envelope after condensing on the relatively cooler surface, eventually creating a dark film that contributes to lumen depreciation (over time, less light is emitted from the lamp). This is the process of blackening. In a halogen lamp, the evaporated tungsten molecules combine with oxygen and halogen to form tungsten oxyhalide molecules. As the tungsten oxyhalide molecules circulate in the envelope, the heat from the filament break them down as they near the filament. The tungsten is then redeposited on the filament, and the oxygen and halogen molecules are free to start the process all over again (Figure 13-2).

Figure 13-2 The halogen cycle extends the life of a halogen lamp. (1) Tungsten is boiled off the filament and becomes vapor. (2) Halogen gas combines with tungsten vapor to form a salt compound. (3) Convection currents circulate the compound until it comes in contact with the filament. (4) The heat of the filament breaks down the compound and the tungsten is redeposited on the filament. (5) The halogen molecule becomes free to renew the cycle.

The halogen cycle is not a perfect process, however, because of the non-uniform distribution of tungsten during the redeposition process. In the end, a weak spot in the filament causes it to break, bringing the lamp life to an end. Also, the cycle only works when the lamp is operated at its rated voltage; when it is dimmed, the halogen cycle ceases to work, leading to lamp blackening. Therefore, it's a good idea to run halogen lamps at full for about 5 minutes at the end of a show in order to "scrub" the envelopes.

The more highly reactive the halide additive, the more effective the cycle. The more reactive halogens produce a stronger bond with the tungsten and oxygen. It takes a higher temperature to detach them; therefore, the tungsten is only deposited on the hottest part of the filament, which also happens to be the thinnest part of the filament. The downside is that the more reactive halogens also attack the quartz envelope and filament, so there must be a compromise. Fluorine and chlorine are the most reactive halogens, but they are too corrosive for the envelope and filament. Bromine is the most common additive in halogen lamps, followed by iodine. Even with these less reactive additives, they still attack the filament near the pinch where it is relatively cool, an effect called the beaver attack. Other elements are also typically combined with halogens to form a salt additive. For example, dysprosium bromide is often used as an additive in halogen lamps because the dysprosium adds spectral lines to enhance the quality of the light.

The halogen cycle also allows the lamp to be operated at higher temperatures since the filament is constantly being rebuilt. The higher operating temperature translates to a brighter and whiter light output. Halogen lamps are normally enclosed in a small quartz capsule, enabling them to be very compact.

Color Temperature

Any discussion of lamps would be incomplete without mention of color temperature. Color temperature is a function of the spectral power distribution of light, or the balance between the different wavelengths across the visible light spectrum.

Natural visible light is made up of a continuous spectrum of wavelengths from 400 to 700 nm. In terms of the color spectrum, it contains every color in the rainbow, from red to ultraviolet (Figure 13-3).

400nm   700nm

Figure 13-3 Natural visible light ranges from ultraviolet (wavelength about 400 nm) to red (wavelength about 700 nm).

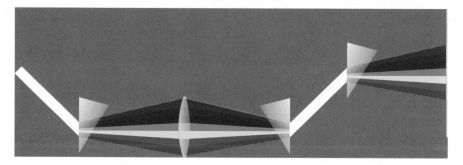

Figure 13-4 In 1665, Sir Isaac Newton's *experimentum crucis* proved that sunlight is made up of a continuous spectrum of color by breaking it into its component colors and recombining them with a pair of prisms. A shaft of light from a hole in a window shutter passes through a glass prism, causing it to break into its component colors. The spectrum is then focused by a convex lens and passes through a second prism, which reconstitutes the white light. The light is then diffracted through a third prism, again splitting it into its components and projecting them onto a white screen.

In 1665 Sir Isaac Newton used a prism to break sunlight into a spectrum of colors and then recombined the colors into white light with a second prism (Figure 13-4).

This is one of the keys to understanding color temperature. Color temperature is a measure of the balance between the red and blue components of a given light source. Light with a higher color temperature contains more blue light, while light with a lower color temperature contains more red light.

For example, consider that you're a blacksmith and you have an iron in the fire. When you first put it in, the iron is cold and black. The hot fire begins to heat it up, and as it heats, you observe that it starts to glow. As the temperature of the iron increases, it goes through a range of colors. When it first starts to glow it looks red. Then, as it heats up more, it turns orange, then it turns yellow, and when it gets really hot it looks white. If the iron were to get any hotter it would melt. The reason that there is a dominant color at a certain temperature is because the intensity of the wavelengths, or colors, varies across the spectrum. At first, most of the heat energy radiates in the lower part of the spectrum, causing the iron to emit more red wavelengths than any other. As it gets hotter, the energy shifts up the spectrum, causing it to emit a little less from the red end of the spectrum and a little more from the blue end of the spectrum (Figure 13-5). The result is that the light shifts from red, to orange, to yellow, and finally to white. If the iron could withstand higher temperatures, then it would eventually start to look more bluish.

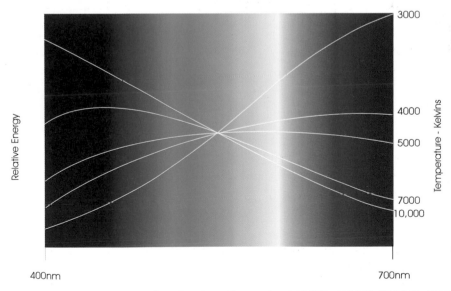

Figure 13-5 Spectral power distribution charts for 3000 K, 4000 K, 5000 K, 7000 K, and 10,000 K.

This is referred to as color temperature because there is a correlation between the color of the light emitted by incandescence and the temperature, in Kelvin, of the incandescing object. Color temperature uses the Kelvin scale, which is a temperature scale named after British physicist Lord William Thompson Kelvin. The Kelvin scale is also known as absolute temperature because 0 Kelvin is the coldest possible temperature. By analyzing the color temperature of light being emitted from a star, scientists can determine the surface temperature of that star.

Tungsten is used for the filament of incandescent lamps because it has a relatively high melting point of about 3672 K (3399°C) compared with other metals such as nickel (1725 K) and steel (1644 K). Most stage and studio incandescent lamps have a color temperature of about 3200 K, which is about the maximum operating temperature for the reliable long-term operation of a filament lamp (Figure 13-6).

400nm   700nm

Figure 13-6 A stage and studio incandescent lamp exhibits a color temperature of about 3200 K.

Incandescent Lamp Efficiency

Of the light emitted by an incandescent lamp, only about 10% of it is in the visible range. Stage and studio incandescent lamps have a luminous efficiency, or efficacy, of about 20 to 30 lumens per watt. The vast majority of the light generated by an incandescent lamp is heat radiation or infrared energy. This is a major consideration in the design of installed lighting systems because it affects the HVAC (heating, ventilation, and air conditioning) system. (See Chapter 27, Design Issues, Thermal Load Calculations section.)

Dimming Incandescent Lamps

Dimming an incandescent lamp is a simple matter of lowering the voltage to the lamp or, in the case of theatrical dimmers, chopping the sine wave midcycle to reduce the duty cycle of the current waveform. The main component of a theatrical dimmer is some variety of electronic switching, usually either a triac or an SCR (silicon controlled rectifier). These are electronic components that can switch current on or off by means of a low-voltage control signal. By turning on the voltage at some point during the sine wave (forward phase control), the duty cycle of the sine wave can be varied according to the percentage of the cycle that it was on versus the percentage that it was off (Figure 13-7).

This has the effect of lowering the RMS value of the voltage and dimming the lamp. However, as the voltage drops, so does the current and, thus, the color temperature. If dropping the color temperature with the dimming intensity is unacceptable, then mechanical dimming can be used.

The latest dimming technology uses insulated gate bipolar transistors (IGBT), a type of switching device that is similar to a field effect transistor (FET). They essentially chop the input voltage into thin slices of varying amplitude to recreate a sine wave (Figure 13-8). The amplitude of the output sine wave can be controlled very precisely, thus controlling the level of dimming. The advantage of IGBT dimming is that it reproduces a sine wave instead of a chopped sine wave. As a result, it produces no lamp vibration of "filament sing," resulting in a very quiet dimmer. It is also more efficient than a conventional dimmer because it doesn't need a choke coil, which introduces inefficiency and heat losses.

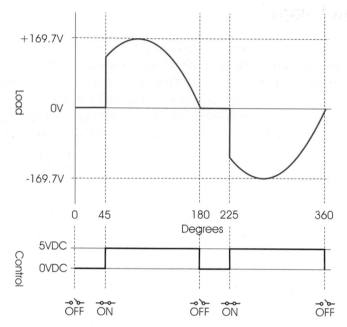

Figure 13-7 By switching on the voltage to a lamp during the sine wave, the RMS voltage to the lamp can be varied, thus dimming the lamp accordingly.

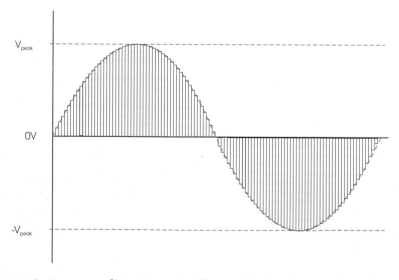

Figure 13-8 A sine wave dimmer varies the amplitude of the output sine wave by chopping the voltage into thin sections of varying amplitude and recreating an amplitude-controlled sine wave.

Discharge Lamps

Discharge lamps are far more common in automated lighting than incandescent lamps, primarily because they are more efficient and are able to produce far more lumens per watt, plus they have a relatively small light source so it's easier to design more efficient optics around them. Unlike an incandescent lamp, a discharge lamp has no filament. Instead, it has a pair of electrodes that sustain an arc in the gap between them. The arc emits visible light in much the same way that the arc of a welder produces a brilliant light.

Anatomy of a Discharge Lamp

The parts of a discharge lamp are shown in Figure 13-9. The electrodes are made of tungsten and are enclosed in a hermetically sealed quartz envelope. The envelope is filled with a cocktail of gas, metal, and salts. The gas aids in starting the arc. When a high voltage is applied to the electrodes, the gas ionizes and creates a path of low impedance across the gap, causing the arc to jump the electrodes. Once the arcing process begins, the heat from the discharge vaporizes the metals and they become the primary source of illumination. The salts enhance the quality of the light produced by the lamp by adding lines of emission. Each metal and salt component provides a series of emission lines at various wavelengths that contribute to the spectral distribution. In an MSR (medium source rare earth) type lamp, for example, dysprosium iodide emits many spectral lines, which helps to improve the color rendering of the lamp. Caesium (cesium in North America) iodide is also added to help widen the arc and, secondarily, to add more spectral lines. Mercury bromide helps keep the salts from attacking the bulb wall and the tungsten electrodes.

Some very high-pressure lamps, such as the UHP lamp, have no salt additives, with the exception of mercury bromide. The extremely high pressure inside the envelope causes the mercury to emit more spectral lines, producing acceptable white light. This is a relatively new technology that works well with lamps up to 250 watts; researchers are working on ways to increase that limit.

The electrodes are electrically connected to the lamp socket by a foil made of molybdenum doped with yttrium (to prevent corrosion). The molybdenum foil, or moly foil, is a good conductor, with a coefficient of expansion

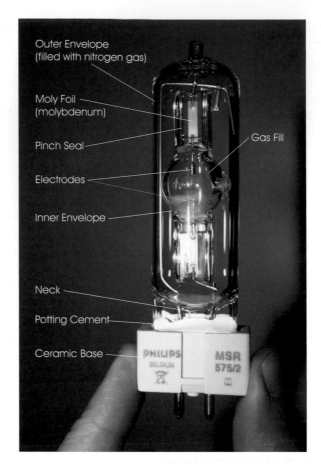

Figure 13-9 A typical single-ended discharge lamp.

that closely matches that of the quartz envelope. That makes it suitable for conducting current through the quartz with a minimum amount of stress between the foil and the quartz. If it were to expand and contract at a different rate than the quartz, it would separate from the quartz and cause the seal to leak and the lamp to fail. As it is, the pinch seal is the weakest link in a lamp. One of the biggest problems is that the quartz doesn't "wet" molybdenum, so it's difficult to seal at the edge of the foil. For that reason, the foil is constructed with tapered edges so that they are as thin as possible. Even with the seal as tight as possible, the foil tends to oxidize with use. As the oxidation grows and creeps along the foil (it's sometimes visible as a darkening of the foil, but it requires very close inspection), it causes expansion and can crack the quartz. The problem is addressed by plating the molybdenum with materials such as chrome to help prevent oxidation. This process is what Philips calls P3 technology. A similar process from Osram is marketed as XS technology.

MSR lamps usually have an outer envelope with a nitrogen gas fill. It acts as an insulator to keep the operating temperature stable. HMI type lamps usually don't have an outer jacket.

Starting a Discharge Lamp

A discharge cold lamp exhibits high impedance across the electrodes. Certain conditions must exist for the arcing process to begin. First of all, the electrodes must be close enough and the voltage must be high enough for the arc to jump the gap. If the electrodes are too far apart, the arc cannot get started. By the same token, if the voltage is not high enough, it cannot initiate the arc.

The lamp design determines the electrode spacing, or the length of the arc gap compared to the length of the arc tube. Medium arc lamps can have an arc gap of about 3 to 10 mm, while a short arc or a compact arc lamp can have a gap from 0.3 to 25 mm. The starting voltage is also a function of lamp design but is typically several thousand volts. A lamp circuit in a fixture is designed to meet the criteria for the starting voltage for a particular lamp with a lamp starter, or ignitor, that generates the required voltage according to the lamp specifications.

The pressure and temperature in the lamp also affect the ability of the lamp to initiate an arc. When starting with a cold lamp, it takes several thousand volts to start a discharge lamp. The ignitor in a discharge lamp circuit is designed to provide the initial high starting voltage. When the ignitor receives the signal to start the lamp, it places a high voltage across the electrodes for a short period of time. The high voltage ionizes the gas in the capsule, causing the impedance across the gap to drop. If the conditions are right (short enough gap, high enough voltage, low enough temperature), then an arc will jump across the electrodes and close the circuit, and current will begin to flow. If the arc fails to connect, then the ignitor will continue to output a high voltage pulse until it successfully starts the arc or until the fixture shuts down the ignitor. When the ignitor is trying to start the lamp, an audible zapping sound can be heard. After the current starts flowing, the ignitor drops out of the circuit and the voltage normalizes at approximately 70 to 90 volts.

When the lamp strikes and the current begins to flow, the lamp begins heating up. It takes approximately 5 minutes, depending on the lamp size, to reach its full operating temperature.

Hot Restrike Lamps

Once the operating temperature has been reached, the increased temperature makes it much more difficult to start the arcing process. If a discharge lamp has been operating for at least several minutes and goes out, it has to cool for about 5 minutes before it can be started again unless it is designated as a hot restrike (HR) lamp and the lamp circuitry is designed to support HR lamps. An HR lamp circuit is designed to apply much higher voltage, approximately 10 times the normal starting voltage, to strike the lamp. An HR lamp is designed with a much bigger base and electrodes to prevent arcing across the pins and to withstand the higher starting voltage.

Discharge Lamp Characteristics

Gas discharge lamps have a distinctively different quality than incandescent lamps, primarily because, unlike an incandescent lamp, a discharge lamp has a discontinuous spectrum. The discharge produces a series of wavelengths in the visible spectrum that, taken as a whole, are perceived as white light. The spectral content has a major influence on the color rendering and the color temperature.

Spectral Power Distribution

The spectral distribution of a discharge lamp shows a series of emission lines at different wavelengths, each of which is a contribution from one of its additives (Figure 13-10).

Because of the discontinuity of the spectrum, discharge lamps have a unique spectral quality that is unlike that of natural light. The additives aid in shaping the spectral distribution and influence the color temperature and color rendering by enhancing certain colors in the spectrum to simu-

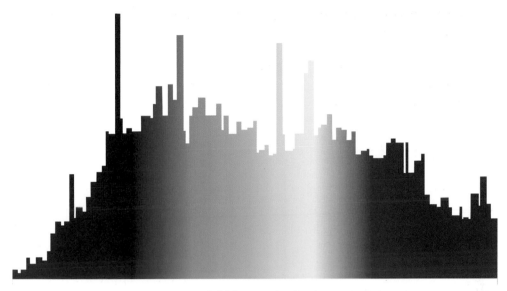

For illustration purposes only - not to scale.

Figure 13-10 The spectral power distribution of a discharge lamp is not continuous as in an incandescent lamp. Instead, it exhibits peaks and troughs at various wavelengths.

late the spectral distribution of natural light. Even though the spectral distribution has these peaks and valleys, the human eye perceives the light as white light with a continuous spectrum. For that reason, we can correlate it to an equivalent color temperature, called the correlated color temperature (CCT) (Figure 13-11). However, even though the CCT might be the same as the color temperature, the way it renders colors could be very different. Therefore, it is important to consider not only the CCT of a discharge lamp, but also the color rendering index (CRI), which indicates on a scale of 0 to 100 how natural a colored object looks when illuminated by the light.

The discharge lamps most commonly used in automated lighting have a CCT of about 5600 K or higher. Some are as high as 7800 K, which automated lighting manufacturers tend to favor because a higher CCT appears to be brighter to the eye. Discharge lamps tend to emphasize the blue end of the spectrum because they are more efficient at higher color temperatures. Consequently, most automated fixtures are very good at rendering colors in the high end of the spectrum, like ultraviolet and deep blue, and they are not so good at rendering colors in the low end, such as deep red.

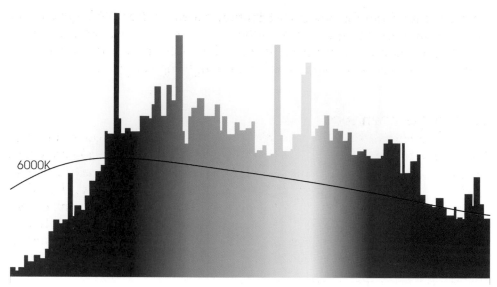

For illustration purposes only - not to scale.

Figure 13-11 The human eye perceives the spectral power distribution of a discharge lamp, within certain limits, as white light with a color temperature that correlates to that of a continuous spectrum light source. This allows us to measure it as a correlated color temperature (CCT). This is true as long as the CCT is not too far away from the natural spectral distribution of incandescent light (or the black body line).

The Effects of Lamp Strikes

The ignition of a discharge lamp is a violent event. The extremely high voltage causes the atmosphere inside the capsule to break down and become conductive, facilitating the flow of current to start. When the arc jumps the gap and makes contact with the electrode, it impacts the electrode so hard that microscopic bits of the electrode are blown off. The arc pits the electrodes and wears them down. Eventually, repeated lamp strikes cause the electrodes to erode, and the gap grows over time until it is too large for the arc to jump. At that point the lamp reaches its normal end of life. It has been estimated that each lamp strike consumes approximately 3 hours of lamp life.

Discharge Lamp Efficiency

Discharge lamps have relatively high luminous efficiencies, typically in the range of 80 to 100 lumens per watt. Increased efficiency has huge implications on everything from the power distribution system to the HVAC system. For an equal amount of light, a more efficient system requires smaller feeder transformers and cable, fewer breakers and branch circuits, and less HVAC. It also reduces ongoing energy costs of both lighting and HVAC.

Lumen Maintenance

As a lamp is operated, two things happen to it over the course of time. First, some of the tungsten from the electrodes evaporates and condenses on the inner wall of the envelope, causing blackening. Second, as the quartz envelope goes through repeated cycles of heating and cooling, the molecules begin to reform in a crystal structure, lose some of their transparent properties, and become more opaque. This is the reverse process of fusing silicon into glass, or vitrification. As the quartz envelope devitrifies, it depreciates the lumen output by blocking some of the visible light. Thus, the aging lamp experiences lumen depreciation.

In addition to losing some of its light output, an aging discharge lamp also loses some of its color temperature. An HMI lamp loses approximately 1 to 1.5 K per hour of operation, while an MSR lamp loses approximately 0.5 to 1 K per hour of operation. Thus, if an HMI lamp starts out with a color temperature of 6000 K, then after 750 hours of use its color temperature will be between 5250 and 4875 K. If an MSR lamp starts out with a color temperature of 6800 K, then after 750 hours its color temperature will be between 6425 and 6050 K. Most shows with more than a couple of automated lights exhibit several different color temperatures across the rig. When all the lights are in white is when it is most obvious.

Bulb blackening and devitrification are not to be confused with the cloudy appearance that some discharge lamps exhibit when they are turned off and the salts and metals condense on the inner envelope (Figure 13-12). The gray and black ash-like coating will evaporate when the lamp is turned and heated to its normal operating temperature.

Also, it's virtually impossible to tell by looking at a discharge lamp whether or not it is a good lamp. Because there is no filament, you can't test it for continuity like you can an incandescent lamp, nor does the presence of dark matter on the inner envelope indicate a lamp failure. Unless there is an obvious malfunction, such as a broken envelope or a fallen electrode, the only way to know if a discharge lamp works is to test it in a known good lamp circuit.

Figure 13-12 When a discharge lamp is turned off and allowed to cool, the metals and salts condense on the wall of the inner envelope and create a cloudy appearance. This is normal.

Lamp Life Ratings

When a lamp manufacturer provides specs on a lamp, they will include a specification on the average rated life in hours. To the end user who might have paid a couple hundred dollars for a single lamp, this might offer some sense of security. But the meaning of average rated life is often misinterpreted. To rate the average life of a lamp, a manufacturer operates a sample batch—it might be 100 lamps—under very controlled conditions. The rated voltage, the ambient temperature, and the number of lamp strikes are all maintained very accurately. When exactly half of the sample batch reaches the end of life, the manufacturer calls that length of time the average rated life. It may be that 49 of the 100 lamps die after only 100 hours and the 50th doesn't die until after 1000 hours; they will still be rated at an average life of 1000 hours. Of course, that's an extreme case, but it is not uncommon for one lamp in a batch of 16 fixtures to fail after only a couple hundred hours even though it is rated for 750 hours. By the same token, it is also not uncommon for several of those 16 lamps to continue to operate well beyond 750 hours. The output will suffer due to lumen depreciation and color temperature depreciation, but in some applications that is not critical.

Discharge Lamp Hazards

Several years ago a technician was working on an automated fixture in a shop. He had to make an adjustment inside the fixture and then test it to see if the adjustment was correct. Each time he opened the fixture to adjust it, the safety interlock switch on the access panel would kill the power to the lamp for safety reasons. So in order to test the results he would have to wait 5 minutes for the lamp to cool and restart. After a few unsuccessful attempts at adjusting it properly he became impatient and decided to bypass the safety interlock switch. He wedged the panel in the housing so that it allowed access to the inside of the fixture but still kept the safety switch closed. He spent a few more minutes adjusting the fixture until he got it just right, then he went about his business. Later that night when he tried to go to bed his eyes started burning. He described the feeling as if the insides of his eyelids were sandpaper, and every time he blinked he was in excruciating pain. He went to the emergency room, where they told him the light had burned his retinas. They gave him liquid drops to numb his eyes. The real culprit? Ultraviolet radiation from the MSR lamp.

Discharge lamps emit a large amount of UV, which is harmful to the eyes and skin. The light coming out of the fixture is filtered through a series of lenses and UV/IR filters so that it is not as harmful as the unfiltered light emitted from the bare lamp. In fact, compliance labs test these fixtures to ensure that they are safe. But precautions should be taken to avoid direct exposure to the lamp. If you insist on working around an operating discharge lamp, wear welder's goggles or similar protection.

Even if you protect your eyes against the harmful effects of UV radiation, keep in mind that discharge lamps also pose a minor explosion hazard. With the exception of xenon lamps, most discharge lamps are under very little pressure at room temperature. But when the lamp is operating, the intense heat builds enormous pressure inside the arc capsule. Should the vessel rupture it could explode, sending shards of glass flying. Lamp explosions are rare, and the lamp housings of automated lights are built to contain such explosions, but anyone working around them should be aware of the hazard.

Discharge lamps commonly used in automated lighting also contain small amounts of mercury. An MSR lamp contains $0.05\,mg/m^3$ of mercury, the total of which is less than the amount of mercury found in a mercury thermometer (about $0.7\,g$). Nevertheless, it still poses some environmental issues, however slight. According to the Material Safety Data Sheet (MSDS) on the Philips Lighting website, "small numbers" of MSR lamps "placed in ordinary trash may not appreciably affect the method of lamp disposal." However, it is highly recommended that spent discharge lamps are disposed of in a responsible manner, preferably through a recycling program. More information about recycling discharge lamps, including where to recycle, can be found on the websites of the International Association of Lighting Management Companies (www.nalmco.org) and the Association of Lighting and Mercury Recyclers (www.almr.org).

Should you happen to break a discharge lamp and spill the contents, there are some precautions you should take. The following information is reprinted from the U.S. Environmental Protection Agency website http://www.epa.gov/epaoswer/hazwaste/mercury/spills.htm

What never to do about a mercury spill:

- Never sweep the area with a broom. Sweeping breaks the mercury into smaller droplets, further contaminating the room and the broom.

- Never use an ordinary household vacuum cleaner to clean up mercury. Vacuuming vaporizes the mercury and increases the concentration of mercury in the air that can result in poisoning.

- Never pour mercury down the sink drain. It may stay in the plumbing.

- Never wash mercury-contaminated clothes in the washing machine. Mercury can contaminate the washing machine.

- Never walk around if your shoes or socks may be contaminated with mercury. That will spread the mercury droplets all over the house.

- Never use household cleaning products to clean the spill, particularly products that contain ammonia or chlorine. These chemicals will react violently with mercury, releasing a toxic gas.

How do I clean up a small mercury spill?

Before beginning the clean up, change into old clothes and shoes that can be thrown away if they get contaminated with mercury. Note: If you are wearing gold jewelry, either remove the jewelry or wear good protective gloves. If the liquid mercury contacts the gold jewelry, the mercury bonds permanently to the gold and ruins it. Wearing gloves is a good idea to prevent mercury from lodging under the fingernails while cleaning.

1. Increase ventilation in the room with outside air and close the room off from the rest of the house. If available, use fans for at least one hour to help ventilate the room.
2. Pick up the mercury with an eyedropper or scoop up beads with a piece of heavy paper (e.g., playing cards, index cards).
3. Wide sticky tape such as duct tape can also be used to pick up any glass particles and mercury beads.
4. Powdered sulfur (which can be purchased at garden supply stores) can be used to bind any remaining mercury. When the sulfur combines with mercury the sulfur turns from the usual yellow color to brown. Continue to use sulfur until there is no longer a color change. Keep in mind that sulfur can be irritating to the skin, nose, throat, and eyes. Sulfur may also stain fabrics.
5. Place the mercury, contaminated instruments (dropper/heavy paper), and any broken glass in a plastic zipper bag. Place this zipper bag in a second zipper bag and then in a third zipper bag (triple bag), tightly sealing each bag with tape. Place the bags in a wide-mouth, sealable plastic container.
6. Throw away everything that may have been exposed to the mercury including towels, bedding, and clothes if they were contaminated.

7. Call your local health department for the nearest approved mercury disposal location. If disposal at such a location is not possible, dispose of the plastic container according to state and local requirements.
8. If weather permits, leave windows open for approximately 2 days to make sure the area is completely ventilated.
9. Wash hands very well with soap and water afterward. Shower well if you think any mercury touched other parts of your body.

CHAPTER 14

The Optical Path

Of the original phenomena, light is the most enthralling.—Leonardo da Vinci

All luminaires are *not* created equal. Even those using the same lamp source can produce varying results in terms of efficiency and light output. The optical path, and everything in it, determines the amount of light a fixture collects from the lamp source and effectively uses. That includes the lamp, reflector, filters, patterns, effects, mirrors, lenses, and the exit glass (if any).

The most fundamental aspect of automated luminaire design is that of the lamp, reflector, and lens combination. Most everything else is secondary to the efficiency of the design. The selection of a lamp source is often a matter of choosing from what's available from lamp manufacturers, though some automated lighting manufacturers like to use propriety lamps in order to control the lamp replacement sales. This can be as simple as renaming an existing lamp or modifying the base of an existing lamp to make it exclusive to their socket. It is the rare occasion, such as in the case of the HPL (Source Four) lamp, when a major lamp redesign comes from anyone outside of the lamp manufacturing industry, although it is not uncommon for lighting manufacturers to develop and advance lamp technology in collaboration with lamp manufacturers. But most often, a lamp is chosen and the luminaire and optical design is built around the lamp.

In addition to the lamp, the reflector geometry and construction have a tremendous influence on several characteristics of the luminaire, including the intensity, efficiency, uniformity of the beam, and quality of the image projection in the case of a profile fixture. The choice reflector in an optical design is a trade-off between efficiency, uniformity, imaging properties, cost, size, and weight. All of these considerations influence the choice of reflector geometry and construction, and some of these decisions are based on whether the luminaire is a profile spot or a wash fixture.

Specular Reflection

Light is electromagnetic radiation that behaves as both a particle and a wave. Scientists refer to this phenomenon as particle–wave duality. The wavelength of visible light is measured in nanometers or 10^{-9} meters (0.000000001 m). This is such a small unit of measure compared to the size of real-world optical components like reflectors and lenses that, for the purposes of analyzing optical systems, we can think of light as a ray rather than a wave. It's easier to use a ray, which can be represented by drawing a straight line from the source in the direction of travel, and ray tracing to understand optics.

All reflectors, regardless of their geometry, present a specular or mirror-like surface, which reflects light uniformly. When light strikes a specular surface, it is reflected at an angle equal to the angle of incidence (the angle at which it strikes the surface of the reflector relative to the normal or perpendicular to the surface) (Figure 14-1).

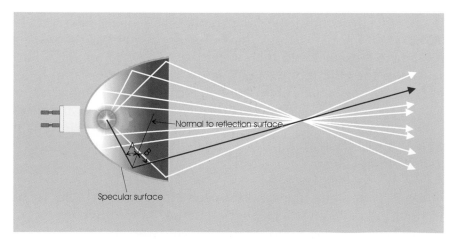

Figure 14-1 When light strikes a specular surface, such as a polished reflector, it is reflected at the same angle at which it strikes relative to the normal or perpendicular to the surface.

This principle is important because it dictates the path of the light from the source to the reflector and back through the optical path. The other important determining factor is the geometry or the shape of the reflector.

Reflector Geometry

There are at least three reflector geometries that are commonly used in the lighting industry: the parabolic reflector, the elliptical reflector, and the spherical reflector. Each has unique characteristics, advantages, and disadvantages.

The Parabolic Reflector

A parabola is a mathematic function describing the square of a number. If you plot the x- and y-axis of the equation $y = x^2$, then the result would be a parabola. The geometry of a parabolic reflector is like a parabola revolved about its center, or a paraboloid (Figure 14-2).

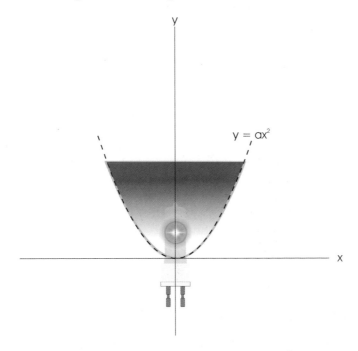

Figure 14-2 A parabola is described by the equation $y = x^2$. A parabolic reflector has the profile of a paraboloid of revolution.

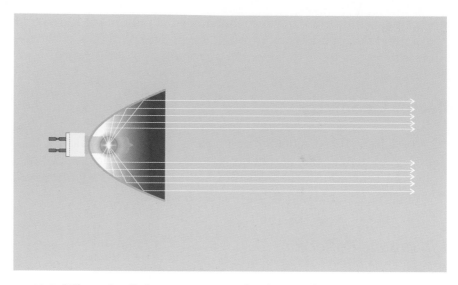

Figure 14-3 When the light source is at the focus of a parabolic reflector, the reflected light is emitted in parallel rays.

If the light is an ideal point source and is located at the focus of a parabolic reflector, all of the light collected by the reflector will be redirected in parallel rays away from the reflector (Figure 14-3).

Although PAR (parabolic aluminized reflector) cans are very common in entertainment lighting, parabolic reflectors in automated lighting are rare. Because the parallel rays produce a very large diameter beam, it is costly to build a dichroic color changing system for lights with a parabolic reflector. The Vari-Lite VL500 is an example of such an automated luminaire. Also, because the rays are parallel, there is no focal point at which a pattern can be imaged for projection. Syncrolite (www.syncrolite.com), Skytracker (www.skytracker.com), and other searchlight manufacturers use parabolic reflectors and gel scrollers for changing colors.

The Elliptical Reflector

An ellipse is a mathematic function described by the following equation:

$$1 = \frac{x^2}{a^2} + \frac{y^2}{b^2}$$

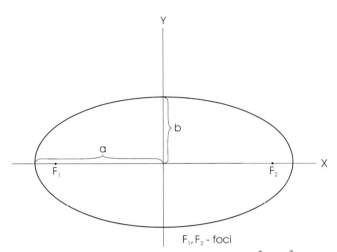

Figure 14-4 An ellipse described by the equation $1 = \dfrac{x^2}{a^2} + \dfrac{y^2}{b^2}$ has two foci and eccentricity defined by the quantities a and b.

If you plot a graph of x versus y on a Cartesian plane, you will get an ellipse.

The degree to which an ellipse deviates from a perfect circle is called the eccentricity and is a function of a and b. The larger one quantity is with respect to the other, the more eccentricity in the ellipse.

The geometry of an elliptical reflector is like half of an ellipse revolved about its vertex, or an ellipsoid (Figure 14-5). If the light were an ideal point source located at the focal point of the elliptical reflector, then all of the light collected by the reflector will be redirected and converged at the focal point of the optical path (Figure 14-6).

Optical engineers who are more concerned with focal distances often use the following relationship to help design an elliptical reflector:

$$r = f \times \frac{(1+e)}{(1+e \times \cos \alpha)},$$

where r is the distance from the focus to the reflected surface, f is the distance from the focal point to the center of the reflector surface, e is

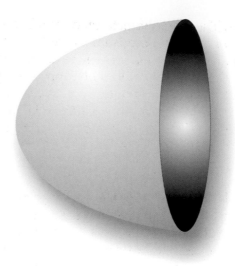

Figure 14-5 By revolving half of an ellipse about its center, the geometry of an elliptical reflector is formed.

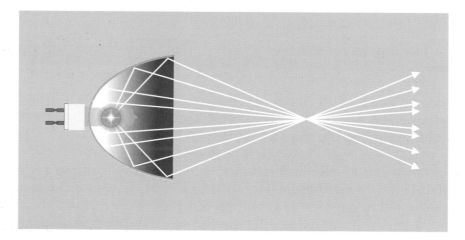

Figure 14-6 When a light source is located at one focal point of an elliptical reflector, all of the light collected by the reflector is redirected and converged at the other focal point on the optical path.

eccentricity, and α is the angle between the axis of the reflector and the direction of the light ray.

Ellipsoidal reflectors are very commonly used in automated lighting, mostly with single-ended medium source arc lamps such as the Philips

MSR and MSD lamps. They are characterized by relatively high efficiency compared to spherical reflectors because they capture a higher percentage of incident light in a useful manner. At the same time, elliptical reflectors tend to produce a peaked beam profile with a hot spot in the center. As a result, there is a fall off of intensity on the edge of the beam. Also, because the light source is not an ideal point source, the projection image is slightly defocused at the edges when the center is in focus. It's difficult to image a pattern that is sharp both in the center of the projection and on the edges of the projection.

The perception of brightness of a luminaire is as much a psychological phenomenon as it is a physical one. When there is a relative hot spot in the center of a beam, there is less contrast between the edge of the beam and the surrounding darkness, creating the perception of less intense light. By contrast, a more uniform beam looks brighter because the edge contrast is higher. For that reason, in a side-by-side comparison between a luminaire with an elliptical reflector and one with a spherical reflector, with all other things being equal, the more uniform beam, which is almost always the one with the spherical reflector, will appear to be brighter. The only sure way to determine the absolute brightness is with an illumination meter. There are many other factors, such as color temperature and angle of incidence, which will influence your perception of brightness as well.

The Spherical Reflector

The geometry of a spherical reflector is like a quarter of a circle revolved around its vertex. It's similar to a quarter or half of a spheroid. If the light were an ideal point source and was located at the center of the spheroid, then all of the light collected by the reflector would pass back through the light source (Figure 14-7). If, instead, the light source is located at a distance halfway between the center of the sphere and the reflector, then the light near the axis will be reflected as a collimated beam with parallel rays. The light that is farther away from the axis produces a spherical aberration, causing the reflected light to diverge from the parallel.

In profile fixtures with spherical reflectors, condenser lenses are almost always used. A condenser lens condenses the parallel rays of light and converges them at a focal point (Figure 14-8). They are also almost always used with double-ended lamps.

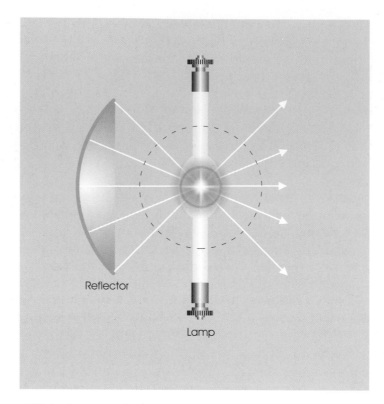

Figure 14-7 If light from an ideal point source is located at the center of a spherical reflector, the reflected light will pass back through the light source.

Several Italian manufacturers of automated luminaires, such as Clay Paky, Fly, and SGM, employ spherical reflectors and condenser lenses in their automated lighting products. They are characteristically very uniform in the beam profile, and they tend to produce very nice projected images with very good center-to-edge focus. They also give the appearance of a very bright beam because of the beam uniformity. They are generally less efficient than fixtures with elliptical reflector systems because the small size of the spherical reflector doesn't capture as much useful flux from the light source.

Reflector Materials

Besides the reflector geometry, the type of material from which the reflector is made has a big impact on the efficiency of the optical system. There

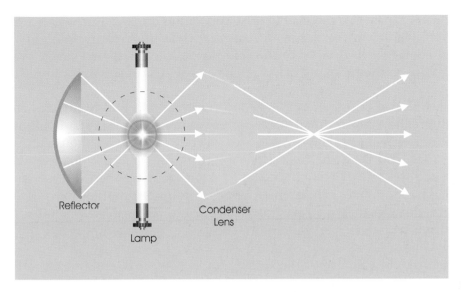

Figure 14-8 A condenser lens is almost always used in conjunction with a spherical reflector. It serves to condense the rays of light and make them converge at a focal point.

are primarily two types of reflector materials commonly used in automated fixtures: aluminum and glass.

Aluminum reflectors are relatively inexpensive and lightweight. They are most commonly found in moderately expensive and less expensive models, and they were used almost exclusively in early automated lighting fixtures (except fixtures like the VL1, which used an HTI with an integral dichroic reflector). An aluminum reflector is made on a lathe by the process of metal spinning. A disc of aluminum cut to the required diameter is placed on a lathe. A mandrel is also placed on the lathe, which is the same contour as the inside of the reflector. It is used to shape the aluminum as it is spun on the lathe. A follower applies pressure to the aluminum disc and forms it over the mandrel.

Once a reflector is formed, it is usually electropolished to make it more specular. Electropolishing is the opposite of the process of electroplating. To electropolish a reflector, the reflector is connected to the positive terminal of a DC power supply and placed in a temperature-controlled bath of electrolyte. The negative terminal of the power supply is connected to a cathode (the reflector acts as the anode) and placed in the bath. When the voltage is raised it creates a current, and in the process, microscopic particles of aluminum are removed from the reflector, creating a highly polished surface. The quality of the reflector and the polished surface varies according to the time and effort spent on the manufacturing processes.

Glass reflectors are generally made of borosilicate glass with a dichroic coating. They can be relatively expensive, depending on the volume of production and the economies of scale. They are heavier than aluminum reflectors, and they are most often found in higher end automated luminaires, although that is changing to some degree. There are some less expensive automated luminaires appearing on the market with dichroic glass reflectors, mostly of the spherical variety, since they are smaller than an elliptical reflector and therefore cheaper to produce in glass.

A dichroic thin-film optical coating provides an excellent, though still not perfect, reflective surface. It is much more efficient than an aluminum surface, maintains more optical integrity, and produces a better projection image. It also allows much of the infrared energy, or heat, of the incident light to pass through the reflector and out of the back of the luminaire. For that reason, many luminaires with dichroic glass reflectors have a large heat sink on the back of the fixture that can get very hot.

Infrared Filters

Heat is one of the primary causes of failure in electrical, electronic, and electromechanical systems and thus is a prime consideration in the design of automated lighting. The extreme temperatures generated by the light source have to be managed in order to strike a balance between producing the maximum light output and totally destroying the luminaire, or elements of it, in the process.

Infrared (IR) light is pure heat energy. An IR filter is most often the first element in the optical train that is used as line of defense against heat in an automated luminaire. It acts as a barrier between the lamp source and the electronic, mechanical, and electromechanical systems in the fixture.

An IR filter is a specialized optical thin-film filter through which visible light passes relatively unimpeded while the longer IR wavelengths are rejected. An IR filter is sometimes referred to as a hot mirror since it reflects heat and passes "cold" visible light. IR energy ranges from about 700 nm to 1 mm, so the ideal IR filter is a low-pass filter with a cutoff at around 700 nm.

Mechanical Dimming

Automated luminaires with gas discharge lamps are incapable of complete electronic dimming because the arc will extinguish if the voltage across the electrodes falls low enough. Some automated fixtures are equipped with special power supplies that are able to dim the lamp 40% in order to pulse (strobe electronically), save energy, reduce heat, and extend lamp life.

Most automated lights are equipped with a mechanical dimmer that can dim between 0 and 100%. Most often, a mechanical dimmer comprises one or two aluminum dimming flags that are progressively moved into the optical path, blocking a larger and larger portion of the light as they dim. The design of the dimmer varies from manufacturer to manufacturer and from model to model, but the leading edge of the dimmer flag normally has some sort of serration or pattern to make the dimming curve smoother and more effective. For example, a Cyberlight has a "bear claw" design dimmer that squeezes down the aperture area as the dimmer is rotated into the optical path (Figure 14-9). Other designs range from a curved surface that approximates an iris as the two flags meet in the center to serrated edges on two dimmer flags.

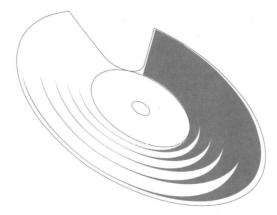

Figure 14-9 This "bear claw" mechanical dimmer is one example of a gradient density filter.

Some of the latest models of automated lighting feature a glass mechanical dimmer made of aluminum-coated borosilicate glass. By etching a gradient pattern in the aluminum-coated glass, it is easier to achieve a smooth dimming curve because of the high-resolution capabilities of the lithographic (etching) process.

In order to create a smooth dimming effect, it is important that the dimmer is not in or near the focal plane of the optical path. Otherwise, the edges of the dimmer will be imaged in the field and it will not be a smooth and uniform dimming effect.

Mechanical dimming has one distinct advantage over electronic dimming: it maintains a consistent color temperature over the range of dimming. Electronic dimming of incandescent lamps warms up the light source as it dims. Dimming discharge lamps usually increases the color temperature because some salts cease emission as the temperature drops, and those tend to be the salts that emit more red. However, mechanical dimming very often does not produce the ideal dimming curve. The limited size of most automated luminaires results in a relatively short gradient for the range from full to complete blackout. As a result, the last few steps of a mechanical dimmer can produce a noticeable difference between steps. Even more disconcerting is the nonuniformity that some mechanical dimming systems exhibit, especially in the last few steps before black. The quality of most mechanical dimming systems ranges from extremely poor to acceptable, with only a few that are excellent.

Optical Thin-Film Filters

One of the most important enabling technologies in an automated luminaire is the optical thin-film filter. An optical thin-film filter is a multilayer coating of microscopically thin dielectric material deposited on a glass substrate designed to change its optical properties. There are many types of optical thin-film filters, including hot mirrors, cold mirrors, dichroic filters, and metallic mirrors.

The manufacturing process starts with the selection of substrate material. Many dichroic filter manufacturers use 1.1 mm (0.043 inches) to 1.75 mm (0.069 inches) thick borosilicate glass. Trade names such as Borofloat, Corning 7059, and Corning 1737 glass are commonly used for dichroic filter substrates. The glass can withstand very high temperatures and it has a low coefficient of thermal expansion, both of which are important characteristics in this application. The refractive index is also important, as we shall soon see.

The glass is normally manufactured in large sheets that have to be cut to size before it is coated. There are two common methods of commercially cutting glass: the scribe and break method and the water jet cutting method. In the scribe and break method, a carbide steel cutting head is used to score the glass and then it can be broken along the score. When a precision score and break machine is used, it produces a clean finish and no additional processing is required. Otherwise the edge may have to be polished or finished. In the water jet cutting method, a fine jet of extremely highly pressurized water mixed with a fine abrasive grit is sprayed through a nozzle to cut the glass as the nozzle moves over the material. Water jet cutters produce a smooth edge and require no finishing. Both the water jet cutter and the precision score and break machine produce very little waste because the cuts are computer controlled and very precise; however, the water jet cutter can cut very intricate shapes and curves, such as concave cuts, which are difficult to cut on scribe and break machines. A scribing machine can cut at speeds of up to 10 to 15 inches per second (25.4 to 38.1 cm/s), while a water jet cutter is about 10 times slower.

Several filters can be cut from a single substrate after it is coated. The size of the substrate varies according to the capacity of the coating equipment, but substrates can range from about 17 to 30 inches, although such large substrates are rare. In preparation for the coating process, the glass is cleaned in a clean room environment to remove any oil, residue, or dust from the glass manufacturing and cutting processes. Foreign matter on the surface of the glass during the coating process can cause defects including pin holes and adhesion problems.

The Deposition Process

Once the glass is cut and cleaned it is loaded into a vacuum chamber where it is coated in a process known as deposition. There are at least three methods of depositing a thin-film coating: physical vapor deposition, chemical vapor deposition, and sputtering. Each process takes place in a vacuum chamber. At the top of the vacuum chamber is a "planetary," which holds multiple glass substrates. The planetary spins each substrate and rotates them all, much like the planets spin on their axes and rotate around the center of the solar system, to aid in coating them uniformly. At the bottom of the chamber is a pair of crucibles that hold the raw materials used to coat the glass. In a typical coating process, one of the crucibles contains silicon dioxide crystals, which have a relatively low index of refraction, and the other contains titanium dioxide pellets, which have a very high index of refraction. Before the deposition process begins, the chamber is pumped down to a near perfect vacuum.

In the physical vapor deposition (PVD) process, the thin-film coating is applied by vaporizing the target materials (SiO_2 and TiO_2), whereupon they diffuse onto the surface of the relatively cooler substrates. The target materials are vaporized by bombarding them with an electron beam one at a time. The beam slowly scans the material, imparting enough energy to melt and eventually evaporate it. As it evaporates, it diffuses throughout the chamber and condenses on the surface of the glass (and everything else in the chamber). While a fine layer of the material builds up on the substrate, a laser beam is reflected off the revolving glass to measure the thickness as determined by the index of refraction. At a predetermined thickness, the first crucible is closed and rotated out of the path of the electron beam while the other is opened and brought into the path of the beam. The second material is then evaporated and deposited on top of the first layer until the second layer is the proper thickness. Layers are deposited in alternating order in the proper thicknesses until a prescribed filter is completed.

The chemical vapor deposition (CVD) process is similar except that instead of using an electron beam to bombard the target materials, they react chemically and decompose onto the substrates. In the sputtering process, the target materials are bombarded by ions, which causes them to vaporize. When the gas molecules of the target material collide with the substrates, they condense back into a solid.

The number of layers and the thickness of each layer vary according to the specifications of the filter. There can be as few as seven layers, as in a yellow filter, or as many as 40 or more layers, as in an indigo filter.

Thin-Film Interference

Dichroic filters work by the principle of interference: some wavelengths pass through the filter unimpeded, some cancel each other out, and others

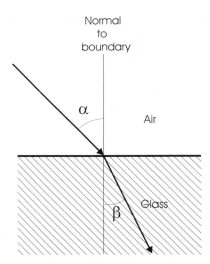

Figure 14-10 Snell's law dictates the angle of the refraction (β) of light when it passes between two media with different indices of refraction. When light passes between a medium with a lower index of refraction to a medium with a higher index of refraction (for example, from air to glass), then the ray bends toward the normal to the surface boundary. The degree to which it bends depends on the exact wavelength of the light. In this example, the angle of incidence (α) is greater than the angle of refraction (β).

are reflected away from the filter. At the beginning of this chapter we learned that the law of reflection dictates that when light is reflected, the angle of reflection is equal to the angle of incidence. Snell's law dictates what happens to light as it passes from one medium to another (Figure 14-10). If the two mediums have a different index of refraction, then a portion of the light is reflected and a portion is refracted. The portion of the light that is refracted bends in a predictable direction. If it passes from a medium with a lower index of refraction to a medium with a higher index of refraction, then it will bend toward the normal to the surface of the medium. The angle between the direction of travel and the normal to the surface of the medium is called the angle of refraction.

When light strikes the surface of a dichroic filter at a 90-degree angle, the following sequence of events takes place:

1. A portion of the incident light is reflected and a portion passes into the first layer of the coating. The portion that passes keeps traveling

in the same direction (the angle of refraction is 0 because it strikes the medium at a 90-degree angle).

2. When the light encounters the next interface, the interface between the first and second layers, a portion of that light is reflected and a portion is passed on to the second layer. The reflected light is directed 180 degrees away from the incident light.

3. The reflected light travels in the opposite direction through the first layer again where it encounters the interface between the first layer and the air. Again, a portion is reflected and a portion is passed along to the air. Due to the thickness of the first layer, which is about a quarter of a wavelength of a given color of light, the reflected light is now traveling alongside the first reflection except it is half a wavelength out of phase. You may think of this as two waves of equal amplitude traveling in the same direction, but with the second launched so that the peak of the second wave coincides with the trough of the first wave. The result is that the two cancel each other out (Figure 14-11). This is precisely what happens between the two reflections caused by the first layer of the dichroic filter.

4. The same process takes place in the second layer and each subsequent layer after that.

A dichroic filter manufactured with very precise tolerances of each layer can be "tuned" to cancel certain wavelengths and pass others, resulting in a filter that produces the desired color (Figure 14-12).

Filter Types

There are at least four types of optical thin-film coatings: low-pass, high-pass, bandpass, and notch filters (Figure 14-13).

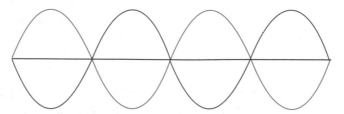

Figure 14-11 The sum of two waves of equal amplitude and frequency but 180 degrees out of phase with each other is 0.

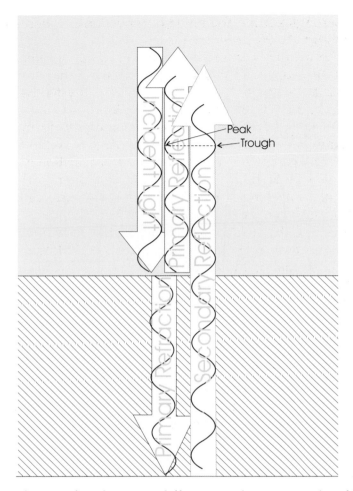

Figure 14-12 The interface between different mediums in a thin-film coating causes a portion of the incident light to reflect and a portion to refract. The primary reflection is in phase with the incident light, while the secondary reflections are designed to be completely out of phase with the primary reflection at the desired wavelength, thus canceling them out. Multilayered filters produce multiple secondary reflections, each of which contributes to phase cancellation. The surviving wavelengths produce the desired color.

The pass region for each type of filter is defined by its cutoff point, or the wavelength at which the filter passes 50% of the peak light energy. The slope of the cutoff determines the level of contamination from bordering colors and influences the saturation of the filter.

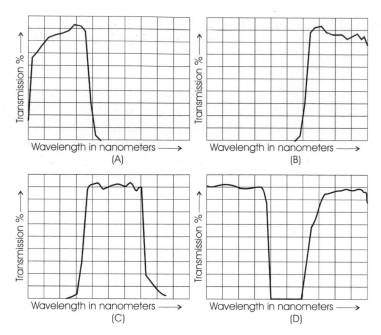

Figure 14-13 (A) High-pass filter. (B) Low-pass filter. (C) Bandpass filter. (D) Notch filter.

Optical thin-film filters make automated lighting, as we know it, possible. Without the high-temperature glass substrates it would be difficult, if not impossible, to manage the heat and alter the characteristics of the beam to produce color change and pattern projection. A gel filter could never withstand the heat produced by a typical automated luminaire lamp source without the protection of an IR filter. Nor could a gel filter live in the housing of an automated luminaire for any useable length of time to make them practical for use in automated lighting.

The ETC Source Four Revolution is an example of a modern automated fixture that uses a gel scroller for color change. It was designed with a gel scroller because the fixture is intended for use primarily in the theatre, where designers are more critical of color and demand more subtle color changes. But optical thin-film coatings have many unique characteristics that make them the overwhelming choice for automated lighting (Figure 14-14). Some of these characteristics include the following:

- Efficiency: An optical thin-film filter can reach efficiencies of 90% or better in the pass band. The efficiency of a gel greatly depends on the color, but it can range from 25 to about 90%. There is little question that a luminaire with an optical thin-film filter is far more efficient than one with a gel.

- Color saturation: An optical thin-film filter is highly selective, with a sharp cutoff between the pass band and the rejection band. A gel, on the other hand, is much less selective and allows much of the bordering color to "contaminate" the purity of color. This, however, is not always the desired effect, as some applications call for less pure color and more pastel color.

- Color stability: An optical thin-film filter degrades very little over time, even with excessive use. A show will look pretty much the same after years of operation when thin-film filters are used. A gel will fade with use, and darker colors will fade more quickly than lighter colors.

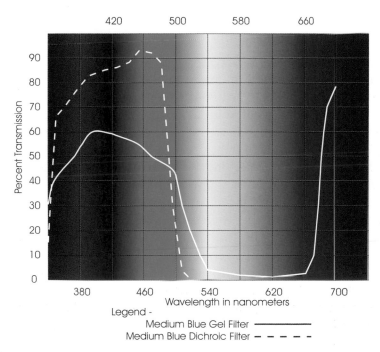

Figure 14-14 A dichroic filter is more efficient, produces more saturated color, and lasts much longer than a gel filter.

For these reasons, optical thin-film coatings play a major role in automated lighting not only for hot mirrors, glass gobos, antireflective coatings, and metallic mirrors, but also as color media.

Color Selection

A dichroic filter is an optical thin-film filter that separates the incident light into two or more colors. When the light strikes a dichroic filter, one color is transmitted through the filter and a different color is reflected away from the filter. The wavelengths of the transmitted light will vary according to the angle of incidence, as will the reflected wavelengths; the greater the angle of incidence, the greater the color shift from normal.

Vari-Lite patented the use of pivoting dichroic filters in automated lighting in 1983, precluding any other manufacturers from using pivoting dichroic filters but not from using them normal to the optical path. Consequently, almost all of the early automated lighting systems, aside from the Vari-Lite fixtures, used a dichroic color wheel for color selection.

Color Wheels

A color wheel is one method of changing color in an automated luminaire (Figure 14-15). Color wheels are commonly made of stamped aluminum, stainless steel, or carbon steel, with a number of apertures along its perimeter, all but one of which has a dichroic filter fastened to it. The open aperture is for no color. Color selection is accomplished by rotating the color wheel until the dichroic filter with the desired color is in the optical path. Some color wheels have a spring-loaded fastener that allows each filter to be removed and replaced, while others are fastened permanently with silicone. The size of the apertures depends on the luminaire optics and the size of the beam. The smaller the aperture size for a given amount of light, the higher the energy density and the greater the heat load that is placed on the optical elements. If the energy density is too great, then the optical components, including the dichroic filters, are at risk for failure.

The location of the color wheel in the optical path is critical. It should be located away from the focal plane so that the imperfections in the dichroic filters do not image in the beam. If the color wheel is too close to the focal plane or if the focus mechanism has a range that reaches the plane of the

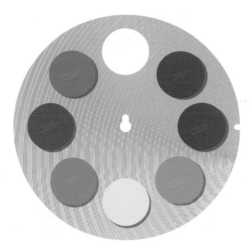

Figure 14-15 A dichroic color wheel is one of the most common types of color selection systems in automated lighting.

color wheel, then every pinhole, scratch, and abrasion will show up in the projected image.

A color wheel is a simple and effective way to provide remote color selection. The aluminum wheel is easy to design and fabricate, and the code to control it is easy to write. The downsides are that color selection is limited to the number of apertures in the color wheel and there is a stark transition between colors. When the color changes from a color on one side of the wheel to one on the other, it has to pass through every intermediate color in between, producing a sort of color strobe. Some color wheel designs have evolved into trapezoidal-shaped filters to minimize the dark space between filters and maximize the useable filter area. This design also provides for the ability to project split colors using adjacent colors.

Color Combining

One of the limitations of using a color wheel for color selection is that the number of colors is limited to the number of apertures in the color wheel. Most automated fixtures with a color wheel have between eight and 12 available colors, including white. Some automated luminaires have a second color wheel to extend the range of available colors (Figure 14-16). The

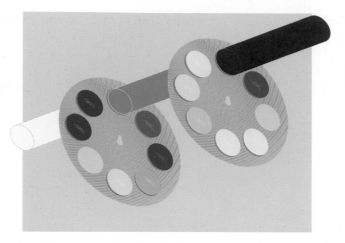

Figure 14-16 By adding a secondary color wheel with carefully chosen colors, the number of available colors in an automated fixture can be multiplied.

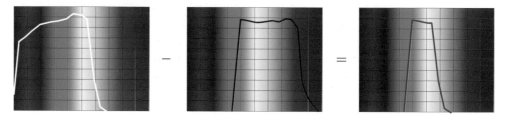

Figure 14-17 The intersection of the bandwidths of the primary and secondary filters determines the results of combining color filters.

secondary color wheel modifies the resulting color by effectively narrowing the bandwidth of the first color selection by overlapping the two filters.

The colors on a secondary color wheel have to be carefully selected to maximize the variation of colors on the primary color wheel. The filters on the secondary color wheel are often wideband color correction filters that double as color correction in addition to color-modifying filters (Figure 14-17). If the overlapping filters do not alter the resulting bandwidth then there is no change in color. On the other hand, if the two overlapping filters have no bandwidth intersection, then almost no light or color is produced, often resulting in a dim UV effect. If the colors on the secondary color wheel are carefully chosen, the number of available colors in a luminaire can be multiplied. For example, a fixture with eight colors on the primary wheel, including white, and four colors plus white on the secondary wheel will produce 40 colors (not all of which are guaranteed to be discernable), provided that the four secondary colors are carefully chosen. But even with an extended range of colors, combining color wheels still results in a limited range of color selection and there is a hard transition between colors.

Color Mixing

A better way to extend the range of available colors is by using CMY color mixing. CMY color mixing is a subtractive method of color mixing using three gradient density filters: one cyan, one magenta, and one yellow (Figure 14-18). Each of the three filters is made of a glass substrate with a thin-film coating that is etched or cut into a shape to form a gradient density pattern. The patterns differ from model to model, but the principle is the same. By slowly varying the orientation of a color mixing wheel with a stepper motor, the gradient gradually increases or decreases the density of the color in the optical path. Thus, the saturation of the selected color can be varied between zero and full. Adding a second or third filter subtracts from the pass band and alters the color. In some automated luminaires, a fourth wheel with a gradient density pattern made of aluminum acts as a dimmer. This is sometimes referred to as a CMYK system, which

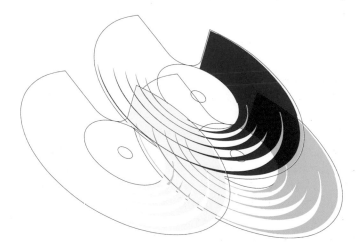

Figure 14-18 Three gradient density color wheels, one cyan, one magenta, and one yellow, can be used in a CMY color mixing system to produce a wide range of colors.

is the four-color offset printing term for Cyan-Magenta-Yellow-blacK. Like a color wheel, the gradient density CMY color filters must be located away from the focal plane or the gradient pattern will image instead of mix.

By using CMY color mixing, almost any color in the visible range can be rendered. Typically, however, very deeply saturated primary colors like blue, red, and green are very hard to come by in a CMY color mixing system. For that reason, many automated fixtures with CMY color mixing also have a supplementary color wheel with saturated colors. The advantages of using CMY color mixing include a wide selection of colors and a very smooth transition from color to color.

Gobos

Gobos are not unique to automated lighting; they have been around for decades. But what is unique in automated lighting is the ability to change gobos remotely. A gobo is simply a pattern that is inserted in the focal plane of a luminaire in order to project an image. There has been much conjecture about the origin of the term gobo. It has been theorized that it's a contraction of "goes before optics" or "goes between optics."

Automated lighting fixtures have used gobo wheels to facilitate gobo change almost since their inception. But the advent of the digital light (see Section 7: Digital Lighting) may one day relegate gobo hardware to lower end, entry-level automated lighting. Until then, the gobo wheel will continue to be the dominant method of gobo change.

Metal Gobos

There are at least three varieties of gobos: aluminum gobos, stainless steel gobos, and glass gobos. The simplest, least expensive way to manufacture gobos is to etch an aluminum gobo wheel with several gobos in it, each of which corresponds to an aperture with a diameter of the appropriate size for the optics of the luminaire (Figure 14-19). This type of gobo wheel typically has anywhere from 5 to 12 or more gobos.

Although an etched metal gobo wheel is relatively inexpensive to produce, it is not without its disadvantages. The gobos are fixed (nonrotating) and nonreplaceable, and the resolution is very limited due to the limited

Figure 14-19 An etched metal gobo, typically fabricated from aluminum, is the simplest and least expensive way to manufacture gobo wheels.

strength of the aluminum alloy. There is no means for suspending an "island" in an etched metal gobo; therefore, patterns like a "tunnel" must have "bridges" to support the center island. As a result, gobos in an etched wheel are generally very basic designs with little intricacy in which every piece must be connected to the whole of the wheel. They are also inherently black-and-white projections, although some color can be added by gluing bits of dichroic glass to them or they can be combined with color media to produce one color and black projections.

Stainless steel gobos have some of the same characteristics as aluminum gobos, but they do offer some advantages. Because of the thin-gauge metal used to make stainless steel gobos, they are always used in conjunction with an aluminum or steel gobo wheel to hold them in place or, in the case of a rotating gobo wheel, a carrier that holds individual gobos. That means they are individually replaceable, allowing the designer the opportunity to introduce some level of customization in a lighting design; they don't have to look like every other automated light of the same model. Also, stainless steel has a greater tensile strength than aluminum, which means that stainless steel gobos can have finer supports and higher resolution. Thus, they can have a lot more detail, such as leaves and vines. There is, however, a trade-off between the level of detail and the life of the gobo. The more detail and the finer the cuts, the quicker a gobo will warp and burn. In short-run shows this is less of an issue, but in permanent installations it is a prime consideration. Stainless steel gobos suffer from the same lack of color as stamped gobos except that it is difficult to glue dichroics to them because of the limited surface area. In a stamped gobo wheel it doesn't matter if the dichroic filters and glue don't fit within the aperture, but in an interchangeable gobo it does.

Glass Gobos

Glass gobos offer the most advantages in terms of resolution and color, although they can be relatively expensive, depending on the number of colors in the gobo. There are several different types of glass gobos, including black-and-white, grayscale, single-color, multicolor/multilayer, and multicolor/single-layer gobos.

A glass gobo is manufactured by etching away the dichroic coating on a dichroic filter (Figure 14-20). The image that is to be made into a gobo

Figure 14-20 A single-color glass gobo is made by masking and etching a pattern onto a dichroic filter.

first has to be digitized using a graphics software program and is then output to film. The film is used as a mask to expose and set a chemical called photoresist, which is used to protect the dichroic filter from the etching chemicals that etch away the thin-film coating. Depending on the particular process, the film can be a photo positive, in which case it passes the light used to set the photoresist, or it can be a photo negative, in which case it blocks the exposing light. Before being exposed, the dichroic filter is coated with the photoresist in its uncatalyzed state. By projecting a film of the image onto the dichroic filter using a UV light, a pattern in the form of the projected image is catalyzed on the dichroic filter, thus setting the stage for the next step in the process. UV light exposure hardens or sets the photoresist, and once it is set it protects the dichroic coating from the etching chemicals while the unexposed photoresist is etched away along with the dichroic coating. The remaining catalyzed photoresist is subsequently removed with another chemical that removes it without damaging the remaining dichroic coating. The final product is a glass gobo with a dichroic coating in the pattern of the original image.

If the process is started using an ordinary single-color dichroic filter, then the final product will be a single-color glass gobo. Some multicolored glass gobos are made by stacking two or three single-color glass gobos in the proper alignment and banding them together. This method is obviously more labor intensive and costly than a single-color glass gobo, and, depending on the image, some of the details may not focus well because of the separation of the image planes, which is equal to the thickness of the glass.

There is at least one method of manufacturing full-color glass gobos on a single substrate using four-color separations. The method involves coating and etching each of the four color separations individually. After the first color is coated and etched, the glass is returned to the vacuum chamber and the second color is deposited on the gobo and then etched. This process is repeated until all four colors have been deposited and etched. Four-color separations involve the colors cyan, magenta, yellow, and black. For the color black, aluminum is used in the deposition process, which blocks light and produces the black.

Black-and-white glass gobos are manufactured using the same process except they are etched on aluminum- or chrome-coated substrates. If they are etched with gradient density dots, then they can produce grayscale shades of light and dark.

The etching process is very precise and is capable of producing very fine resolution. Some commercial gobo manufacturers boast resolution of up to 20,000 dpi, but the final product is dependent upon the quality and resolution of the original artwork and digitizing equipment and processes.

Glass gobos are generally very durable and heat resistant, but they are not indestructible. Like dichroic filters, they must be used properly in order to maintain them intact. Some manufacturers like Apollo say that they should always be put in the optical path with the coated surface toward the light source to minimize the heat in the glass. Others, like High End Systems, advise putting the glass gobo in with the coated side away from the light source to more evenly heat the glass, rather than heating only the portions through which the light passes. Uneven heating produces a differential in heat that can lead to stress cracks. You should always read and follow the instructions from the manufacturer of the particular glass gobo you are using.

It's not easy to detect which side is the coated side, but you can tell by holding a pointed object such as the tip of a screwdriver or a pencil up to the glass to see if the reflected image touches the object. If they appear to touch, then that is the coated side; if there appears to be some separation, then it is not the coated side (Figure 14-21).

Front Surface Mirrors

Front surface mirrors are designed with the reflective coating on the front surface of the glass substrate, as opposed to a second surface mirror, in which the back of the substrate is coated. The advantage of front surface mirrors is that they prevent secondary reflections caused by the interface between the air and the glass substrate because the light never reaches the glass. They are also more efficient for the same reason. They are typically coated with aluminum and overcoated with silicon dioxide to help protect the relatively soft aluminum coating. The overcoating also helps improve the durability of the glass and seals the aluminum, making it easier to clean. The efficiency of an overcoated front surface mirror is close to 90%.

Antireflective Coatings

Some higher quality lenses and optical glass have an antireflective (AR) coating to help improve the efficiency of the light transferred through the

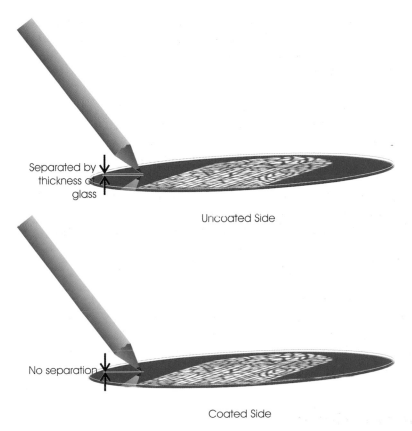

Figure 14-21 To determine which side of a dichroic filter or glass gobo is the coated side, touch one of the surfaces with a pointed object. If the reflected image touches the object, then that is the coated side.

coated material as well as the imaging quality. AR coatings are made with the same vacuum deposition process used for making any other optical thin-film coating, except the coating is made of multiple layers of magnesium fluoride. The index of refraction for magnesium fluoride at 550 μm is 1.38, which is in between that of air (~1.0) and crown glass (~1.5 at 550 μm). When light strikes the interface between the air and the AR coating at a normal to the substrate, it is partially reflected away from the glass. When it strikes the interface between the AR coating and the glass substrate, another part is reflected away from the glass. Because the difference in the indices of refraction between the air and the coating is similar to the difference in the indices of refraction between the coating and the substrate, the reflections are equally strong. If the thickness of the AR coating is about a quarter of a wavelength of the reflected light, then the two reflections will be 180 degrees out of phase and the reflections will cancel each other out, thus eliminating them.

Effects

In addition to color changers and gobos, other effects that may or may not be found in an automated luminaire include textured glass, moiré effects, strobing, "animation," irising, color correction, prisms, frost, and beam shaping.

Lenses

In automated luminaires, the optical design makes use of lenses to shape and control the size, imaging, and focal length of the optical system. Different types of lenses serve different purposes, and their optical characteristics are determined by the type of glass from which they are made (which determines the index of refraction) and their contour. The choice of lens in a particular application is determined in the design phase by considering efficiency, image quality, and cost.

There are several types of lenses, the most common of which are spherical lenses because their surfaces, both front and back, are formed in the shape of a portion of a sphere. Each of the surfaces is classified according to the contour of its front and back surfaces. If the surface curves outward from the center of the lens, then it is a convex surface. Conversely, if the surface curves inward toward the center of the lens, it is a concave surface. If the surface of the lens is flat, it is a plano surface. The front and back surfaces can have different contours, which gives rise to at least five varieties of lens as shown in Figure 14-22.

If the surface is convex, then the focal length is considered positive; if it is concave, then the focal distance is considered negative. This is important to remember during lens calculations.

If a lens is convex, then a parallel beam of light passing through the lens will converge at the focal point (Figure 14-23). For this reason, a convex lens is a converging lens.

Convex-Convex Plano-Convex Concave-Concave Plano-Concave Convex-Concave

Figure 14-22 Common lens profiles.

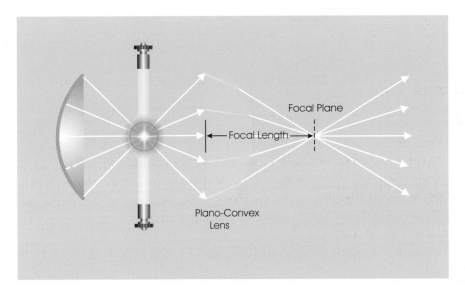

Figure 14-23 A lens with a convex surface focuses a collimated beam of light at the focal point of the lens.

If a lens is concave, then a parallel beam of light passing through the lens will diverge (Figure 14-24). For this reason, a concave lens is a diverging lens.

If the front and back surfaces are not the same type, then the focal length can be calculated using the following equation:

$$\frac{1}{f} = (n-1)\left\{\frac{1}{R_1} - \frac{1}{R_2} + \frac{(n-1)d}{nR_1R_2}\right\},$$

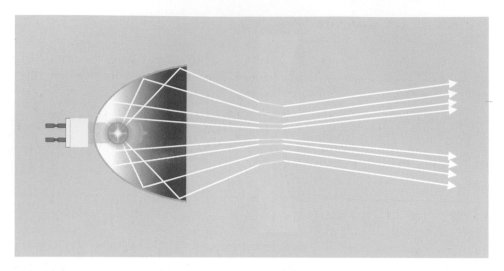

Figure 14-24 A lens with a concave surface spreads or diverges a collimated beam of light passing through it.

where f is focal length, n is the index of refraction of the lens material, d is the thickness of the lens, R_1 is the radius of curvature of the front surface, and R_2 is the radius of curvature of the back surface.

If d is relatively small compared to R_1 and R_2, then the focal length can be estimated as

$$\frac{1}{f} = (n-1)\left\{\frac{1}{R_1} - \frac{1}{R_2}\right\}$$

This approximation works for thin lenses.

Once the focal length of a lens has been determined, then the lens power can be determined by the following equation:

$$\text{Lens power} = \frac{1}{f}$$

The focal length is positive for converging lenses and negative for diverging lenses. The unit of measure for lens power is an inverse meter (1/m, or m^{-1}) and is called a diopter.

Spherical Aberrations

It turns out that a lens with a spherical surface is not ideal for projecting an image because it produces a blurry image, or what is known as an aberration. The spherical aberration is caused by the fact that the rays of light away from the center of the lens focus on a slightly different plane than those near the center (Figure 14-25). Aspheric lenses do a better job of producing crisp, sharp images, but they are harder to manufacture and more costly than spherical lenses.

Chromatic Aberration

Another type of lens aberration is called a chromatic aberration, which is caused by the natural dispersion of the lens material. Because the index of refraction of glass varies with the wavelength, when white light strikes a point on the lens, it tends to disperse like a prism. The result is that the edge of the image shows a rainbow of colors ranging from red to blue.

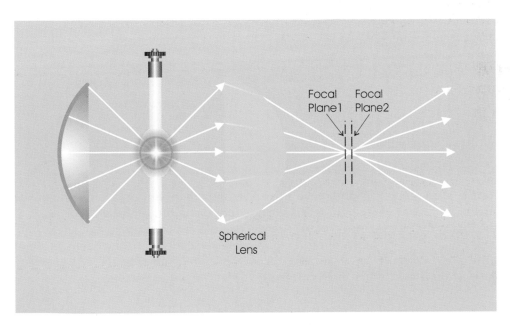

Figure 14-25 A spherical lens has a slightly different focal plane for rays that are away from the center of the lens, producing a slightly blurry image due to spherical aberration.

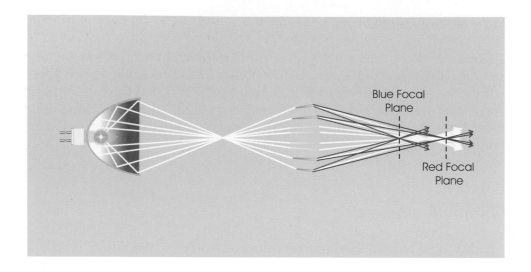

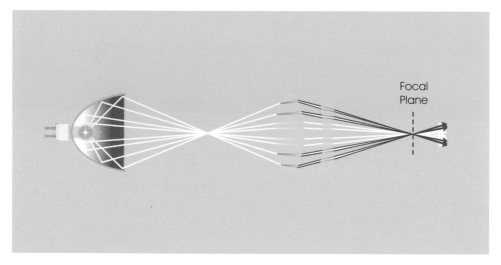

Figure 14-26 Top: The difference in wavelengths between opposite ends of the spectrum causes white light to disperse with red and blue at the extreme ends of the focus. Bottom: An achromatic doublet (shown with its component lenses: one convex-convex lens made of crown glass and one concave-concave lens made of flint glass) corrects the chromatic aberration by recombining the red and blue ends of the spectrum at the focal plane.

Chromatic aberration can be corrected to some degree by the use of what is known as an achromatic doublet or achromatic lens (Figure 14-26). An achromatic lens is actually two lenses (sometimes three), one convex lens made from crown glass and one concave lens made from flint glass, bonded together with optically clear cement. The concave lens diverges the various wavelengths in the opposite direction from the convex lens, resulting in a more uniform focal plane for all wavelengths.

SECTION 5
Communications

CHAPTER 15

DMX512

Those parts of the system that you can hit with a hammer (not advised) are called hardware; those program instructions that you can only curse at are called software.—"Levitating Trains and Kamikaze Genes: Technological Literacy for the 1990's" by Brennan, Richard P.

Years ago, before there was a digital lighting control standard, automated lighting manufacturers were left to their own devices in the area of control and control protocol. Some used digital signals for control, and others used 0–10 volt analog control or some other analog scheme. As a result, almost every automated lighting controller was proprietary to one type of fixture and every fixture was wired directly to the controller or to a repeater box. Cross-pollination among different manufacturers' gear required the use of converters and adapters. Analog control cables were fat bundles of wire that amounted to a wire per parameter per fixture. In those days, automated lighting was pretty much limited to four or five parameters, but even small analog systems had big wiring requirements, and most analog controllers were limited to eight or 16 instruments. The connectors alone took up quite a bit of real estate on the backs of analog controllers.

The area of control of automated lighting was, in the early days, one of the limiting factors of the technology. As far back as the 1930s, when George Izenour first attempted to build an automated lighting system, he cited the need for a control system that could handle a large number of control channels. In the 1960s, the commercialization of the transistor made possible the use of digital control, but it was not very practical to implement because there were no standards in hardware or software. But a development in the 1980s changed all that.

In the years leading up to 1981, there was a popular movement toward building small, personal computers. In 1981, IBM broke open the

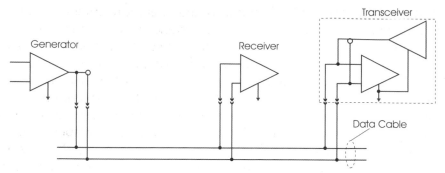

Figure 15-1 A DMX512 receiver has differential input to amplify the difference in the voltage between the two input terminals.

In its most basic form, the physical layer of a DMX512 system comprises a differential line driver, a terminated transmission line, and at least one differential receiver. A differential line driver is usually an operational amplifier (op amp) that amplifies the difference in the voltage between the two input terminals (Figure 15-1). For example, if the voltage on pin two is −5VDC and the voltage on pin three is +5VDC, then the differential is 10VDC. The 0V reference is the ground, or pin one.

A DMX512 transmitter (controller) generates the control signals and feeds them to the line driver. The line driver communicates with the receivers on the data link through a cable or network of cables.

Data Cable

A DMX512 system consists of a controller or controllers, receivers, a network of distribution medium like cable, wireless, or fiber, and sometimes data amplifiers, splitters, and/or combiners. Although wireless transmission and fiber are sometimes used for data distribution, they are only a physical layer carrying a translated version of DMX512. The DMX512 protocol calls for distributing data with copper cable. The integrity of a DMX512 distribution system can be compromised by using cable that is inappropriate for high-speed data distribution. Unfortunately, some manufacturers have made it all too easy to choose the wrong cable by using connectors that are commonly used for audio cable, which is most often high-capacitance cable and not suitable for digital signals. The appropriate cable has certain characteristics that make it appropriate for high-speed data transfer.

According to the TIA/EIA485 standard, the interconnecting media should be paired cable with a characteristic impedance of 120 ohms. The characteristic impedance of a cable is the impedance of an infinitely long length of that particular cable. It is determined by the physical properties of the cable, including the wire gauge, the thickness of the insulating material, and the type of shielding it uses. A data distribution network should have a uniform characteristic impedance to minimize signal reflections that could cause data errors. If a signal encounters a change in impedance along the signal path, some of the electrical energy is reflected back to the source. The amount of reflection depends on the difference in the impedance, but in general, the greater the difference, the greater the reflection. When a data signal is reflected, it mixes with the original signal and the receiver sums the two data signals, often resulting in corrupted data. The fixtures near the center of the data run are often more susceptible to data problems of this sort for two reasons. First, the reflections near the end of the run are more in phase with the original signal and therefore cause less of a differential. As the reflection travels farther away from the source, it becomes more out of phase, thus presenting a bigger problem. Second, by the time the reflection reaches the opposite end of the data link, it has lost some intensity due to the resistance in the line. To eliminate data reflections at the end of a data run, a 120-ohm terminator should always be used. A terminator is simply a 120-ohm, 0.25-watt resistor placed across pins two and three and across pins four and five (if applicable). It absorbs the electrical energy at the end of the data link and minimizes reflections.

In addition to having a characteristic impedance of 120 ohms, the ideal data cable should be a low-capacitance, twisted pair cable with an overall foil shield and braid shield. It should be at least 24 AWG or larger for longer runs to keep the voltage drop across the run as small as possible.

The capacitance of a cable is important in high-speed data transmission because it affects the waveform. A digital signal is a square wave, like that shown in Figure 15-2.

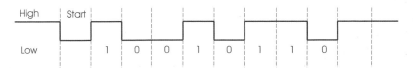

Figure 15-2 A DMX512 signal is a series of high and low voltages, which makes a square wave.

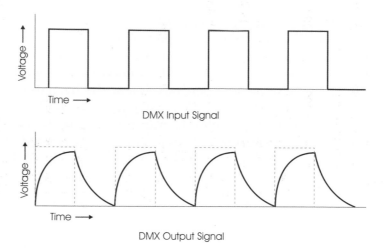

Figure 15-3 A high-capacitance cable like microphone cable distorts a DMX512 signal by rounding the corners.

When a cable is connected to a transmitter, it looks like a capacitor to the source. When the voltage goes high, it takes time to charge the "capacitor" in the cable. Thus, the voltage rises slowly as it fills the capacitor with energy. Consequently, when a square wave is input to the cable, if the cable has a high capacitance, then the slow charge on the cable changes the waveform from a square wave to a sawtooth wave (Figure 15-3).

Problems with high-capacitance cable may not be apparent in smaller systems, which leads some people to believe that it's okay to use for DMX512 applications. But high-capacitance cable degrades DMX512 signals and make for an unstable system whether or not it's readily apparent. It's a good practice to get in the habit of using low-capacitance cable because the problem will manifest itself when it is least expected and when it is most critical!

There are a number of cable manufacturers who make cable specifically for DMX512 and high-speed data applications. Listed in Table 15-1 are some of the more popular ones.

You should take care to make sure a cable is plenum rated, such as Belden 89841, when it is being installed without conduit in plenum. In the construction industry, a plenum is a ceiling cavity or a raised floor cavity, and a plenum rating means that it meets certain criteria for fire resistance and smoke emissions. Most of the portable cables used in the touring industry are not plenum rated.

Table 15-1 Commercially available DMX512 cable.

Type	Pairs	Impedance (Ω)	Gauge (AWG)	Jacket	Capacitance (pf)	Shield	Temp (°C)
Artistic Licence DataSafe 2	1	90	22	PVC	20	Inner: Al/Mylar 100% Outer: tinned copper braid 85%	−30 to 75
Artistic Licence DataSafe 4	2	90	22	PVC	20	Inner: Al/Mylar 100% Outer: tinned copper braid 85%	−30 to 75
TMB ProPlex PC222P	1	80	22	Polyurethane	22	Inner: Al/Mylar 100% Outer: tinned copper braid 85%	−40 to 105
TMB ProPlex PC224P	2	110	22	Polyurethane	22	Inner: Al/Mylar 100% Outer: tinned copper braid 85%	−40 to 105
Creative Stage Lighting DuraFlex 22/2WS-D	1	100	22	PVC	15	Inner: Al/polyester 100% Outer: tinned copper braid 90%	80
Creative Stage Lighting DuraFlex 22/4WS	2	100	22	PVC	15	Inner: Al/polyester 100% plus drain Outer: tinned copper braid 90%	80
Belden 9841	1	120	24	PVC	12.8	Al. foil-Polyester tape/tinned copper braid	−30 to 80
Belden 9842	2	120	24	PVC	12.8	Al. foil-Polyester tape/tinned copper braid	−30 to 80

DMX512 over CAT 5

In October 2000, a Task Group of the ESTA Control Protocols Working Group commissioned an independent study of the feasibility of using low cost Category (CAT) 5 cable instead of EIA485 rated data cable. After collecting and examining the data, the group concluded that "in most respects, unshielded twisted pair (UTP) and shielded twisted pair (STP) CAT 5 cable can be expected to perform at least as well as EIA485 cable for DMX512 applications" (see http://www.esta.org/tsp/working_groups/CP/ DMXoverCat5.htm). That's good news for designers and installers of permanent installations, because the cost of CAT 5 cable is considerably less than that of DMX512 cable. Using construction grade CAT 5 cable in portable applications is not recommended, however, because the jacket is neither rugged nor flexible enough to withstand the rigors of temporary applications. In fact, the Standard for Portable Control Cables for use with ANSI E1.11 (DMX512-A) and USITT DMX512/1990 Products (E1.27-1) specifically disallows portable CAT 5 cable for portable DMX512 applications. In permanent installations, CAT 5 cable used for DMX512 applications can be terminated with terminal blocks or standard DMX512 connectors. RJ45 connectors can be used if they are not accessible to unauthorized personnel, i.e., if they are internal to the chassis.

DMX Connectors

The original DMX512 standard specified the use of five-pin XLR connectors, although only three of the five pins were used; the other two were reserved for an optional second data link, which is seldom implemented. For that reason, there is no physical reason for disallowing three-pin XLR connectors, other than the fact that they are not to spec. They work fine, but the DMX512 standard called for five-pin connectors. But several automated lighting manufacturers decided that they would use three-pin XLR connectors because they are cheaper than five-pin connectors and three-pin XLR cables were more readily available at any music store in the form of microphone cables. There are still several, mostly lower end, automated lights and dimmer packs using three-pin XLR connectors for DMX512 connections. This can lead to problems, as we will soon see.

The standard also specifies that female connectors are to be used on the transmitter or console and male connectors on the receiver or load end. You can easily remember which gender is the output and which is the input if you think in terms of an extension cord, which has the same gender rules. If you plug an extension cord into a wall outlet, then it is hot. If the output of the extension cord was a male connector, then you would be walking around with a hot male connector, which could easily come in contact with you or someone else—a very uncomfortable experience, to say the least! Thus, the output is always a female connector, which is much safer. The same applies to DMX512 connectors. If you have ever spent hours pulling DMX512 cable only to find out you ran it the wrong way, then you'll appreciate the analogy and you'll never forget it.

The pin out of a DMX512 connector (Figure 15-4) is designated as follows:

- Pin 1: Common (shield)

- Pin 2: Data complement (data 1–)

- Pin 3: Data true (data 1+)

- Pin 4: Optional second data link complement

- Pin 5: Optional second data link true

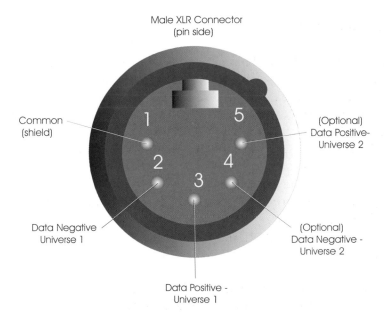

Figure 15-4 DMX512 five-pin XLR pin designations.

Termination

Termination is a very important part of a reliable DMX512 data distribution system. Every data link in the system and every output in a data distributor must be terminated properly in order to ensure the integrity of the data and prevent it from becoming distorted by signal reflections.

Terminating a data link is as simple as inserting a data terminator at the end of each run or in the output of each empty data distributor output. The terminator matches the impedance of the cable and looks to the transmitter or controller like an infinite length of cable. In effect, it absorbs rather than reflects the energy of the signal as it reaches the end of the line. Without a terminator, the data line is open and looks to the controller like an infinite impedance, which is something akin to a brick wall in terms of signal flow. When a signal encounters infinite impedance it is reflected back down the line toward the transmitter. In the process it causes interference with the original signal, and the data become garbled and could be lost.

Smaller DMX512 networks with few fixtures and short runs sometimes function sufficiently without termination, leading some people to believe that they are unnecessary. But even small systems without termination can be unstable, and the slightest change might cause them to function erratically. It's a good practice to always terminate data runs, large and small.

Automated lighting can behave erratically on an unterminated data line. The light might flicker, or, if it's a moving mirror fixture, the mirror might glitch. It can happen to any fixture in the data link, not necessarily every one and not always the last in the link.

A data terminator can be easily built by soldering a 120 ohm, 0.25-watt resistor between pins two and three and between pins four and five of a five-pin XLR connector (Figure 15-5).

Building a Data Network

A DMX512 network can be simple, as with a single controller and a single fixture, or it can be very large and complex, with multiple data lines, data splitters, controllers, and more. Regardless of the size of the system, the fundamentals are the same. Each load is connected in a daisy chain fashion,

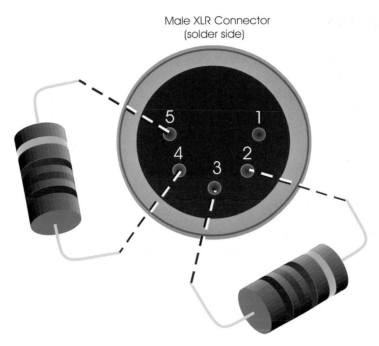

Male XLR Connector
(solder side)

Figure 15-5 A data terminator serves to stabilize a DMX512 system by preventing signal reflections at each open data port. It's easy to build a data terminator by soldering a 120-ohm, 0.25-watt resistor between pins two and three and between pins four and five of a male five-pin XLR connector.

with the output from one fixture connected to the input of the next fixture, and so on. Up to a total of 32 fixtures may be connected on a single data link, provided that they each comply with the EIA485 specifications for a "unit load" describing the characteristics of the receiver. Most dimmers and automated lights comply. There is also a limit to the maximum length of the total cable run for each data link. An EIA485-compliant data link can operate up to 1 km (3281 feet), but it is recommended to keep it below 500 m (1640 feet).

The stub of cable inside a fixture or dimmer used to connect it to the data line is purposely kept as short as possible to make it appear as a lumped load. If the stub length is too long, it has the same effect as a "wye" cable or a twofer, both of which will cause instability in the network.

A wye cable should never, under any circumstances, be used to split a data signal because it can cause signal reflections and corrupt the data. If more than 32 loads need to be connected to the system or if the total data run is over 500 m (1640 feet), then the most reliable way to do so is to use a data distribution amplifier or a data repeater.

A data amplifier accepts an input through an EIA485 receiver and boosts the signal with an EIA485 transmitter. An amplifier may have a single input and a single output, as in a repeater, or it may have multiple outputs, as in a data splitter amplifier or data distribution amplifier. Either way, it allows for the continuation of a data link beyond the recommended maximum length by regenerating the signal from the input to the output. The signal can be amplified several times if necessary as long as the amplifiers are fast enough to reproduce digital signals accurately. If the amplifiers are too slow they can cause errors across multiple repeaters.

DMX512 Data Protocol

The transmission and receipt of DMX512 data mean nothing without a common understanding of the representation of the data. This is the purpose of the data protocol: to define a standard way of representing data and packaging it in a format that can be easily exchanged, interpreted, and understood.

DMX512 is a serial protocol, which is why it can be transmitted across one pair of wires. It is also an asynchronous protocol, which means that packets of data are not transmitted at regular intervals but only when an update is needed or at a maximum of 1 s, whichever comes first. Also, the data are not clocked by a separate timing circuit. For that reason it requires a signal, called a Reset signal, to be sent to the receivers to indicate that a new data packet is about to come down the line. Once the Reset signal is sent and some housekeeping is taken care of, then the values for each of a maximum of 512 "dimmers" can be sent in sequential order, starting with dimmer one. Each set of data updating the dimmer values is called a packet. The values are coded in binary and range from 0 to 255 decimal. How the dimmer levels are interpreted is up to the receiver. For example, the value 10 (decimal) sent to dimmer six could be an intensity value of 4% or it could mean "open the shutter" to an automated luminaire. The data are transmitted at a rate of 250 kilobits per second.

Like every part of the data packet, the Reset signal has specific requirements to which it must adhere. It has to start with a high-to-low data transition and then stay low for at least 88 µs. When a Reset signal is transmitted, the receivers know to expect the start of a packet transmission.

After the Reset signal comes the Mark After Break, which is a high value that must be held for at least 8 µs but less than 1 s (the entire packet time has to be less than 1 s, so the Mark After Break time needs to be considerably less). The Mark After Break serves to separate the Reset signal and the Start code.

The Start code is used to define the meaning of the data in the rest of the packet. In both the original DMX512 standard and in the 1990 update, the only defined Start code was the Null Start (all zeros), meaning the packet contains dimmer level information. Other Start codes (1 through 255 decimal) could be registered with USITT by manufacturers for proprietary use.

Every packet has to start with the Reset, Mark After Break, and Start code sequence before it can transmit the data. The data values are formatted in frames of 11 bits: one Start bit, which is a low bit, eight dimmer level Data bits (least significant bit to most significant bit), and two Stop bits, which are high bits (Figure 15-6). Each bit takes 4 µs for a total frame time of 44 µs.

A controller does not have to transmit 512 channels of data; it may transmit as few as one channel or as many as 512 channels. If fewer than 512 channels are needed, then only the required channels may be sent, as long as the total packet length is 1196 µs. When DMX512-A was approved, then the minimum packet length for receivers stayed at 1196 s, but the minimum packet length for transmitters became 1204 µs.

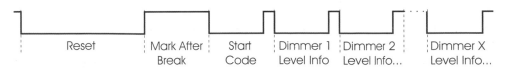

Figure 15-6 A DMX512 packet begins with a Reset signal, a Mark After Break, and a Start code followed by the actual data. Each data frame is transmitted sequentially starting from one up to a maximum of 512. The frame consists of a Start bit, eight Data bits, and two Stop bits. In the illustration, all channels are at zero.

CHAPTER 16

DMX512-A

When I am working on a problem I never think about beauty. I only think about how to solve the problem. But when I have finished, if the solution is not beautiful, I know it is wrong.—Buckminster Fuller (1895–1983), architect, engineer, inventor, philosopher, author

DMX512 was conceived as a unidirectional communications protocol, and for almost 20 years it served its purpose effectively. But the increasing power and sophistication of controllers coupled with the increasing size and complexity of lighting systems have afforded the opportunity and created the desire to incorporate bidirectional communications between the controller and the loads under control. In fact, some manufacturers built proprietary bidirectional communications capability into some of their equipment before it became a formal standard. Now that it has been standardized, sending and receiving information to and from controllers and devices are going to change how we build and program automated lighting systems. DMX512-A is a new standard that, among other things, formalizes bidirectional communication capability in DMX512.

In 2004, the ANSI Board of Standards Review approved a modified DMX512 standard authored by the Control Protocols Working Group of ESTA, which is made up of industry volunteers who are manufacturers, consultants, theatrical dealers, and end users. The standard, known as E1.11, Entertainment Technology—USITT DMX512-A Asynchronous Serial Digital Data Transmission Standard for Controlling Lighting Equipment and Accessories, broadens the DMX512 standard to provide for the physical means to facilitate bidirectional communication. To distinguish it from previous versions of the standard, equipment that is compliant with E1.11 is supposed to be marked DMX512-A or USITT DMX512-A.

Much of the standard was unchanged from its previous version. It's still an eight-bit asynchronous serial data transmission using standard universal asynchronous receiver transmitter (UART) chips that are commonly used in RS-485 serial data ports, and it still uses the same timing and protocol as before. The difference is that the Start code, which was formerly restricted to the null set, or all zeros, is now expanded to cover a range of purposes. Alternate Start codes other than the null set are now used to tell the receivers the purpose of the next packet of data that is about to come down the data line. In addition, there are now five allowable configurations of the data link (interconnecting cable), including the use of two-pair cable for dual DMX512 universes.

Alternate Start Codes

A Null Start code is still used to signify that a packet of data contains dimmer level data (or any parameter level data), ensuring compatibility with legacy (existing) equipment. If the Start code is anything other than the null set, it is known as an Alternate Start code (ASC). There are 256 possible Start codes, each signifying a unique instruction.

Reserved ASCs

A number of ASCs were set aside by the standards committee to deal with commonly occurring tasks. For example, if a console operator wants information from a particular fixture, for example, the status of the menu display, then a message is sent to the fixture requesting that bit of information. The information will most likely come back in the form of ASCII text, so before the fixture sends the data it will send the ASC 17h (17 hexadecimal). That alerts the receiver, in this case the console, that the packet of data about to follow will be ASCII text. Since the text might cover more than one page, the first packet after the ASC 17h indicates the page number of the text transmission. It can be between one and 256 pages in length. The second packet indicates the number of characters to expect for each line of text, and the third packet starts the actual text transmission. Each subsequent packet continues the ASCII text until it reaches the 512th packet or until the packet contains all zeroes, indicating the end of the text message.

Another reserved ASC is a test packet (55h) that transmits a series of data slots with the same value (55h) to test the timing of the receiver. The ASC CFh is a System Information Packet (SIP) that provides for sending "checksum" data to test the integrity of data that have been sent. It essentially adds the value of the bits sent in a previous data packet and compares the sum to the expected value. If they match, then there is a high probability, though not a certainty, that the data are not corrupt. This is very important in certain applications. For example, when you are upgrading the software in a fixture, if the software upgrade is not completed correctly it could render the fixture unusable. So checking the integrity of the data before implementing the upgrade is very important. In the past, if a fixture had flash memory, it could be updated by the use of special black boxes or upload boxes that had to be connected to the data line, but the controller had to be taken offline. The DMX512-A implementation makes it possible for the controller to handle upgrades or be left online while another device performs the upgrade.

Proprietary ASCs

The ASCs that have not been reserved by the standards committee can be registered by a manufacturer as a proprietary ASC that can be used to send custom information over the data link. For example, if a manufacturer builds a fixture with a unique function, they might request a proprietary ASC in order to handle the control of that function. When a manufacturer requires a proprietary ASC, they must first register for a Manufacturer ID. Registration requests for ASCs, Manufacturer IDs, and Enhanced Functionality protocol must be sent to the ANSI E1 Accredited Standards Committee through ESTA, and it's their sole discretion whether or not to assign them, depending on the availability of unused and unassigned ASCs.

Enhanced Function Topologies

When the original DMX512 protocol was implemented in 1986, it allowed for an optional second data link on the fourth and fifth wires in a five-wire cable. It did not, however, spell out how to use the second data link, and, as a result, there were several different implementations used over the years, some of which were compliant with DMX512 and others which were not. DMX512-A changed the requirements for the second data link, and in the process it has disallowed some of the existing implementations that were not in compliance. There are now four different standardized ways of using the second data link. These implementations are known as Enhanced Function Topologies, and each one has an EF number. Their uses are described in the following sections, and their allowable topologies are summarized in Table 16-1.

Enhanced Function 1

EF1 is a data link that transmits half-duplex EIA-485 compliant data on the primary data link and does not use the secondary link at all. A half-duplex signal is one that can transmit data in only one direction at a time. When one end of the data line is in transmit mode then the other has to be in receive mode and vice versa; it cannot simultaneously transmit and receive data. The direction of data transmission in an EF1 topology is controlled by the ASC.

Enhanced Function 2

EF2 is a data link that transmits data only on the primary data link and receives data only on the secondary data link. The primary link is a dedicated unidirectional send line and the secondary link is a dedicated unidirectional receive line. The combination of send and receive data pairs makes up a full-duplex data link.

Table 16-1 Allowable topologies in DMX512-A.

Topology	Description
EF1	Primary link: half-duplex send or receive ($\uparrow\downarrow$)
	Secondary link: not connected (NC)
EF2	Primary link: unidirectional send ($\uparrow$)
	Secondary link: unidirectional receive ($\downarrow$)
EF3	Primary link: unidirectional send ($\uparrow$)
	Secondary link: half-duplex send or receive ($\uparrow\downarrow$)
EF4	Primary link: half-duplex send or receive ($\uparrow\downarrow$)
	Secondary link: half-duplex send or receive ($\uparrow\downarrow$)

Reproduced with permission from ESTA.

Enhanced Function 3

EF3 is a data link in which the primary can transmit only unidirectional data but the secondary link can transmit or receive in half-duplex mode. The bidirectional data on the secondary link is controlled by the ASC.

Enhanced Function 4

EF4 allows for two half-duplex data links, one on the primary data link and the other on the secondary data link. In both cases, the return of data is under the control of the ASC.

Bidirectional Distribution Amplifiers/Return Data Combiners

The use of a bidirectional data link necessitates the need for specialized distribution amplifiers when more than one DMX512 output from a single universe is required. When a data link is used for both transmitting and receiving, the distribution amplifier must have the ability to control the direction of the flow of data. In addition, the data returning from each output have to be combined on a single return data link to the controller in such a way as to prevent data collisions. One protocol that prevents such collisions is part of the Remote Device Management (RDM; see Chapter 17) scheme.

Termination

In addition to using specialized distribution amplifiers, care must be taken to properly terminate both ends of a bidirectional data line. The terminators are the same as for a unidirectional DMX512 terminator (120-ohm, 0.25-watt resistor between data negative and data positive).

Isolation

Until DMX512-A became the standard, isolation of the DMX512 ports was not required. The standard said that "suitable optical isolation, transformer isolation, or other means may be employed," but no provisions or

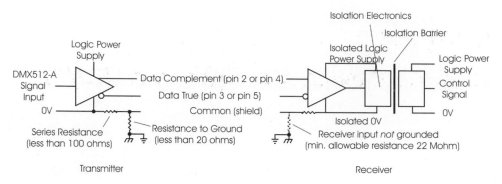

Figure 16-1   The preferred topology is a grounded transmitter and an isolated receiver. Reproduced with permission from ESTA.

guidelines were given. That was changed in DMX512-A. The preferred method is for the transmitter to reference earth ground and for the receiver to be isolated, which provides for a grounded shield but prevents ground loops caused by differences in the ground potential between the transmitter and receiver (Figure 16-1).

CHAPTER 17

Remote Device Management (RDM)

If you have an apple and I have an apple and we exchange these apples then you and I will still each have one apple. But if you have an idea and I have an idea and we exchange these ideas, then each of us will have two ideas.— George Bernard Shaw

If DMX512-A is the highway on which information travels between a controller and a fixture, then RDM is the car that shuttles some of the data passengers back and forth. After several years of development by the ESTA Controls Protocols Working Group, Remote Device Management (RDM) was recently adopted as a standard. RDM is a protocol that is used in conjunction with DMX512-A in order to configure, monitor, and manage the devices on the network. It is an extension of DMX512 and it defines the housekeeping and message structure that controllers and devices on the DMX512 link use to exchange information. After the controller "discovers" which devices are on the data link, then it can configure, monitor, and manage each of them by using RDM commands.

This protocol will change the way we work with automated lighting and other devices. Instead of configuring all the devices in the shop or on the ground before flying them in a rig, it will soon be possible to manage DMX512 address assignments and fixture personalities from behind a console. Better still, RDM will eliminate the need to climb a truss or bring a truss in because the DMX512 addresses were not set properly.

Unlike DMX512, RDM is a bidirectional protocol, and it has an error checking scheme. In DMX512, new data is sent a maximum of 44 times per second, depending on the number of channels involved. If one or two data packets are corrupted, then the data will be refreshed very quickly and few problems are likely to be encountered. If an RDM packet is corrupted, it could alter the meaning of a text message or it could corrupt a software upgrade. Therefore, a checksum is included in each RDM transmission to ensure the integrity of the data. A checksum is a crude way of validating the data received by a device. It adds the value of each bit in the data packet and compares it to the checksum value. If they correspond, then there is a high likelihood, though not a complete certainty, that the data is valid. It's a bit like a driver counting the number of passengers at the beginning and end of a trip to verify that they were all safely delivered. If the number at the end of the trip matches that at the beginning of the trip, it's a safe bet they are the same passengers who started the trip.

The RDM Physical Layer

The physical layer of RDM—the physical components, wiring, and connections—is a subset of the Enhanced Functions of DMX512-A; more specifically, RDM calls for the use of Enhanced Function 1, a half-duplex signal on the primary data link (pins 2 and 3). The direction of the data transmission is controlled by the Alternate Start code, which can only be initiated by the controller and not the device under control. Such a system is known as a polled system, because the controller has the ability to ask each of the receivers whether they have anything to report. Only the controller can poll the devices on the data link and not the other way around. In an RDM system, the secondary data link is not used.

The RDM Discovery Process

In order for the controller to communicate with the devices on the data link, it must first know which devices are connected to the link and how to get a message to each one. The first task when an RDM-capable controller goes online is to seek out each RDM-capable device by a methodical process known as discovery. Since the DMX512 address can be the same for more than one fixture, sending RDM messages by using the DMX512 address could cause problems; if more than one fixture responds to a command then the data will collide and become meaningless. Therefore, every RDM-compliant device is required to have a unique ID (UID) that is stored in the memory of the device. The UID differs from a DMX512 address in that a DMX512 address is temporarily assigned in the field and it can be changed by the user, while the UID is permanently assigned in the factory by the manufacturer and cannot be changed. The UID comprises a 16-bit Manufacturer ID assigned to the manufacturer by ESTA and a 32-bit Device ID assigned by the manufacturer. The complete 48-bit UID is used in the discovery process for the purpose of identifying each device on the line.

The discovery starts with a methodical search of UIDs using a binary search tree (Figure 17-1).

The controller first sends a "Discovery Unique Branch" message to a subset of the search tree using a targeted range of UIDs. The first targeted range of UIDs is the lower half of the search tree; the second targeted range is the upper half. After the first Discovery Unique Branch message and its target UID are sent, all the devices on the line whose UID is equal to or greater than the target UID send a response back to the controller. If there is more than one responder in that range of UIDs, then there will be data collisions and the data will not necessarily be valid, but the controller will then know there are responders in that range. It will then store those locations to memory and continue its search.

If only one response is received, then the sum of the binary digits is compared to the checksum received in the response. If they correspond, then the controller records the UID as a valid responder. The controller then

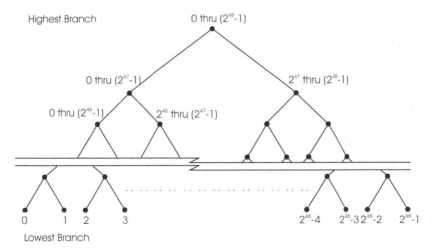

Figure 17-1 The RDM discovery process methodically searches every branch of a binary tree, starting from the highest and dropping to the lowest, to find all RDM-capable devices on the data link. Reproduced with permission from ESTA.

sends it a Mute command to stop it from responding to any more discovery commands. The same branch is subsequently tested again to see if any further responses are received.

If the checksum is not valid, then it is assumed that is because multiple responders have caused a data collision and invalidated the checksum. Now the controller knows that there are multiple responders in the target range and it requires a narrower search. The discovery then continues by narrowing the search range to half of the previous range. When the discovery reaches the end of the sequence of UIDs on all adjacent branches, it then drops down to the next lowest branch and continues its search. When it reaches the lowest branch of the search tree, then there will be only two possible UIDs left. The controller will then mute one of them and wait for a response from the other. After receiving its response, the controller notes its UID and continues until all responders have been discovered.

If there are no responders to the original message then the controller stops looking in that range of UIDs and moves to the adjacent branch to continue the discovery. It continues until it exhausts the entire range of UIDs and completes its search.

RDM Parameter Messages

Once the controller completes the discovery process, it can send and receive messages to the devices on the data link using their UIDs. It can communicate with each device individually or it can broadcast messages globally to every device on the data link. When a controller sends an RDM message, it is identified as such by its Alternate Start code (ASC). Then and only then can a responder generate an RDM response. A responder cannot send an RDM message without first receiving a message from the controller.

An RDM parameter message can be either a Get command or a Set command. A Get command is a request for information about a parameter, and a Set command is used to change the setting of a parameter in a device. Each parameter is uniquely identified and called by its PID (parameter ID).

RDM messages fall into one of 10 categories, as outlined in the following sections.

Network Management Messages

The Communication Status parameter is a central repository for a fixture to keep error messages associated with a fixture in order to analyze the integrity of the network. When an operator wants to look at the cumulative error data, a Get Communications Status command is sent and the fixture responds with the information. Examples of errors that would generate a network management message include a message that ends before the message length field is received, a message length that doesn't match the data received, and a checksum failure.

Status Collection Messages

When a fixture has information to send about its status or one of its parameters, it has to wait until it is polled by the controller. Until then, that information is deferred and held in the message queue. There are five commands related to the collection of status messages: Get Queued Messages, Get Status Messages, Get Status ID Description, Clear Status ID, and Get or Set Sub-Device Status Reporting Threshold. When the controller sends any one of these commands, then the fixture sends the requested information. The Status ID Description has to do with the severity of the message—either an error, warning, or advisory—and the Clear Status ID clears the status message queue. Set Sub-Device Status Reporting Threshold limits the length of the message a subdevice can send.

An example of a Get Queued Message might be when the DMX512 start address of a device has been changed at its menu display and the fixture wants to report the new start address to the console.

RDM Information Messages

RDM Information Messages give the user specific information about the fixture and which parameters it has that are supported by RDM. The Get Supported Parameters command and the Get Parameter Description command fall under this category. Once the controller has obtained all of the RDM-supported parameter messages from a device, it can then use Get and Set commands to control those devices.

Product Information Messages

Product Information Messages provide details about a variety of fixture-related information. The Get Device Info command retrieves information about the fixture RDM protocol version, model ID, product category, software version ID, number of consecutive DMX512 slots (DMX512 "footprint"), DMX512 personality, DMX512 start address, number of subdevices, and the sensor count. In addition, the Get Product ID command can call up myriad details about the device, including the type of lamp it uses, whether it's a projector, atmospheric generator, dimmer, scenic drive, or data distributor, and much more.

DMX512 Setup Messages

DMX512 Setup Messages relate to a number of issues related to a fixture's DMX512 configuration. They include retrieving or setting the DMX512 personality of a fixture, retrieving a description of a particular personality, retrieving or setting the DMX512 start address, and retrieving information about the number and types of DMX512 slots (or channels) and their descriptions. This feature allows the operator to change some settings from the console that, without RDM, would have to be changed at the fixture.

Sensor Parameter Messages

If a device has sensors, such as temperature, voltage, current, etc., then the Sensor Parameter Messages allow the controller to exchange information about them. These messages include retrieving descriptions of sensors, getting or setting sensor values, and recording sensor values. The recording function might be useful for monitoring changes in sensor values.

Power and Lamp Setting Parameter Messages

Power and lamp settings can be retrieved and manipulated with this group of RDM messages. All of the functions related to the fixture and lamp operation, such as the number of hours the device has been operated, number of lamp hours, number of lamp strikes, current lamp status, lamp on/off mode, and number of power on/off cycles, can be retrieved and/or set using these messages. The lamp mode is commonly used to determine under which conditions the lamp will turn on.

Display Setting Parameter Messages

Some devices have onboard displays that can be manipulated by the user; those manipulations can take place with RDM Display Setting Parameter Messages. For example, the display can be inverted in the event that a device is also inverted, or the display can be dimmed or turned off completely.

Device Configuration Parameter Messages

Certain devices are configurable with regard to common traits such as pan and tilt. The Device Configuration Parameter Messages concern such things as inverting pan and/or tilt, swapping pan and/or tilt, and accessing or changing an onboard real-time clock.

Device Control Parameter Messages

Various functions that are used with some devices are grouped into the Device Control Parameter Messages. These include a method of identifying a device, resetting a device, finding the power state of a device, performing a self-test, describing the self-test functions, and recording and playing back onboard presets. For example, the Get/Set Identify Device command is used to physically identify a device. Any device that receives this command will respond by flashing or making an audible sound.

The commands listed here are not a complete list, but a sample of some of the functions that RDM will enable. As manufacturers take advantage of the protocol the list of commands will be expanded to meet the needs of the end user.

CHAPTER 18

Architecture for Control Networks (ACN)

Without deviation from the norm, progress is not possible.—Frank Zappa

When a group of lighting professionals came together under the auspices of USITT to create a standard for DMX512 protocol in 1986, automated lighting as we know it was in its infancy. Only a handful of companies around the world manufactured automated lights, and most of them only rented them; they weren't for sale. In addition, when a client hired an automated lighting system, they often had to hire a programmer/operator, too. Clients were bound by the terms of the contract to use specially trained personnel to set up and operate the automated lighting system. Therefore, there was little need to integrate automated lighting systems with conventional lighting; they were built and used as stand-alone systems. Under those circumstances, a universal control standard for automated lighting was superfluous. Instead, such systems used proprietary digital control protocols or 0–10 V analog control. Consequently, the control of automated lighting was not a consideration for the creators of the original DMX512 standard.

But automated lighting took root very quickly, and as it spread and became more commonplace, it began to be used in a size and scope that had not previously been imagined. When end users demanded more specialized control for larger, more complicated systems, independent console manufacturers sprang up to meet the need. Suddenly the idea of using DMX512 for automated lighting control made sense. When automated lighting manufacturers embraced DMX512, the way DMX512 was used changed dramatically. The number of channels in a typical DMX512 system doubled or tripled overnight. A typical lighting rig with 48 channels of dimming now needed 128 or 256 more DMX512 channels to control 8 or 16 automated lights. When lighting designers began to push the envelope with automated lighting, specifying rigs with hundreds of automated lights that used multiple universes of DMX512, consoles began expanding their outputs beyond the limitations of a single DMX512 universe by offering multiple DMX512 ports for systems that required more than 512 channels of DMX512.

In 1999, when Light & Sound Design (now part of PRG) displayed the first "digital light," called the Icon M, at the LDI show, it had a significant impact on the use of DMX512. The ill-fated[1] product used the Texas Instruments DMD to project "soft gobos"—gobos that could be created with software rather than hardware—and animation (see Section 7, Digital Lighting). Although the product was never mass produced for sale, it did spawn a whole new generation of DMX512-controlled media servers that, once again, expanded the use of DMX512. One of the first such products, the High End Systems Catalyst, uses over 40 channels of DMX512 for each of up to eight layers for a total of 320 DMX512 channels. Compare that with at least 30 or more channels of DMX512 for a top-of-the-line "conventional" automated light and you can begin to see how the demand for DMX512 channels has changed. At the same time, LEDs hit a price point and a level of brightness that made them attractive to the entertainment lighting industry, and LED video displays and quasi-video displays have gained tremendous popularity in the market. As a result, many automated lighting consoles are now being tasked to drive displays as individual pixels or through DMX512-controlled media servers, causing an explosion in the consumption of DMX512 channels. Clearly a new protocol is desired, if not completely necessitated, in the industry.

In the late 1990s, even before the digital lighting phenomenon, ESTA began the long process of developing a new standard for the control of entertainment lighting and devices. The new standard, E1.17, commonly referred to as Architecture for Control Networks (ACN), is still under development and is currently in its third public review. It is expected to be finalized by the middle of 2006.

The ACN Suite of Protocols

ACN is not a single protocol like DMX512, but a suite of control protocols and languages that work together in order to distribute data for the control

---

[1] Sadly, the Icon M was never mass-produced, nor was it ever offered for sale. The original lot of 16 units was used on a few tours, including a Korn tour, but although millions of dollars were spent to develop the product, it was never fully realized.

of entertainment technology over a network. It is designed as a flexible system that can adapt to a number of hardware environments as well as to advances in technology. For that reason, the functions of the suite are split up according to function and divided into layers, each of which concerns a narrow portion of the entire process.

Because it is bidirectional, not only can a controller send data to a fixture, but also the fixture can send information back to the controller. (RDM has also adopted this bidirectionality; however, it is limited to relatively simple, nontime-critical responses regarding status and configuration. See Chapter 17, Remote Device Management.) For example, the controller might ask the fixture for its current address or its current operating temperature, and the fixture can respond by sending the correct data back to the console. ACN uses portions of TCP/IP (Transmission Control Protocol/Internet Protocol), and as such, it is has similarities to the Internet and to local area networks (LANs). It is strictly a software protocol, not a hardware protocol, and it does not specify how to build infrastructure, such as the cables, hubs, and connectors, that are needed to physically transmit data. It does not specify the type of cable or the type of connector to use, as does DMX512. Instead, it relies on existing technology and infrastructure, such as Ethernet, Wi-Fi, Firewire, and optical fiber, to carry the data where they need to go. It can take advantage of existing infrastructure as well as off-the-shelf accessories, such as routers, switches, bridges, and hubs. It will accommodate several controllers functioning on the network at one time, thus allowing several programmers to program a show simultaneously in a multiuser programming environment. Alternatively, it will allow the network to be subdivided, allowing, for example, a controller in one hotel ballroom to control the lights in that room while another controller in another ballroom simultaneously controls the lights in that room. It will also accommodate the use of remote focus units or remote consoles that can be plugged into the network at various locations. In general, it will allow a lighting control network to behave and operate in a manner similar to the Internet. And, in fact, it is designed to operate just as effectively over an application-specific network, such as a network of consoles, as it will over an existing LAN or WAN infrastructure, including the Internet. An operator should be able to work over a network thousands of miles away from the system with the same effectiveness (minus the live visuals) as if working in the same room as the system.

Unlike DMX512, ACN is a scalable protocol, meaning that a system can be designed for any system, large or small, using any number of addresses or channels up to 4,294,967,295 (32 bits). It is a "plug and play" system with a utility that monitors the data link and discovers which devices are connected and functioning in the system. Each device is monitored, managed, and controlled using a Device Management Protocol (DMP) by "getting" information from it and "setting" the values of certain properties within it. Anytime a new device is added, it will be automatically configured after the system discovers and recognizes it. If the system has not seen such a device before, its properties may become known to the system by asking the device for its DDL (Device Description Language) file, a file that describes the device using a DDL, which is part of the ACN protocol. Every device must have a DDL file, and it must provide it to a controller upon request.

ACN Elements

At the heart of the ACN architecture are three main elements: the DDL, the DMP, and the Session Data Transport Protocol (SDT).

Device Description Language

DDL is a text language for describing the characteristics of a device, its properties, and how they are used to control that device. The essential job of DDL is to describe the model of a device representing its functions as a set of variables or properties so that a console will know how to control and monitor it. A DDL description tells the controller what the device does, which variables or properties are involved, and the behavior of those properties. For example, in an automated light that can pan 540 degrees, the root property is the automated light (the "parent" property), and the pan function is one of its "child" properties. The maximum allowable pan value (540) is a child property of the pan function. How the maximum value (540) to be interpreted is a function of the "behavior" tagged to that property. For example, 540 could be degrees or it could be stepper motor steps. A root property can have several child properties, such as pan, tilt, color, or gobo, each of those properties may have several child properties, and so on. The entire hierarchy of properties defines the device in terms of a written model.

There is a DDL specification within the ACN protocol that describes the allowable behaviors associated with the device properties. This standard set of behaviors will grow as new innovations in technology are developed and introduced.

The device model is written in a subset of XML, or Extensible Markup Language, which is a standard for describing data in such a way that it can be understood by computers and humans alike. For example, the following information is a portion of DDL describing the pan and tilt properties of an automated luminaire. The first line indicates that it is a DDL document. The second line indicates that the text is defining a device. The third line is a comment to help the operator (not the machine!) understand what is to follow. The fourth line assigns a label to the property being described. The fifth line is the access protocol. The sixth line indicates the end of the description of that property.

```
(this is the root property)
<device>
<! - - description of an automated luminaire - ->
<property label = "Automated Luminaire">
<protocol protocol = "ACN-DMP-1" address = "1">(this is
   the access protocol)
<property>
```

The protocol interface is that part of DDL that helps map it to various protocols. If the property in question is, say, the intensity of a device, the protocol interface gives the controller the proper information it needs to use a particular protocol such as DMX512 or DMP.

Device Management Protocol

Once the controller discovers a device and recognizes its properties through DDL, it can then interact with it. DMP is the portion of the ACN suite that is used to configure, monitor, and control the properties of each of the devices on the network. It provides the address structure to identify those properties and the messaging structure used to manipulate them. It does its job by "getting" and "setting" the values of the properties of the devices.

There are several primary DMP messages and response messages. Some messages of interest include Get_property, Set_property, Subscribe,

Unsubscribe, and Event. Get_property and Set_property are the two main messages via which properties of a device are read and written to. Subscribe and Unsubscribe are tools for monitoring changes to properties of interest to the controller. When a property of a device changes, it generates an event with the new property value to send to those controllers that are subscribed to that property.

Some of the response messages include Get_property_reply, Get_property_fail, Set_property_fail, Subscription_Accept, and Subscription_Refuse. When a controller sends a Get_property, the device must respond with either a Get_property_reply containing the requested value or a Get_property_fail message. A Set_property_fail message is sent in response to a Set_property_with_reply request from the controller that could not be carried out along with a reason why it failed. Subscription_Accept and Subscription_Refuse messages must be sent in response to a Subscription_Request from the controller. If a controller is subscribed to a property then it will receive all events generated by that property.

All communication in ACN occurs between components. When a Get_property or Set_property message is sent by a controller, it must first specify the component to which the message is targeted, and then it must specify the address of the property within that component. The controller knows about the component through ACN discovery, and it knows which properties are available within that component by recognizing the type of device or reading the DDL of a newly encountered device. The format of DMP messages is detailed in ANSI BSR E1.17 *Multipurpose Network Protocol Suite—Device Management Protocol* and is beyond the scope of this book.

Session Data Transport

SDT is a protocol for sending data between ACN components (controllers, devices, and monitors). Part of its job is to package multiple short messages into a single packet to make more efficient use of network bandwidth. SDT also provides dynamic and multicast reliability that the TCP/IP transport protocol does not provide. DMP defines the format and meaning of data and SDT transports the data where they need to go.

SDT messages must conform to the ACN Package Data Unit (PDU) structure as defined in ANSI BSR E1.17 *Multipurpose Control Protocol Suite—E1.17*

"ACN" Architecture. This structure is used throughout ACN and simplifies decoding the protocols. When SDT transports client data to multiple members within a session, each client block is wrapped up and addressed to the intended receiver. The address of the sender of the ACN packet is found at the top-most level within the packet, as is the length of the packet. A packet is made up of a continuous list of PDUs, each of which must follow a specific PDU format as defined by the ACN architecture document. Packets are sent within a session by a session leader, which sends the packet to the members of the session. A group of session membership messages are used to set up and manage the session. They include Join, Join Refuse, Join Accept, Leave, Leaving, Connect, Connect Accept, Connect Refuse, Disconnect, and Disconnecting. There are a number of other types of session messages including Reliable and Unreliable Session Data Wrappers, which do the actual work of carrying the transported data, a Session Parameters message, which allows the tweaking of various values related to the operation of the session, a NAK message, which triggers the resending of missed packets, and request and reply messages for communicating which sessions an ACN component participates in.

When a message is sent from a leader to a member, it is said to be traveling downstream; when it goes from a member to a leader, it is traveling upstream. Multiple sessions can operate simultaneously, and any component may be a leader, a member, or both. Each session is identified by a Component ID (CID) and a session number. A summary of SDT messages is shown in Table 18-1.

The ACN Transport

ACN uses a subset of the TCP/IP suite of protocols for internetworking, or interconnecting dissimilar computer systems. The main protocol used by ACN is one within TCP/IP called User Datagram Protocol (UDP), which is used to send short messages of up to approximately 1500 bytes, known as datagrams, between components of ACN. (Note that UDP allows for datagrams of up to 32K bytes; however, packets larger than 1500 bytes or so become fragmented and lead to performance degradation. For this reason, ACN disallows these large datagrams.) These datagrams are not necessarily sent or received in order, nor does UDP provide for any reliability; datagrams can go missing without any notification. But UDP does, however, provide for a fast and efficient means of transport with an

Table 18-1 Session data transport message summary. Reproduced with permission from ESTA.

Channel Data Wrappers	Symbol	Contains PDU Block	Sent to Ad Hoc Address in SDT Base Layer PDU	Sent to Destination Address in SDT Base Layer PDU	Sent to Destination Address in Wrapper PDU	Sent to Source Address in SDT Base Layer PDU
Reliable Wrapper	REL WRAP	✓		✓		
Unreliable Wrapper	UNREL WRAP	✓		✓		
Channel Membership						
Join	JOIN		✓			
Join Refuse	JOIN REFUSE					✓
Join Accept	JOIN ACCEPT					✓
Leave	LEAVE				✓[4]	✓
Leaving	LEAVING				✓[4]	✓
Channel Parameters	CHANNEL PARAMS				✓[4]	
Reliability and Sequencing						
Acknowledge	ACK				✓[4]	✓
Negative Acknowledge	NAK			✓[3]		

Continues

Table 18-1 *Continued*

Channel Data Wrappers	Symbol	Contains PDU Block	Sent to Ad Hoc Address in SDT Base Layer PDU	Sent to Destination Address in SDT Base Layer PDU	Sent to Destination Address in Wrapper PDU	Sent to Source Address in SDT Base Layer PDU
Acknowledge						
Session Membership						
Connect	CONNECT				✓	
Connect Accept	CONNECT ACCEPT				✓[4]	
Connect Refuse	CONNECT REFUSE				✓[4]	
Disconnect	DISCONNECT				✓	
Disconnecting	DISCONNECTING				✓[4]	
Client Protocols						
Client Protocol		✓[2]			✓	
PDUs						
Diagnostic						
Get Sessions	GET SESSIONS		✓[1]			
Sessions	SESSIONS					

[1]Sent to source address of packet containing *Get Sessions* message.
[2]Depends on client protocol specification.
[3]Sent to channel downstream for NAK suppression.
[4]Sent outbound on reciprocal channel, but association field indicates intended inbound channel.

efficient use of bandwidth. ACN adds reliable transfer and the ability of the session leader to know which packets have been received by each session member on top of UDP.

Network Media

ACN does not specify any physical layer (Figure 18-1). Instead, it is an application program that sits on top of an underlying network technology, such as Ethernet (IEEE 802.3), wireless Ethernet or Wi-Fi (IEEE 802.11), Firewire (IEEE 1394), modem, serial links, and high-speed links used for backbone distribution, such as ATM, SONET, and FDDI. Many automated luminaires are already hard-wired with RJ-45 connectors, which are commonly used with Ethernet, Art-Net, and similar network applications using shielded twisted pair (STP) or unshielded twisted pair (UTP) cable.

In summary, the DDL, the DMP, and the SDT work together to set up and control devices on an ACN system. Each protocol handles a portion of the job and works independently of each other so that they can be adapted and upgraded without affecting the overall system. Data are sent over the network using UDP to package datagrams and send them quickly and efficiently.

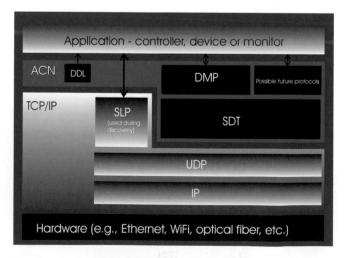

Figure 18-1   The structure of the ACN architecture. Reproduced with permission from ESTA.

The complete ACN suite of protocols is very complex and involved. A complete dissertation on each of the protocols is beyond the scope of this book. For more information, see the complete documents describing the standard. Electronic and printed copies of American National Standards Institute (ANSI) standards are available on the ESTA Foundation website (http://www.estafoundation.org/pubs.htm) or through ANSI (http://webstore.ansi.org/ansidocstore/dept.asp?dept_id=3004). Printed copies are available through USITT (http://www.usitt.org/bookstore/go.php?to=ItemList&category=ESTA%20Publications) or through PLASA (http://www.lsionline.co.uk/books/result.asp?cat=Standards).

CHAPTER 19

Menuing

Understanding is a kind of ecstasy.—Carl Sagan

The first moving lights needed no addressing capabilities because they were each individually connected directly to the console with bundles of wires, with each pair controlling a single attribute with a 0 to 10V control signal. As controllers became more sophisticated and moved to a digital multiplex control format, it necessitated the need for a fixture addressing system so each fixture could decode the digital signal to determine whether or not to respond to any given command. Most of them used (and some still use) a dual inline package (DIP) switch system that allowed the address to be set manually in the field. The address is configured by turning individual switches on or off in a binary offset fashion. For example, if all the switches are off (0000) then the starting address is 1 (binary offset of 1, as you don't usually have a fixture "0"). Some fixtures had the ability to respond to different protocols since there was no standard at the time, and some added options, such as pan and tilt swap, that gave that particular fixture its own unique personality. Thus was born the first automated lighting menuing systems, which allow a fixture to be set up and configured according to the requirements in the field.

As automated luminaires become more and more sophisticated, their menuing options and personality traits are becoming increasingly complex and more numerous. Many of the new automated lights introduced in the industry in the past few years offer very little in the way of new and innovative effects; manufacturers are mostly repackaging existing effects in unique combinations. The innovations are coming mostly in the areas of price breakthroughs, size and weight breakthroughs, and advanced software features. As a result, menuing systems are growing in popularity and menuing features are expanding. Ironically, these innovations are becoming increasingly unnecessary, as advances in console technology and increasingly sophisticated control protocols are making most of the

Figure 19-1 A typical automated lighting menu display.

functions of a menuing system redundant. When RDM and ACN are fully implemented, menuing systems may become unnecessary except for specialized functions such as self-testing and preproduction preparation.

Almost all the automated luminaires manufactured today, even some of the less expensive ones, have an LCD, LED, or vacuum fluorescent display (VFD) to address and configure the fixture. Most menu displays have a three- or four-character alphanumeric LED readout with three or four navigation buttons. Some are moving toward a multiline LCD display, and more advanced digital lights typically have a small thin film transistor (TFT) active matrix display with video capability.

Every manufacturer has a proprietary menuing system—there is no standard for menu labels or functions—but there are many common elements that are fundamental to every moving light (Figure 19-1).

Some of the more typical menuing functions are the following:

- Addressing: Typically, addressing the fixture is the highest priority of the display menu and appears in the lowest branch of the menu options tree. Changing the DMX512 address is usually accomplished by pressing the enter button and scrolling up or down until you come to the desired starting DMX512 address. Some manufacturers allow you to set the address by fixture number rather than by the DMX512 address. In that case, there might be a letter designator, such as the letter "F" before the address. The processor in the fixture converts the fixture number to the appropriate DMX512 starting address by calculating the number of DMX512 addresses required for each fixture and multiplying by the fixture number and adding 1. For example, if the fixture has 16 parameters and uses a slot of 16 DMX512 addresses, and the fixture number is set to 8, then the starting address is 113.

- Pan Invert, Tilt Invert: In some instances it might be useful to change the pan and/or tilt orientation so that they are more easily programmed. For example, if a row of fixtures is laid out symmetrically between stage left and stage right, then panning the stage left fixtures onstage results in the stage fixtures panning off stage. By inverting the pan in the stage right fixture, the same panning action will result in all fixtures panning onstage. Also, if some fixtures are standing on the floor and some are hung off of the truss, then the truss fixtures will be inverted relative to the floor fixtures. When the truss fixtures are tilted downstage, then the floor fixtures will tilt upstage, and vice versa. By inverting the tilt in either the floor fixtures or the truss fixtures, they will tilt in the same direction.

- Vector Mode/Tracking Mode: When an automated fixture is refocused, there are two ways in which it can move: it can receive a command that contains its final ending coordinate and a speed in which to move, or it can receive a continuous stream of data controlling every step of the pan and tilt motors along the path to the end point. If it only receives an end position and a speed, then it is in Vector mode. If the controller dictates every step of pan and tilt, then it is in Tracking mode. The advantage of using Vector mode is that the fixture will calculate the time it takes to move the required distance and will ensure that the pan and tilt movements are timed to start and stop at the same time. The advantage of using Tracking mode is that the controller can handle the timing using cross-fades, and in some instances it's easier to program. Very often, automated lighting manufacturers use a combination of tracking and vectoring in a fixture. For example, the Martin MAC fixture, in certain modes, average the last few DMX512 values it receives to ensure smooth pan and tilt.

- Blackouts During Fading: Some fixtures offer the ability to black out the color wheel and/or gobo wheel when it is changing colors and/or gobos. Often the strobing effect produced by a color or gobo wheel is a distraction, and by blacking out the wheel during movement it produces a more subtle effect.

- Display Orientation: If the fixtures are rigged in a truss, just as most of them end up, then not only is the fixture inverted, but so is the display. By inverting the display, it is once again oriented with the gravitational pull of the earth so you don't have to hang upside down on the truss to understand the cryptic lettering.

- Lamp Control: Many automated luminaires have a feature that allows the lamp to be turned on and off remotely by sending it a DMX512 control signal. Without that feature, if you wanted to turn the lamp on or off you would have to switch the power or climb the truss to do so. But in some instances it might be preferable to have the lamp turn on automatically when power is applied to the fixture or when the fixture senses the presence of a DMX512 signal. For example, if the system is to be run by a novice operator or one trained in operating conventional lighting, then they might not be familiar with the procedure for striking the lamps. In that case, a menuing option to set the means by which the lamp comes on would be useful, and many automated luminaires have that feature. Typically, the options are the following:

  - *Auto on:* Lamp comes on automatically when the fixture is powered up.

  - *DMX control:* The lamp can be turned on and off via DMX512 from the console.

  - *DMX presence:* The lamp automatically turns on when it senses the presence of a DMX512 control signal and automatically turns off after a prescribed period, usually a few seconds, in which the DMX512 control signal is turned off.

- Monitoring: There are a number of items that are useful to monitor during the life of an automated luminaire. Many menu systems offer the opportunity to display certain types of information about the operation of the fixture, some of which is user resettable and some of which is not. These might include the following:

- *Total time a fixture has been operated:* This is typically not user resettable.

- *Resettable operation time:* This can be used to monitor certain durations such as the amount of time a rental fixture is on over the span of the rental.

- *Lamp on time:* This is useful for monitoring the operation time of a lamp. It can be used, for example, to find out if a lamp failed prematurely. It is typically resettable and should be reset when a fixture is re-lamped.

- *Number of lamp strikes:* In addition to the number of hours a lamp has been operated, the number of lamp strikes also affects the lamp life. This item is normally resettable and should be reset each time a fixture is re-lamped.

- *Fixture temperatures:* This feature can be used to monitor the internal temperature in various parts of a luminaire. For example, very often there is at least one temperature sensor in the head and at least one in the base of a moving yoke luminaire. If a lamp continually douses on its own, then the temperature should be checked to see if the fixture is overheating.

- *DMX512 values:* Most automated luminaires have the ability to display the current DMX512 for each parameter in the fixture. This allows you to troubleshoot the fixture and controller.

- *Software versions:* By displaying the software version currently loaded in the fixture, you can discern whether or not it is up-to-date.

- Control: Some automated luminaires have onboard programming with the ability to operate without an external controller in stand-alone mode in a master–slave configuration. There might be one or more programs that can play in sequence, and they might be triggered automatically, through programmable timed cues, or by an audio trigger.

- Fan Speed: In some cases the fan noise from a group of automated luminaires is too loud for a particular passage or quiet period. Some fixtures have the ability to control the fan speed in order to reduce the fan noise for a short period of time. If the internal temperature of the fixture exceeds the maximum allowable limit, then the fan speed control is overridden by the fixture and the speed is brought back to maximum.

- Self-Test: In the event that a luminaire malfunctions, it is helpful to test the fixture independently of the controller to help isolate the problem. That's when a self-test routine comes in handy. When you place a fixture in self-test mode, it will perform a routine that tests each parameter in sequence, allowing you to identify problems with the fixture.

- Reset: The reset function allows you to re-home each of the parameters in a fixture. It should be used in the event that a parameter is obviously out of position.

- Error Messages: The display in most automated luminaires serves as an indicator in the event that an error occurs. Depending on the sophistication of the menu system, there might be an extensive error message system including such errors as overtemperature, lamp ignition failure (typically because of the cool-down period), wheel position errors, sensor failures, and more.

These are a few of the more typical menuing functions. Some automated luminaires have more features and functions, while others have fewer.

When RDM and ACN (see Chapter 17, Remote Device Management and Chapter 18, Architecture for Control Networks) are fully implemented, then many or all of these functions will be accessible and resettable from the controller. Networking is a powerful feature that decentralizes control of the fixture and allows you to fully control it from either end of the net. Instead of climbing the truss to set the fixture address or change its personality, the lighting operator can handle it from the front of house. That's not to say that in the future the menuing system of automated luminaires will go away, because it probably won't. It will just be available on both ends of the data line.

SECTION 6

Maintenance and Troubleshooting

CHAPTER 20

Preventive Maintenance and Troubleshooting

Inanimate objects can be classified scientifically into three major categories; those that don't work, those that break down and those that get lost.—Russell Baker, Pulitzer Prize-winning newspaper columnist

When automated lighting systems were in their infancy, two things were certain: they were sure to impress and they were sure to break down. The MARC 350 lamp, which was originally designed for 16-mm movie projectors, was a popular lamp source for automated lighting in the early 1980s because it has an integral dichroic reflector, a high color temperature, and a relatively small arc. But it also required the use of an electronic switching power supply, which, at the time, proved to be relatively unreliable in automated lights. The lamp also suffers from relatively short lamp life and the color temperature varies quite a bit over the life of the lamp. Later on, some automated lighting manufacturers began using HTI lamps and magnetic ballast power supplies, which have fewer components and are much more reliable in this application. But the lamp life of the HTI lamp is also relatively low, and, because they require considerable cooling, the fans tend to be large and noisy.

When the original Clay Paky Golden Scan was introduced in the late 1980s, it was one of the first, if not the first, automated luminaires to use an HMI lamp, and it was a vast improvement over the existing lamp technology. HMI lamps have been used as a daylight source in the film industry for a long time. These lamps are used in automated lighting primarily in their double-ended form with spherical reflectors and condenser lenses. They are typically extremely reliable, they have a relatively long life (1000 hours or longer), and they are easier to cool because the pinch seals are farther from the arc and a spherical reflector exposes more of the lamp to forced air currents.

Shortly after the introduction of the Golden Scan, Philips introduced the MSR lamp, which was an evolution of the Philips Tin Halide (SN) lamp.

By adding dysprosium instead of tin, the color consistency was vastly improved and thus the MSR lamps were born. They found their way into the Coemar product line as well as into High End Systems Intellabeam fixtures. MSRs are packaged in single-ended envelopes,[1] which facilitate the use of elliptical reflectors and provide much more efficient optics. In the beginning they were more difficult to manufacture because they are compact and the chemistry was new, so the early lamps were not as reliable as the lamps of today.

Today, many automated luminaires use either MSR or HMI lamps (or their long-life equivalents). As lamp technology has improved over the years, premature lamp failures have become less of an issue, but power supply circuits are still the hardest working systems in an automated luminaire. They carry the most current, produce most of the heat, and are among the most common sources of failure.

Lamps and power supplies aside, there were numerous opportunities for trouble to find its way into an automated lighting system. Sometimes the motors would fail from repetitive high-speed operation, and sometimes the ribbon cables connecting the motors, which flex back and forth and twist round and round hundreds of thousands of times, would break. Other times the motor drive chips, which carry the current to drive the motors, would burn up, the connectors carrying current to the power supply and lamp would melt, or a software glitch in the EPROM would lock up the fixture. At times the problem would be something as simple as a mechanical fastener failure, and at other times it would be something as perplexing as the contamination of the quartz in the lamp envelope during the manufacturing process. And there were many times when a malfunction was purely a mystery.

But the enthusiasm for automated lighting was never dampened. Users of automated lighting simply factored in the failure rate and compensated by carrying more spare parts and entire fixtures as spares. Formulas were loosely developed whereby a spare fixture was allotted for a given number of working fixtures, so, for example, if a show had 24 fixtures there might be four spares for a total of 28 fixtures. Distributors carried huge inventories of spare parts, and road technicians jockeyed for truck space and carried portable "hospitals" laden with spare parts.

------

[1] Philips literature refers to MSR lamps as single-ended lamps, but technically they have a double-ended arc tube inside a single-ended outer envelope.

Complicating matters for the lighting crew was the fact that, in the early days, Vari-Lite literally cloaked their lighting hospitals to keep their technology secret for fear of being pirated. Only Vari-Lite-trained technicians were allowed to see the inside of their fixtures, much less learn how to maintain and repair them. Consequently, Vari-Lite required a technician to accompany each and every automated lighting package that went out the door, adding to the cost of the system. The art of maintaining and repairing automated lighting was a closed shop.

The good news is that the reliability of automated lighting fixtures has improved tremendously over the past 20 years. Whereas it used to be common to find failure rates as high as 10% and sometimes as high as 100% in the first year of operation, now the failure rate of most fixtures is much lower, perhaps as low as 1 or 2%. Reliability is largely model dependent and, to some extent, manufacturer dependent, but overall the technology is far more proven and reliable than it used to be.

Still, considering the huge numbers of automated lighting in the field, failures are inevitable. The older a fixture is, the more likely it is to be in need of maintenance and/or repair.

Common Sources of Problems: Heat, Gravity, Age

Heat is one of the main enemies of electronics and automated lighting. Every bit of power consumed by a luminaire is eventually converted to heat, and the management of heat in a fixture is the key to its longevity and proper operation. Many failures in electronic components can be attributed to excessive heat, which is a natural by-product of the friction produced by resistance to the flow of electrical current. In the real world, every current-carrying device has some element of resistance, however large or small. As the temperature of a conductor increases, so does its resistance. The amount of heat produced is proportional to the resistance and the square of the current.

$$\text{Power loss (heat)} = I^2 r,$$

where I is current in amps and r is resistance in ohms. The amount of energy lost to heat is known as the $I^2 r$ loss.

Electronic components like motor driver chips and microprocessors are designed to operate within certain parameters, including the ambient operating temperature. When the operating temperature exceeds the specified operating range of the component it is subject to failure.

There are a number of reasons why a luminaire might exceed the normal internal operating temperature, but among the most common is the restriction of airflow. Most automated luminaires are cooled by forced air ventilation using one or more fans with an intake, exhaust, and routed airflow path. Should any one of these airflow passages become obstructed, the internal temperature will rise and cause the thermal protection to turn off the fixture or cause the fixture to fail altogether. The most common cause of airflow obstruction is the collection of dust and debris. Regular maintenance that includes cleaning the fixture internally with compressed air will prevent this problem.

CAUTION: It is very important to hold the fan blades stationary when using compressed air to blow out the dirt and dust (Figure 20-1). If the fan is allowed to rotate freely it can generate a back EMF (voltage) that can damage the internal electronics that are in most axial fans.

Figure 20-1 Always hold a fan stationary when using compressed air to blow it free of dust and debris. Allowing the fan to spin freely can damage the fan.

Dust can also cause problems by blanketing components in a luminaire, particularly when fog and haze are used heavily. The residue of fog and haze tends to attract dust and dirt, causing the internal components of a fixture to collect a blanket of dust, thus insulating them from the cooler free air and trapping the heat. The chronic heat buildup can eventually lead to component failure. In addition, dust and dirt that cling to glass trap heat and produce hot spots that can lead to heat stress, possibly cracking the glass. Keeping optical components clean helps prevent heat-related failures.

In certain locations where the ambient air temperature is high or the air circulation is limited, it is a good idea to consider augmenting the airflow as insurance against overheating. For example, if the lights are installed in a plenum, chances are the airflow is limited. Adding a blower or bringing in forced air from outside of the plenum will ensure that the ambient air temperature will stay cooler.

Another common cause of heat damage is electrical connections that are not mechanically sound. For example, if a lamp socket loses its spring tension, then the contacts lose some of their surface connection with the lamp post. When that happens, it tends to cause arcing, which pits the contacts and increases the resistance between the lamp and the socket. Increased resistance produces more heat, which further deteriorates the socket and causes more arcing and pitting. It is a destructive cycle that eventually leads to the failure of the lamp socket.

Another situation causing heat damage is when the terminals of a connector become loose. Almost every automated luminaire uses a variety of connectors to accommodate the easy disassembly of the fixture for servicing. When fixtures are transported, particularly in the case of touring shows, connectors can become loose from excessive vibration. If that happens, the resistance between the cable and the connector increases, which sometimes produces enough heat to melt the connector.

Gravity is also a source of potential problems for automated luminaires, particularly those with heavy components like those found in magnetic ballast power supplies. Often the fasteners for such heavy components as magnetic ballasts and large transformers tend to loosen over time or from excessive vibration or rugged handling. If they break free inside the fixture they can physically damage other nearby components and cause hundreds of dollars worth of damage. Make sure all internal components are secured properly by physically inspecting them and checking their fasteners regularly.

As luminaires age, certain materials naturally break down and cause some components to fail. The most common failures involving aging materials can be found wherever insulating materials are used, such as in the lamination in transformers and stepper motors. These laminations are commonly varnished and tend to break down over time due to heat and thermal expansion and contraction. Also, certain components such as lamp sockets, fans, belts, spring plungers, and power factor capacitors have a finite life span and will need to be replaced periodically. It's difficult to prevent these types of breakdowns and it's difficult to detect them in advance, but you can detect signs of failure, such as cracking belts and the telltale black marks of an arcing socket. Routine inspection of these parts is highly recommended, especially as fixtures age and these types of failures become more common.

Preventive Maintenance

In order to maintain and maximize the life of an automated luminaire, the following steps should be taken:

1. Keep the airflow circulating by making sure that the vents and fans are free of dust and debris. This is particularly important in environments with heavy fog and haze. The mineral oil from haze machines does not evaporate as does the glycol from most fog machines, so an automated luminaire in a heavy haze environment should periodically be cleaned internally to remove the mineral oil buildup. In club environments, the combination of fog fluid and cigarette smoke causes excessive buildup of dust and nicotine, so a heavy cleaning schedule is advisable. Even in cleaner environments, dust tends to build up at the intake of the forced air circulation system, which is normally around the fans. Use compressed air to blow the dust out of the intake vents and fans. Clean the optical components (reflector, filters, lenses, etc.) with a mild detergent. *Do not* use any cleaning solvents because they can damage the thin-film coatings.
2. Use compressed air to remove the dust from all electronic components. Dust can blanket a PC board and act as an insulator, trapping the heat and eventually leading to the failure of the components on the board. Ensure that any heat sinks and current-carrying compo-

nents are free of dust and dirt. Remember to prevent the fans from spinning freely while using compressed air to blow them out.

3. Visually inspect the infrared (IR) filter and confirm that it is intact and not broken or missing. The IR filter is typically the very first optical element after the lamp and its job is to pass as much visible light as possible while reflecting the IR wavelengths (which are pure heat) back to the light source. It is extremely important for the protection of the fixture from heat.

4. Visually inspect all of the fasteners, particularly those that are securing heavy components, such as transformers and ballasts, and make sure they are sufficiently tight. Rough handling can loosen the fasteners securing these components, and if they break free they can cause significant damage to other components. Use Loc-tite or a suitable thread-locking sealant on every fastener.

5. Visually inspect the lamp socket for signs of arcing and belts for signs of cracking.

6. Make sure to pay attention to the manufacturer's recommendations for the orientation of the fixture. Some fixtures can be rigged in any orientation, while others must be restricted to certain orientations. This is normally because of the type of lamp used in the fixture, some of which will fail prematurely if their orientation causes the rising heat to increase the operating temperature beyond the limits of the specifications.

Cleaning Automated Lighting Components

The best way to ensure the long operating life of an automated luminaire is to keep it clean both inside and out. A can of compressed air or an air compressor, some mild detergent, and a soft lint-free cloth are the best tools for maintaining a clean fixture.

Compressed air can be used to remove large particles of dust and debris, but cleaning the optical elements of an automated luminaire requires the use of a cleaning agent and an abrasion-free applicator. Most optical components, like dichroic filters, glass reflectors, and glass gobos and lenses, have an optical thin-film coating that can be damaged by some chemical cleaning solvents that have a high pH. To clean them, use isopropyl alcohol or a mild detergent and a soft, lint-free cloth. Avoid abrasive cleaners that can scratch the coating and cause permanent damage. Some technicians use optical wipes that are impregnated with thin-film-safe cleaning solution in a lint-free wipe, such as a Zeiss wipe. These cleaning aids are designed for camera lenses and modern thin-film coatings found on sunglasses and other consumer optics.

Lubrication

Automated luminaires, by their nature, have many moving parts, many of which require lubrication to reduce friction and wear. The question is whether or not these moving parts ever require relubrication or whether they are self-lubricating. Most moving parts in automated fixtures use long-lasting Teflon-based or graphite-based grease that, under normal circumstances, requires no relubrication during the normal life of the fixture. Other parts have self-lubricating bushings, gears, and bearings made of nylon or Teflon embedded with molybdenum disulfide or mineral oil that require no maintenance.

Troubleshooting

When a problem with an automated luminaire arises during the load-in for a show, the highest priority is to address the problem as quickly as possible in order to maximize programming time and put everyone at ease. For that reason, many productions carry spare fixtures for emergencies. Once a problem fixture is swapped out and a spare is put in its place, then the problem has been addressed.

In the field, it is common to troubleshoot to the board level as opposed to troubleshooting to the component level on a test bench. That simply means that instead of isolating problems with individual components on a circuit board, the entire circuit board is replaced with a spare, then the circuit board with the problem is sent back to the shop or the factory for replacement or repair. Troubleshooting to the component level usually requires an oscilloscope and possibly other more specialized test and repair equipment that an automated lighting technician normally does not carry in the field. Instead, the properly prepared automated lighting tech carries a supply of replacement parts to address common failures in the model and make of automated lighting on the show. Manufacturers of automated lighting normally offer a recommended list of spare parts based on the number of fixtures in the rig. A sample recommended list of spare parts is shown in Table 20-1.

Table 20-1 Most manufacturers offer a recommended list of spare parts based on the most commonly known failures of automated luminaires.

X-Spot Xtreme
80050074 850-watt lamp power supply
99070003 Motor power supply
80010155 Three-phase board
80010153 Two-phase board
80010152 CPU board
80060006 Ignitor
99270075 11.5 mm stepper motor
99270076 15.1 mm stepper motor
99270077 33.8 mm stepper motor
99270078 43.5 mm stepper motor
99270079 50.8 mm stepper motor
99270080 62.5 mm stepper motor
90402024 2.5a SB SMT fuse
90403027 2.5a SB fuse
90402016 5a FA fuse
80430083 Color mix assembly
80430079 Dual litho assembly
80430078 Litho/iris assembly

Troubleshooting Procedures

CAUTION: Before attempting any diagnostics, troubleshooting, or repair, be sure to disconnect power from the fixture. Do not under any circumstances access the inside of an automated luminaire with the power still connected.

Regardless of the nature of the problem encountered with an automated luminaire, the approach to troubleshooting it follows the same pattern. First, the problem should be isolated in the system to the power, control signal, or the luminaire. For example, if the lamp won't strike, then it should be determined whether or not the fixture is receiving power and a control signal with a lamp strike command. The easiest way to accomplish this is to use the onboard menuing system that is built in to most automated luminaires. If the fixture is easily accessed, then using the menu to strike the lamp will confirm whether or not there is sufficient power and removes the controller from the system. The sole exception is that some 208/220V luminaires' menus will function on 120V but the lamp won't strike. In that case, only a voltmeter reading across the power input will determine whether or not the voltage is correct.

If the lamp won't strike from the menu command, then you have isolated the problem to the fixture. The next step is to isolate the problem in the fixture. The most obvious next step in this example is to check the lamp. Unfortunately there is no reliable method of testing a discharge lamp except to place it in a known good lamp circuit; you can't judge its condition by visual inspection or by checking it for continuity because of the arc gap. So the only solution is to replace the lamp with a new one or a known good one and test the fixture again. If it still won't strike, then the problem has to be further isolated. The next step is to consider each element of the circuit in order of probability of failure. In a lamp circuit, the ignitor, the socket, and the ballast or power supply board, depending on whether or not the fixture has a switching power supply, are the only other elements in the lamp circuit besides the fuse.[2] By swapping out these items one by one, starting with the ignitor, and then the ballast or power supply board, the bad component will eventually be found.

If the problem is something other than the lamp, then the same procedure applies: the problem should be isolated to the fixture, then inside the fixture, and finally to the bad part. For example, if everything on a luminaire is working except for one function, say, the color wheel, then the first thing to do is to put the fixture in the self-test mode to see if the problem persists. If it does, then you can be certain it is not a control signal or controller syntax problem. The next step is to isolate the problem inside the fixture. If there is an error message on the menu, it usually indicates a problem with the position sensor, perhaps a dirty optical sensor or a displaced Hall sensor. If there is no error indication, then the problem needs to be isolated to the logic board that generates the control signal, the motor drive chip, or the stepper motor. The quickest and easiest test is to change the motor drive chip. If that doesn't fix the problem then the next step might be to change the logic board. If that still doesn't fix the problem then it's likely that the stepper motor is bad.

---

[2] Technically, if there is a power factor correction capacitor in the fixture, it is part of the lamp circuit. However, if it fails as an open circuit, the fixture will draw more current but it won't prevent the lamp from starting. If it fails as a short circuit, it will trip a breaker or blow a fuse in the fixture.

Troubleshooting to the board level is one part systematic approach and one part intuition. It helps to know which components most commonly fail and what are those components' associated parts. The next few paragraphs describe some of the more common problems that might occur with automated luminaires.

Common Failures

In the realm of automated lighting, there are probabilities and then there are certainties. It is certain that an automated light will eventually experience some type of failure. It is probable that a group of automated luminaires will experience some types of failures more often than others. Generally speaking, those components that carry the highest currents and generate the most friction are, under normal circumstances, the most likely to fail. These include the lamp starter, switching power supplies, motor drive chips, and sometimes ballasts and stepper motors. Moving parts like stepper motors and fans are susceptible to failure, but normally in older fixtures. As fixtures age, some components with a finite life span are susceptible to failure, including lamp sockets, fans, belts, spring plungers, and power factor capacitors. Some of the most common failures are discussed below.

Motor Drive Chips

Other than the lamp and the lamp circuit, stepper motors consume the most power in an automated luminaire. Consequently, the components in the motor drive circuit pass high currents, and the motor drive chips that are responsible for outputting the current to drive the motors are subject to failure (Figure 20-2). The current generates enough heat in the chips that they are usually heat-sinked, either on top of the chip or in the form of large copper traces on the board. Still, they tend to fail often enough that some manufacturers use IC sockets to facilitate their easy replacement, although sockets are becoming less common as more manufacturers are moving to surface mount technology (SMT). Also, socketing a motor drive chip sometimes exacerbates the heat problem because poor contacts with increased resistance produce more heat. A visual inspection will sometimes suffice to determine if a motor drive chip is blown because when they fail they often explode, smoke, arc, or otherwise show visible signs of catastrophic failure. If a motor stops working, as determined by a self-test routine, one of the first things to suspect is the motor drive chip. If a visual

Figure 20-2 Motor drive chips supply the current to drive stepper motors. The photograph shows two PBM 3960 digital-to-analog converter (DAC) and PBL 3771 motor driver pairs.

inspection doesn't reveal any obvious problems, then the easiest field test is to switch the header (cable connector) with a known good motor drive circuit to determine if the good chip will work in the bad circuit and vice versa.

Switch-Mode Power Supplies

In the event that a lamp won't strike in an automated luminaire with a switch-mode power supply and the problem cannot be resolved by replacing the lamp or ignitor, then it is likely that there is a problem with the power supply. Compared to a magnetic ballast power supply, a switch-mode power supply is very complicated, has far more components and component-level troubleshooting, and is more difficult to repair. If you have the luxury of swapping out a bad switch-mode power supply and sending it to the factory for repair, consider yourself lucky. If, on the other hand, you enjoy troubleshooting these power supplies to the component level, then start with the power handling components, which switch the current on and off to regulate the voltage and flow of energy.

Switch-mode power supplies typically use insulated gate bipolar transistors (IGBT) or metal-oxide semiconductor field-effect transistors (MOSFET) to switch the current. You can perform a rudimentary test on an IGBT or MOSFET using a digital multi-meter that has a diode checker, for example, a Fluke 87. This method will only tell you whether the component is functional; it won't tell you whether or not it's within spec.

Caution: Most switch-mode power supplies have large capacitors that can hold a charge for prolonged periods of time. Before analyzing a power supply, be certain that the circuit and the capacitors in particular have been properly discharged. Failure to do so can be dangerous.

A MOSFET has three terminals: a gate, a drain, and a source. For n-type MOSFETs, perform the following checks (Figure 20-3):

1. Remove the MOSFET from the circuit. The gate should be isolated from the drain and the source. To check it, put your meter in the Diode Test mode and clip the red lead to the gate (first terminal). Clip the black lead of the meter to the drain (usually the second terminal of the MOSFET). It should read "OL," indicating an open circuit. If it reads 0.000 or a very small number, then the MOSFET is bad.
2. Move the black lead to the source (third terminal). It should read "OL."
3. Move the red lead to the source and the black lead to the gate. It should read "OL."
4. Move the red lead to the drain and the black lead to the source. It should read "OL."
5. Move the black lead to the drain and the red lead to the source. This is putting a forward bias on the junction between the two. It should read between 0.400 and 0.500 volts. If it reads lower than about 0.4 volts but higher than about 0.3 volts, then there's a possibility that the MOSFET is bad. If it reads lower than 0.3 volts, then there's a very good possibility that it's bad.

An IGBT is similar to an n-type MOSFET, so it can be tested in a similar manner, though the voltages for the forward-biased case may differ.

Printed Circuits Boards

As automated luminaires get more powerful, manufacturing techniques get more sophisticated and the printed circuit boards (PCBs) in them

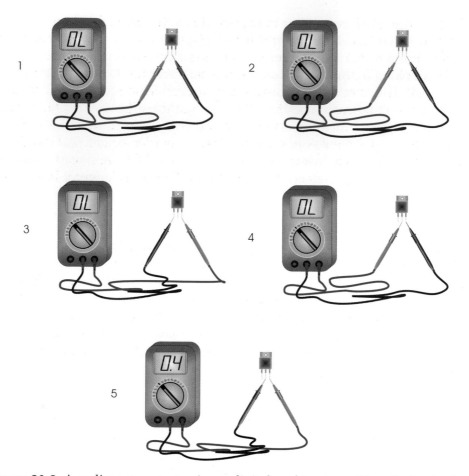

Figure 20-3 A rudimentary test using a digital multimeter with a diode checker can determine whether or not a MOSFET is functional.

become more complex. While a lot of the early models and lower-end models of automated lighting have single-layer PCBs, many of the newer fixtures have very complex, high-density multilayer PCBs. These layers are laminated with glue, and they can be electronically connected to each other through drilled holes called vias. To make the vias conductive they are electroplated or loaded with small rivets. Some of these vias, called blind vias, are exposed on only one side, while other vias called buried vias are completely unexposed to the outer layers of the laminated PCB. These vias make it very difficult to diagnose and repair multilayer circuit boards.

What's more, SMT is starting to replace through-hole technology. Surface mount devices (SMDs) such as ICs and displays are mounted directly on the surface of a PCB and soldered en masse in convey-belted ovens using a reflow solder technique. SMDs are typically smaller than their through-hole counterparts because the leads are smaller. That makes for a smaller package and smaller fixtures, but it makes it more difficult to replace parts. The soldering technique for reworking and repairing SMDs is the same as that for through-hole devices, except that a smaller soldering iron tip is usually necessary. The combination of multilayer PCBs and SMT makes it challenging to diagnose and repair some mother and daughter boards.

Power Factor Capacitors

The purpose of a power factor (PF) capacitor is to counter the effects of the inductance in the magnetic ballast to bring the voltage and current in phase with each other. When a PF capacitor fails, it does not affect the apparent operation of an automated luminaire. It does, however, change the phase relationship between the voltage and the current, and as a result, the current increases in proportion to the phase difference between the two. In a fixture that draws about 12 amps, losing the PF capacitor could raise the current to about 18 amps.

A visual inspection of a PF capacitor is sometimes sufficient to detect its working state because they sometimes physically destruct to some extent when they go bad. On the other hand, sometimes there is no physical evidence of failure. A PF capacitor can fail as a short or an open circuit. If it fails as an open circuit and there is no physical damage, then the only clue to its failure is that the fixture is suddenly drawing significantly more current. In the case that it fails as a short, the fixture will blow a fuse or trip a circuit breaker right away. A continuity checker will immediately tell you if a capacitor is shorting if you place the leads across the two terminals of the capacitor (be sure that the capacitor is discharged before doing this or it could severely damage your tester); if it reads as a short then the capacitor is bad. If it reads as an open circuit right away then it's probably bad, but further testing might be necessary. A capacitor checker is the best way to determine whether the capacitor is still within tolerance. Some digital multimeters have a capacitor checker, but they do not test capacitors at their full rated voltage. They are a good means of finding obvious faults but they can't detect subtle problems. The best way to accurately test a capacitor is to substitute a known good one and compare the current draw of the fixture.

Ballasts

Testing a magnetic ballast in the field is a bit tricky given that most lighting technicians usually carry little test equipment other than a multimeter. To accurately test a ballast (which is an inductor), the inductance and efficiency (or Q) are typically tested at its operating frequency using an impedance analyzer and an oscilloscope because the values are frequency dependent. However, a simple DC resistance field test will give you a general idea of the working condition of a ballast.

When a ballast fails, any one of three things can go happen: it can short circuit, open circuit, or change its value of inductance. If a fixture is dropped and the ballast is jarred or is vibrated excessively, the windings can move, causing a change in value of inductance or causing an audible hum in the ballast. It can also cause a short somewhere in the windings, which may or may not cause complete failure. If an automated fixture begins to draw more current than it normally does and a malfunction of the PF capacitor has been ruled out, or if the lamp will not strike and the lamp and ignitor have been ruled out, then exchanging the ballast with a known good one will tell you whether or not the suspect ballast is out of tolerance.

If the windings of a ballast are stressed and broken or burned, then it will open the coil. If the insulation on the wires breaks down, it will short the windings. If a ballast is suspected of malfunctioning, then a DC resistance check will give a quick indication of an open circuit. After removing the ballast from the circuit, place the leads of an ohmmeter across the terminals of the ballast. If the DC resistance is at or near infinity, then it is an open circuit and the ballast should be replaced. The normal DC resistance reading of a common magnetic ballast in an automated lighting is very low, in the range from a fraction of an ohm to a few ohms. Thus, it is very difficult to distinguish between a good ballast and one with a dead short using only an ohmmeter.

Transformers

A transformer is similar to a ballast except that it has two windings instead of one, unless it's an autotransformer, in which case it has only one winding. Normally when a transformer fails it is immediately obvious: either the transformer will short, in which case the fixture will blow a fuse or trip a circuit breaker, or it will open, in which case the fixture will not power up at all. If the luminaire continually trips a circuit breaker or blows a fuse right away, the first component to suspect is the lamp circuit or the transformer. By disconnecting the lamp circuit and testing the fixture again, you can isolate the problem to the lamp circuit or the transformer. If the fuse blows or circuit breaker trips without the lamp circuit, then it is probably a bad transformer. It can be tested by taking it out of the circuit and metering the primary and secondary windings; they should exhibit resistance in the range from a few hundred ohms on the primary winding to a few ohms on the secondary winding. Of course, an ohmmeter works by using a small DC current to test the resistance, which is quite different than the actual working conditions of a transformer. According to Don Pugh of Light Parts, Inc. (www.lightparts.com), "If there are pinholes in the enamel insulation of the windings, a high AC voltage will jump right through like a trained circus cat."

Fasteners

With heavy components like ballasts and transformers, the mechanical fasteners sometimes loosen over time, particularly in rental or hire fixtures. If they break loose they can physically damage other components in the fixture. They should be checked periodically to make sure all the fasteners are secure. The electrical connections should be checked as well, particularly on spade lug terminals and crimp-on connectors.

Sensors

Optical sensors are generally reliable, but the photoreceptor does tend to collect dust and dirt. If they are allowed to go uncleaned for long periods of time they can cause problems. Magnetic sensors sometimes have problems because of the proximity of the Hall sensor. They have a relatively tight tolerance, and if the long leads on the sensor bend too far away from the magnet, then they can't detect it. If either the optical or the magnetic sensor is malfunctioning, then the parameter in question, whether it's a wheel or an effect, will not be able to find its home position, and in most cases the menu display will indicate a sensor error.

Since the mass commercialization of automated lighting systems, they have vastly improved in reliability and serviceability. They still, however, collect dust, dirt, and fog and haze condensation. And they still require regular cleaning and maintenance in order to operate at peak performance.

SECTION 7
Digital Lighting

CHAPTER 21

Digital Lighting

Once there was a time when the bringing-forth of the true into the beautiful was called technology. And art was simply called techne.—Martin Heidegger, German philosopher

The year 1999 was a watershed in automated lighting. At LDI in November of that year, Light & Sound Design (now part of PRG) displayed the first digital light, called the Icon M. It was a moving yoke fixture that projected "soft gobos"—gobos that could be created with software rather than hardware—and animation created by the use of a Texas Instruments Digital Micromirror Device (DMD) under the control of a microprocessor. It was the first time that the idea of marrying automated lighting and video was presented to the industry, and after it was demonstrated, it was clear where automated lighting technology was going in the next few years.

Technically, an early version of the Icon M called the Medusa had been previewed by a select few individuals in the industry at a private showing at LDI 1998. The fixture was shown sans yoke in order to solicit feedback on the color system and the user interface for controlling images. One of the attendees at the sneak preview happened to be a partner in Wynn Willson Gotellier, which later went on to develop the Catalyst orbital mirror head for panning and tilting video images. In the same year, a lighting designer named Gary Westcott designed a system of Sanyo video projectors fed by content under the control of a Macintosh computer for a small David Bowie tour. He had wanted to use some prototypes of the Icon M, but the manufacturer declined for fear they would tip their hand on the project. Little did anyone realize that the Bowie tour was the precursor to the new age of digital lighting.

The Digital Mirror Device

The DMD chip is the technology that made possible the concept of the Icon M. The DMD is an optical semiconductor with a rectangular array of up to 2 million micromirrors, each measuring about 16 μm on a side, on a chip less than an inch wide (Figure 21-1). The mirrors are so small that it would take 62,500 of them laid end to end to reach a length of 1 m. They are fabricated by a process known as micromachining, in which masks are used to selectively etch away portions of a silicon wafer or to add new layers to construct mechanical and electromechanical systems. The process is very similar to the fabrication of integrated circuits. Such microelectromechanical systems are called MEMS, and they are a type of nanotechnology.

In a DMD, each of the micromirrors is mounted on a hinge that allows them to pivot ±10 degrees. When light is bounced off the micromirrors, it can be reflected in or out of the optical path of a projector by using an electrostatic charge to turn them "on" or "off." In that way, each micromirror in the array acts as a single pixel, turning on or off to create an image.

The intensity of the light is controlled by varying the duty cycle of the pulse-width modulated control signal; the longer the width of the pulse,

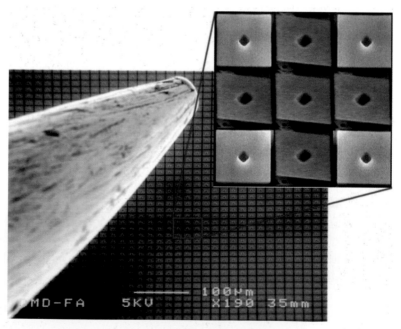

Figure 21-1 A digital micromirror device, or DMD, is a rectangular array of up to 2 million micromirrors, each measuring about 16 μm on a side, on a chip less than an inch wide.

the longer the pixel stays on and the higher its perceived intensity. The frequency of the pulse is much faster than the human eye can detect, and the pulses are "averaged" together by the brain. Color can be added by using three DMD chips, one with red light, one with green light, and one with blue light. The three primary colors are overlaid to produce a full-color picture (Figure 21-2).

Alternatively, a color image can be created by using a single DMD chip and a color wheel with red, green, and blue dichroic color (Figure 21-3). The color wheel rotates at a high frequency, and light pulses are timed to correspond with the desired color. When pulsing a combination of colors such as red and blue, a third color is perceived by the eye.

In the Icon M, the onboard memory could store 1000 soft gobos and a limited number of animated gobos. The Icon M project eventually ran out of money; the original 16 fixtures were the first and last to be produced. They were subsequently added to Light & Sound Design's rental

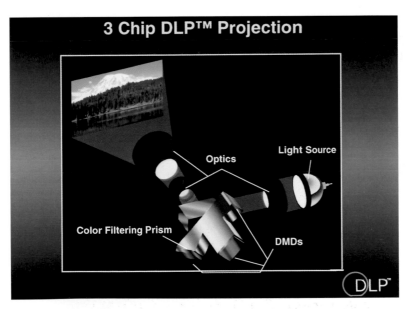

Figure 21-2 A pulse-width modulated control signal with a variable duty cycle controls the intensity of a pixel by turning each mirror on and off repeatedly. The human eye averages the pulses and sees them as a fixed level of intensity. Three DMDs with red, green, and blue light are used to produce a full-spectrum picture.

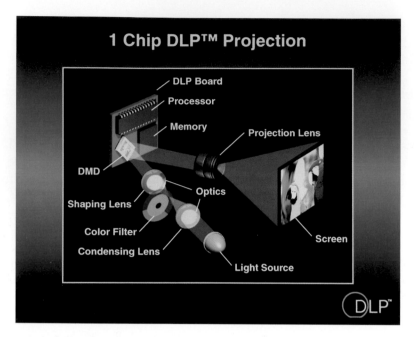

Figure 21-3 A full-color display can also be made using a single DMD chip with a rotating dichroic color wheel. The color wheel spins at a high rate of speed, and the control signal pulses are timed to turn the mirrors on and off to correspond with a particular color.

inventory and have seen action in a few tours, including a Korn tour, but they were never the commercial success that they should have been. They did, however, manage to change the face of the industry, launching the first phase of the movement toward the convergence of lighting and video.

Two years later, High End Systems launched the Catalyst, which was much more of a commercial success (Figure 21-4). The Catalyst system, in its original version, was an orbital mirror head that mounted on the front of a large video projector. A media server running on a Macintosh computer fed a video signal to the remote projector, and the orbital mirror head moved the image around the space. The system was controlled by a DMX console and allowed the operator to call up a still image or an animation, apply certain effects, and position the resulting video image anywhere within the range of the mirror head. Later, the name Catalyst migrated to the media server, and it remains so today.

Figure 21-4 The High End Systems Catalyst was the first stand-alone DMX-controllable media server and orbital mirror head. (Photo courtesy of High End Systems.)

The original Catalyst system used projectors with up to 10,000 ANSI lumens that were very big and expensive. At the time, a typical 10K ANSI lumens projector cost as much as $80,000 or more. The effectiveness of the system couldn't be denied, but it clearly deviated from the trend of automated lighting toward smaller, lighter, cheaper, and brighter luminaires. Still, the Catalyst system raised quite a few eyebrows, and digital lighting was recognized as the "next big thing" in entertainment lighting.

Catalyst served as proof of concept for digital lighting, and several manufacturers took note. Since the introduction of the Catalyst in 2001, several media servers have appeared on the market and the convergence of video and lighting took a giant step forward. The systems approach taken by Catalyst and Icon M was beginning to be dismantled, and manufacturers focused on the first step in the process, that of managing and controlling content—the video information—from a DMX console. In the span of about 5 years, up to a dozen DMX-controllable media servers came on the market, owing much to improvements in Microsoft's DirectX software and the falling cost of high-end video graphics cards. Both were a direct result of developments in the computer gaming industry.

By offering a discrete component of digital lighting as a separate product, manufacturers were free to look at other options for projection and display.

Advances in LED, LCD, and DLP technology significantly increased the number of products with which media servers could be used.

Digital Light Processing and LEDs

Digital Light Processing (DLP) is Texas Instruments' patented projection system, which uses a DMD engine and a dichroic color wheel to produce full-color video. In 1996, TI began licensing the technology to projector manufacturers and shipping in substantial quantities. DLP projectors began appearing on the market in growing numbers a few years later. Around the same time, LEDs reached a price point and intensity that made them attractive to the entertainment market and so began to proliferate. They were soon incorporated into RGB color wash fixtures and as RGB pixels for video and quasi-video displays. Before long, a cottage industry sprang up around the design and manufacture of LED displays and fixtures. LED walls, curtains, modules, and fixtures began to show up in productions of every type. The new displays increased the demand for media servers and control software to manage the growing number of applications for video and quasi-video display.

Liquid Crystal Displays

Today, the quest for the ideal self-contained digital light is still in its infancy. High End Systems offers the DL-1 and DL-2 digital lights, and Publitec offers a moving yoke projector called the Beamover (Figure 21-5). A Japanese manufacturer, Active Vision Co., Ltd., offers the AV4. Each of these digital lights houses an LCD projector in a moving yoke enclosure.

The projectors in the fixtures range in output from 3000 to 4500 ANSI lumens. An ANSI lumen is the projector standard most often used by manufacturers for measuring the light output from a video projector set forth by the American National Standards Institute. It works by dividing the projection into nine equal areas and averaging the luminous flux in lumens in each area to derive the standard measure of brightness.[1]

---

[1] The specification in which the ANSI lumen is defined is no longer supported by ANSI as of 2003; however, it is still in widespread use in the industry and is commonly referred to in projector specifications. The IEC lumen is the current standard for measuring projector brightness; it is virtually identical to the ANSI lumen but is seldom cited in the literature.

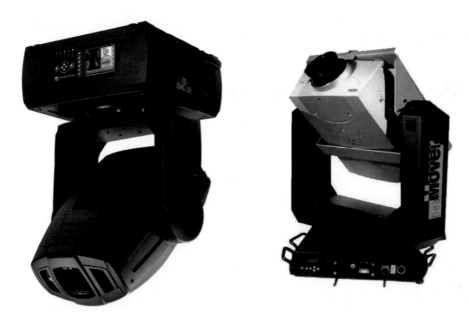

Figure 21-5 Two of the few commercially available digital lights are the High End Systems DL2 (left) and the Publitec Beamover (right).

Perceived Brightness

One of the challenges in digital lighting is deciphering specifications related to brightness and correlating them to our experience with conventional lighting. The industry is used to dealing with illumination in lux and footcandles, and sometimes with luminance in footlamberts or candelas per square meter. Conventional fixture photometric specifications are often presented in the form of a chart showing the throw distance and the resulting beam or field diameter and the illumination in lux or footcandles (Figure 21-6).

Alternatively, a more concise way of expressing the same information is to give the total luminous intensity in center beam candelas from which the illumination in footcandles (or lux in SI units) can be calculated:

$$\text{Illumination} = \frac{\text{center beam candelas}}{(\text{throw distance})^2},$$

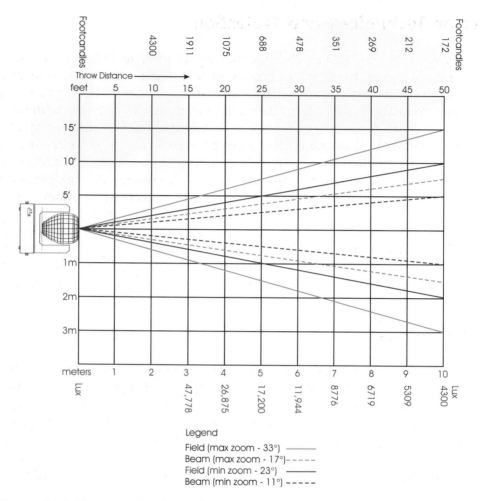

Figure 21-6 Photometric data showing throw distance and the resulting illumination.

where illumination is in lux and distance is in meters using SI units, and illumination is in footcandles and distance is in feet using imperial units.

Video projectors are specified in terms of ANSI lumens, which is only one factor in the influence of the perceived brightness of a video image. Other important factors are the contrast ratio, the ambient light levels, the reflectivity of the projection surface, and the size of the projected image.

Lamp Technology and Projection

Whether they use LCD or DLP technology, the key to reducing the size, weight, and price tag of projection engines has been the increasing efficiency of lamp sources and heat management. In the past, large projectors almost exclusively used xenon lamps because they can be made with very short arc gaps. A short arc gap makes it easier to build an efficient optical system because all of the optical elements—reflectors, apertures, lenses, etc.—can be smaller. But the requirements for a xenon source are more complex: the lamps have to maintain a certain orientation to work properly and they are under extremely high pressure, which makes them very dangerous to handle. For those reasons, metal halide lamps became very popular with manufacturers of small- to medium-sized projectors, but the halides used in making the lamps forced them to use bigger arc gaps. In lamps, the higher the wattage is, the larger the arc gap needs to be. Thus, some of the efficiency is sacrificed for the sake of size, weight, and cost.

The UHP Lamp

In 2001 Philips and Ushio introduced a new lamp with a shorter arc that enables the production of smaller, lighter, and cheaper projectors. The Philips UHP is a mercury discharge lamp with a compact 1 mm arc gap (Figure 21-7). The smaller arc gap provides for a more efficient optical system and more light from the projector. This is accomplished by pressurizing the lamp to more than 200 atmospheres, which changes the spectral distribution, or the colors generated by the lamp. In an ordinary mercury lamp, salt additives produce the red spectral lines to balance the

Figure 21-7 The UHP lamp improves the spectral emission of the mercury by using high pressure.

light between the red and blue ends of the spectrum. Without the additives, the light would be very blue with almost no red light at all. By pressurizing the lamp envelope to an extremely high value, the mercury emits enough red light to produce a fairly balanced color temperature.

Currently, the technology is limited to relatively low-wattage lamps of about 250 watts maximum, but that could change in the near future. When manufacturers become successful at devising and perfecting cooling techniques, that limit is expected to be raised and another quantum leap in performance will be achieved.

As projectors continue to increase in efficiency and drop in size and price, digital lighting will continue to benefit from the advances. Before long, digital lighting will be on the same trajectory as "conventional" automated lighting, with smaller, lighter, cheaper, and brighter technology.

SECTION 8

Automated Lighting Programming

CHAPTER 22

Automated Lighting Programming

The question of whether a computer can think is no more interesting than the question of whether a submarine can swim.—Edsgar W. Dijkstra

An automated light without some means of control is no more useful than a car without an engine. By the same token, an automated lighting controller without programming is no more useful than a car with no gas in the tank. In either case, the car can't get out of the driveway. Programming is one of the most important aspects of automated lighting, and in some cases it's also one of the most overlooked and misunderstood as well. The difference between a well-programmed system and a poorly programmed system has a great influence on the outcome and performance of a lighting system. Automated lighting consoles have evolved into highly effective tools that help the programmer work very quickly and effectively. But the most powerful consoles also require a great deal of study and understanding before the programmer can take full advantage of them. In most show environments, programming time is limited and a great deal of work must be done in a very short amount of time, much of it even before setting foot on the job site. Those programmers who are the best prepared and who can work quickly and accurately are in the highest demand and command the highest compensation. It pays to learn the craft well.

There are a number of automated lighting consoles on the market, each with unique hardware and software. The approach and programming process in different consoles are often very similar, but the terminology and syntax can vary from manufacturer to manufacturer and from model to model. But regardless of the type of console used for a particular application, there are certain common procedures and approaches to programming automated lighting.

Preshow Preparation

Before you even show up at the show site, there is a certain amount of preshow preparation that is in order. As a responsible programmer, you should gather as much information as possible about the show beforehand so that you can make the most of your precious programming time. Programming time is normally expensive, and it often includes the rental of lighting equipment, facilities, and crew. By preparing properly you can help manage costs, prevent budget overruns, and ensure the financial success of the project, which can ultimately lead to more programming work in the future.

Before undertaking a project you should speak to the lighting designer or the party responsible for your being there and find out as much as you can about what is expected of you as a programmer and of the programming itself. You should know, to the extent possible, the expectations of the lighting as a result of your programming, including the all-important question, "How do you know when you're finished?" Is the success of the programming session measured in time, number of songs, number of cues, or some other measure? If there are any benchmarks you should know what they are.

Once you have a good idea of the parameters of the project, then you should set about gathering all the materials you will need for it. That includes a light plot that indicates the numbers and types of fixtures as well as their locations, the DMX512 protocol for each type of automated fixture, the user manuals for the automated lighting, dimmer packs (if there is also conventional lighting) and the console, and any music that you might need for preparation or programming. If you have a laptop, it is a good idea to upload all the files associated with the project and the equipment, including user manuals for the console, fixtures, and dimmers, the latest software upgrades for the console, and the fixture profiles for every fixture in the rig (console specific), and have them ready for easy access. Normally, these include AutoCAD (or some variation thereof) and Adobe Acrobat files, so your computer should have a DWG reader and a PDF reader.

In addition, you should also prepare and/or pack any items that you might need to test the system, focus it, and program the console. Those items might include the following:

- A portable sound system (MP3, CD player, etc.) to play back recorded material to time your cues. You should also have a pair of headphones, not only to hear your music when you're programming, but also to block out external noise. Noise-canceling headphones are great for programming to a music track while the audio crew is tuning the sound system, which is a very loud and distracting procedure.

- A laptop computer to reference light plots, user manuals, important phone numbers, and to take notes. Having Internet access is highly recommended, and many show sites have Wi-Fi set up especially for the crew. You can increase your odds of being connected by outfitting your laptop with a satellite Internet card.

- Floppy discs or the appropriate backup medium for your console.

- If you're also planning to focus the lights, a good light meter, especially if there is video involved. When the video crew questions the light level on stage (as they often do), then you can give them reassurance with confidence by using a light meter.

- A DMX512 tester, especially if you are working with a small lighting crew with few lighting techs.

- Some DMX512 terminators in case the system was not terminated correctly. You should have both five-pin and three-pin terminators in order to be prepared for any situation.

- Five-pin to three-pin adaptors in case you get to the show site and find that the console hasn't been set up and it doesn't mate with the automated lighting control cable. Five-pin is the most common console DMX512 output connector type, but three-pin DMX512 connectors are still commonly used in many automated lighting fixtures.

- At least one good DMX512 cable in case there is a data connection problem. If you ever have a question about the integrity of a DMX512 connection you can temporarily bypass the existing cable and use a known good one. A medium-length cable, about 25 feet, is usually sufficient.

- A permanent marker to mark cables, notes, etc. You might be surprised by how often it comes in handy.

- Notepaper for making programming notes along the way.

- An adjustable wrench to refocus or move lights. It's also a good idea to keep it on a lanyard to secure it to your person, especially when you might be working on the truss or in a lift. Hint: a dual ⅝- and ⅜-inch ratcheted box end wrench works well for tightening cast iron c-clamps. The ⅝-inch end fits the truss bolt and the ⅜-inch end fits the set screw.

- A flashlight to check settings and connections under counters, in the back of racks, and elsewhere.

- A good pair of gloves for handling and refocusing hot lights.

- A thumb drive for file transfers.

Last, before you leave for the job make sure you have a list of important phone numbers, including show contacts and tech support contacts. Having a contact to fall back on in the case of technical problems or programming support is always a good idea.

A very important matter to consider is the ergonomics of the chair, console, and monitor(s) in the system. A programmer often spends hours upon hours behind a console, and small issues with ergonomics can develop into major problems. Your chair should provide lumbar support and the monitors should be placed at eye-level. The console should be accessible without having to reach too far, and during the programming session, the programming portion of the console (as opposed to the playback portion) should be closest to you. The keyboard and mouse should be within arm's reach, especially if they are used often. Some programmers go as far as to buy their own chair and include it in the truck pack. If you have ever suffered from back pain then you'll appreciate the importance of good ergonomics. If you have been fortunate enough to avoid such problems, take care to protect yourself from future problems as you age.

If you have access to a previsualization program like WYSIWYG, ESP, or LD Assistant, then you can do a lot of the programming before arriving on the show site. If you don't, you can still do a certain amount of prep work beforehand by using an offline editor. Many higher-end consoles have offline editors that allow you to do certain housekeeping tasks such as patching fixtures and programming fixture groups and palettes before-

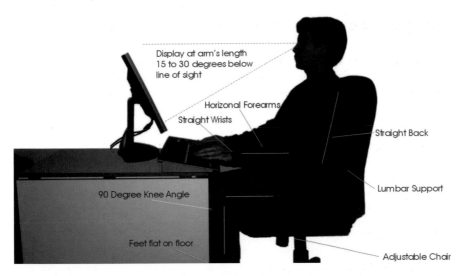

Figure 22-1 An ergonomically correct front of house (FOH) set up is very important for the long-term health of a programmer.

hand. An offline editor is the console software without the associated hardware. It can be installed and operated on a laptop or desktop computer as long as it meets certain minimum hardware requirements. The requirements for most offline editors are minimal and most computers today can handle them with no problems. Offline editors can be used to create, modify, and save shows on disk. Before arriving to program a show, it is a good idea to use an offline editor, if one is available, in lieu of a console, to set up and prepare for a show.

Backing Up

You can save yourself from considerable agony by adhering to one simple and easy-to-follow rule of programming: back up early and often. Countless hours of programming have been lost because the programmer didn't follow this simple rule. Before starting any show, you should be ready to create five or six files and label them "(show name) A" through "(show name) F."

If the console has a USB port you can plug in a small external drive or use a series of thumb drives. If it uses floppy discs then you should have five or six floppies and mark them with a permanent marker with the show name and the letters A through F. The first order of business before starting to program should be to create your first backup and label it "(show name) A." Then place it on the bottom of the stack (if it is a floppy disc). As you progress through the programming session you should pause every 10 to 15 minutes to back up your work. Each successive backup should be stored on the next letter in the alphabet and it should go to the bottom of the pile. Continue in this manner until all the letters are used. At that point you can recycle the used floppies (or files) and store new backups over the old, maintaining the same order.

The purpose of using this progressive backup system is to retain the ability to revert to old backups in case you make a mistake. There are times when you might overwrite important information without knowing it until you have already backed up your show several times. If you only use one backup file then the information is lost as soon as you write over it. On the other hand, if you have several backups, then you can revert to an older one to restore the lost information.

The importance of developing good backup habits can't be overemphasized. If you get in the habit of backing up early and often, it will certainly pay off at some point in your career.

Patching Fixtures

If you have a plot of the show, you can use it to patch the console for the show. Patching fixtures ahead of time helps make more efficient use of programming time while on the show site. If you are using an offline editor the chances are good that it has a fixture library to help make patching the show quicker and easier. Even without an offline editor you can patch the fixtures in the console.

Patching fixtures is typically done in a setup menu where the fixture library resides. When you go into the setup menu you can select the types and numbers of fixtures in your rig and then assign the DMX512 address to each one as shown on the light plot. Automated luminaires need several control channels to control all of its parameters, so the patch normally includes the starting address only. The console often stores the DMX512 protocol (the function of each channel in an automated luminaire, e.g., channel 1 = pan, channel 2 = tilt) for a variety of automated fixtures in its fixture library, so it knows how many channels are required for the particular fixture you are patching (Figure 22-2). When you assign a starting address it calculates the next available DMX512 address. When you patch the next fixture or group of fixtures, if you accidentally overlap DMX512 addresses the console will very often reject your patch assignment and give you an error message.

If the console doesn't have your fixture in its library, then you may have to create a fixture profile in the console. This is typically done in the setup menu, where you can add a new fixture or edit an existing one. To do this you will need the DMX512 protocol for that fixture, which gives you detailed information about the order of the control channels and their functions.

Once the console has been properly patched, you should be able to take control of each fixture individually. You can test your patch by selecting each fixture one at a time and giving it a command that can be visually confirmed. For example, you can bring the intensity to full to confirm that you have control of the correct fixture, which confirms that the fixture is patched to the console and it is addressed correctly.

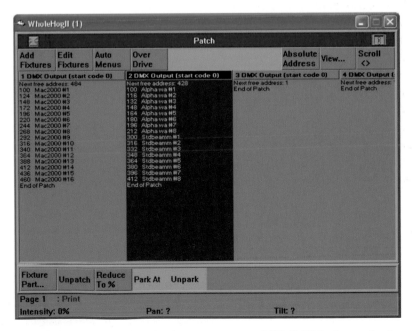

Figure 22-2 An automated luminaire uses several DMX512 channels for control of all of its parameters.

Many automated lighting consoles have a "highlight" feature, which allows you to select a group of fixtures and bring them to full intensity one at a time with the press of a single button. That saves time by negating the need to select each fixture individually, bring it to full intensity, clear it, and move to the next fixture. This feature makes it very easy to select all the lights in the rig and step through them one at a time to check that they are all working properly and that they are patched and addressed correctly.

Preparing Fixture Groups

One of the ways that a programmer can save time is to organize groups of fixtures and record them in the console as a fixture "group." Without fixture groups you have to remember how the fixtures are arranged in a rig and their respective DMX512 addresses or unit numbers. For example, if there are eight automated lights on the upstage electric and you want to change their color, you would have to select each one individually or select them as a range of fixtures. In either case you would have to remember the unit numbers of those eight fixtures, or on some consoles you would have to remember their starting DMX512 addresses. In a WholeHog console, the syntax would be the following:

1. Press the Group button until it toggles to the automated lighting fixture type in question
2. Type "1 THRU 8" and then the Enter key

Selecting the fixtures individually with the above syntax requires at least six button presses. If we take the time to record the eight automated lights on the upstage electric as a fixture group ahead of time, then the same task can be accomplished with one button press. The syntax for recording a fixture group involves selecting the desired fixtures individually and recording them to a Group button.

Taking the time to organize the plot in logical fixture groups and then actually recording them takes extra time on the front end of a production, but it saves much more time in the long run. It's also imperative for "busking" or live playback. (See the section on busking below.)

Preparing Palettes

A palette is a user-programmable memory location that stores the value of a parameter (or parameters) of a fixture for later use in programming. It can be thought of as a lookup table for a parameter recorded in a cue. When a cue is recorded with that palette, it references a specific location in the lookup table and uses that value for the parameter. The advantage of using a palette as opposed to hard coding each and every cue is that, after a parameter is recorded in a palette, it can be called up quickly and easily with the press of one button. That speeds programming every time the same value needs to be called up and recorded. For example, if you select all the CMY color wash fixtures and create a color with 78% cyan, 43% magenta, and 0% yellow, you can then record that color to the color palette and label it, say, Moon Blue. Then you can duplicate that color again at any time by selecting any of those CMY color wash fixtures and pressing the color palette button labeled Moon Blue.

Another major advantage of using palettes is that if a universal change in a parameter is required, then the change can be made in the lookup table rather than in every instance of it in every cue. This can be a huge time saver. For example, if you later decide that you don't like the Moon Blue and want to change it to Congo Blue, then you can simply call up the wash fixtures, create a new color with 100% cyan, 85% magenta, and 0% yellow, then record that color over the Moon Blue color in the color palette and change the label to read Congo Blue. Then every cue that references that color will automatically be updated. Another common example has to do with the position palette. All of the positions on the stage are usually recorded as a position preset. If there is a podium on stage, for example, then it is usually one of the positions recorded in a palette. Without the use of position palettes, focusing an automated light would require the programmer to select that fixture, then take control of the pan and tilt and change their values until they focus on the podium. Depending on the skill of the programmer, it can take from several seconds to a few minutes to position the beam accurately. If several cues target the podium, then each time the programmer will have to repeat the procedure. On the other hand, if the position is recorded as a palette the first time, then it can be repeated with the press of one button. Also, if the stage position of the podium is changed, then the palette can be updated, and each cue that refers to that palette will automatically be updated as well (Figure 22-3).

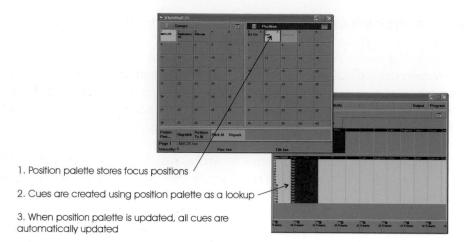

1. Position palette stores focus positions

2. Cues are created using position palette as a lookup

3. When position palette is updated, all cues are automatically updated

Figure 22-3 Palettes are similar to a lookup table used by a cue to obtain a value for a parameter. If the lookup table is updated, then each cue is automatically updated as well.

Palettes can be used for almost any parameter in an automated light. The terminology used by various consoles differs; some refer to palettes as a preset or memory, but the function is identical.

Program Blocking

If you have any collateral material such as a script, recorded or printed music, or a program schedule, then you can prepare in advance by blocking, or diagramming, each segment of the show. Your blocking can include diagramming a song to notate the intro, verses, chorus, bridge, and outro, or it could be more high-level blocking, such as transitions from speaker to speaker in the case of a corporate event. If it is a music show that is to be programmed, then you should listen to the music as much as possible, memorize every nuance of the songs, and block them for reference during programming.

On-Site Preparation

When you show up on the show site, you should make sure that you have drinking water and perhaps some snacks to fend off hunger between meals. Nutrition bars make good portable snacks that can occasionally substitute for a full meal.

The first order of business is to ring out the system and check that every component of the lighting system is working properly. In order to do that, the console should be patched correctly. If you have prepared the patch ahead of time, this will also serve to check the patch.

To ring out the system, turn on the console, load the show, and look at the patch in the Setup menu to confirm that it is patched correctly. Then strike all the lamps and confirm that they are on by selecting each fixture one at a time and bringing the intensity to full. If there is a Highlight feature in the console it will help speed up this process. Check to make sure that there is light coming from the fixture and that one and only one fixture comes on at one time. Unless the light plot calls for doubling circuits or DMX512 addresses, there should be a one-to-one relationship between the control channels and the luminaires. If two lights come on at once, then the electrician patched the dimmers incorrectly, the DMX512 addresses were set incorrectly, or the console was patched incorrectly. Before you raise the issue with the electricians or automated lighting techs, make sure the fault is not in the console patching!

Programming Cues

Once the system has been rung out, then you can begin programming. If you have prepared properly and set up your building blocks ahead of time (fixture groups and palettes), then you can start creating cues. The creation of a cue is as simple as creating a "look" that you want by selecting a fixture, applying a position to it, adding color, gobo, and/or effects, then moving on to the next fixture to repeat the process. Once every fixture in the cue has been positioned and programmed, then the look can be recorded as a cue. In some instances, if you know the timing ahead for that cue you can record it with the cue. In other instances you will have to arrange the cues in a stack and modify the timing at a later time.

Tracking

One of the trickiest aspects for new automated lighting programmers to grasp is that of a tracking console. If you don't pay close attention to the way a tracking console is programmed, then a cue may not execute exactly the same way every time it is called upon unless it is called in the same order every time. If a series of cues is rearranged or if a cue is inserted between two other cues, there is no guarantee it will look the same as it did when it was programmed, so it's very important to understand how tracking works in a console.

Tracking is the way the values for each parameter in a fixture change from cue to cue. In a tracking console, only the *changes* to a parameter are recorded in a cue, not the exact state of every parameter at the time the cue is recorded. If a particular parameter is not changed in a cue then the console stores nothing at all for that parameter. It's a much more efficient way for the console to store data, and it helps during playback when you want to create unique-looking cues by modifying existing cues.

For example, if cue 1.0 is an open spot with no color, cue 2.0 changes the color to blue, and cue 3.0 adds a gobo, then when the cues are executed in sequential order the spot will change from no color to blue and then to blue with a gobo. However, if the cues are played back out of order from, say, cue 1.0 to 3.0 to 2.0 to 1.0, then the spot will go from no color to no color with a gobo, to blue with a gobo, and then to blue spot with no gobo. That is completely different than the looks that were recorded as cues. That's because only those parameters that were changed in each cue were recorded; those that were not changed tracked through from cue to cue.

This is very useful for busking because it gives you the ability to create a look and then modify one aspect of it to create a new cue without changing the entire cue. You could call up a cue with an upstage wash and then change the color without changing the focus, zoom, or any other parameter. Or you could call up a look with gobos projecting on a cyc and then change the gobos, colors, zoom, focus, or any other parameter you care to change.

On the other hand, tracking can cause problems if you expect certain looks to appear at certain times. For example, if you modify a cue by adding strobing and then go to another cue in which you don't want strobing, the shutter function will track through unless it is hard coded with an open shutter. It can be very frustrating when you don't get the results you expect. Only by paying close attention can you prevent these things from happening.

Blocking Cues

In tracking consoles there are special cues that are designed to prevent the values of every parameter from tracking through to the next cue. They are called blocking cues, and they simply take a snapshot of the state of the entire lighting system at the time the cue is recorded and record the state of each parameter. Because blocking cues take more memory, they should be used sparingly and not with every cue in the show. Most automated lighting consoles have a way of recording a blocking cue with a few keystrokes rather than physically setting each and every parameter in the system.

Mark Cues

A mark cue is a special cue that is used to set up the lights to be ready for the next cue to be executed before it is actually executed. It prevents the simultaneous fading of position, effects, and intensity when a cue is executed so that you don't see the colors and gobos changing to the new position. The idea is to set the position, color, gobo, and effects with the intensity set to 0% before the cue is executed. That way, when the cue is executed it simply fades up without any movement or color or gobo change.

Point Cues

Often a cue needs to be inserted between two cues in a stack. One of the fastest and easiest ways to accomplish this is by using a point cue. A point cue is one that is numbered one or two decimal places after the whole number. For example, if you need to insert a cue between cues 1.0 and 2.0, you can record a cue as cue 1.5.

Playback

Once the cues have been programmed, they can be arranged on the console for the most logical method of playback. This is where a great deal of flexibility and personal tastes factor in. While some automated lighting operators like to have all of the cues arranged in one stack to be played back in order by pressing the Go button, others like to spread the cues across several playback faders so they can be more hands-on with the playback. You may also choose to stack all of the cues for one song on one playback fader and use one page of playbacks for the entire show, while others may choose to put each song on a different page.

The program material may lend itself to one method or another. For example, a theatrical production normally takes place in the exact same sequence day after day, week after week, with little or no variation except for timing. A production like this lends itself to a stack with the cues arranged in the order in which they will be played back. On the other hand, a live band might rearrange their set list every night. In that case, a single stack with every cue in the show would be practically worthless. It would make much better sense to arrange the cues by songs and have the ability to call up a song quickly. The organization of cues for playback is a matter of personal preference, and a bit of experimentation will help you find what works best for you.

Precedence

Conventional consoles typically operate on a highest takes precedence, or HTP, basis. That means that if two cues are running concurrently and both are sending an intensity level to the same channel, the channel with the highest intensity wins.

Automated lighting consoles, on the other hand, typically operate on a latest takes precedence, or LTP, basis. In an LTP console, if two cues are running concurrently and both are sending a value to the same channel, then the value that was sent last takes precedence. The logic is that in an automated light, the majority of the parameters have no one value that is more important than any other. For example, blue is no more important than red; a wide zoom is no more important than a narrow zoom. Therefore, the last setting takes priority.

Busking

Busking is a term that means to perform in a public place, usually while soliciting money. It's more common in England, but the production community, which is heavily influenced by the English, has adapted and altered it to mean the act of improvising playback of lighting cues on the fly, often to match the tempo and feeling of the music. It's a common way of operating lights when the program material is unfamiliar, such as during a music festival with many different acts. The key to busking is to set up the console properly so that you can have the maximum amount of flexibility to be able to change looks very quickly and orderly. Typically when a show is to be improvised, then elements of cues are recorded on the playback faders in such a manner that they can be mixed together easily and quickly. For example, one playback fader may contain several different focus positions with an open beam in no color. The next playback fader may contain a stack of different colors or color chases. The next one may contain different beam looks so that they can be mixed with the focus and colors, and so on. Some programmers can set up enough cue elements to busk for hours and seldom, if ever, repeat looks.

Perfecting the Craft

Automated lighting programming is a craft, and like any craft, it can be honed by study and practice. It is one part organization and set up, one part syntax, and one part execution. The more time you can spend behind a console, the more familiar you will become with programming techniques, the faster you will be able to program, and the more you will be in demand as a programmer.

There are several resources to help automated lighting programmers hone their craft. Offline editors can be downloaded free of cost and used to practice programming. In addition, manufacturers and distributors offer training courses designed to introduce a particular console to beginners or to advance their programming skills. Some courses are paid training and some are free to the public. It is in the best interest of console manufacturers to educate users about programming their consoles so they do all they can to encourage new users.

SECTION 9

Lighting Design with Automated Luminaires

CHAPTER 23

Automated Luminaire Types

We eat light, drink it in through our skins. With a little more exposure to light, you feel part of things physically. I like feeling the power of light and space physically because then you can order it materially. Seeing is a very sensuous act; there's a sweet deliciousness to feeling yourself see something.—James Turrell, artist known for his use of light in art

Like any artist, a lighting designer needs a variety of tools with which to ply the trade. As the saying goes, if the only tool in your toolbox is a hammer, everything begins to look like a nail. The one thing lighting designers most desire is the ability to create looks that have never before been seen. If variety is indeed the spice of life, then a variety of looks in a show is the elixir that might prolong a lighting designer's career. Having a variety of lighting instruments with which to create these looks is important. It should come as no surprise that automated lighting luminaire types closely parallel those of conventional luminaires. What works for conventional lights generally works for automated lights.

Moving Yoke Fixtures

Some of the earliest automated lights were moving yoke fixtures, from the first of George Izenour's designs in the early 1950s, to the Century FeatherLites in Studio 8H in the late 1950s, to the first commercially successful automated lights, the Vari-Lite fixtures. Moving yokes have a certain aesthetic appeal that becomes apparent when you first see their choreographed movement with or without any beam intensity. But there are other more practical considerations for using moving yokes as opposed to moving mirror fixtures. The advantages of moving yokes are the following:

- Wider range of pan movement. Most automated lights on the market today offer 540 degrees of pan, which equates to one and a half full revolutions. They are able to cover virtually any position, upstage or down, stage right or stage left, from the lighting grid as long as they have an unobstructed path. There have been a few moving yoke fixtures with continuous pan, including the Laser Systems Gyrolight (Laser Systems is no longer in business) and the Morpheus PanaBeam XR2.

- Shorter optical path. A mirror adds another element in the optical path, which also adds length to the optical path and the fixture. Smaller and more compact fixtures are cheaper to transport and easier to fit in the lighting rig.

- Robotic movement. The synchronized movement of a number of yoked fixtures adds an element of choreography not found in moving mirror fixtures.

On the flip side, there are also some inherent disadvantages to moving yoke fixtures, including:

- Slower movement. A moving yoke has far more mass than a moving mirror fixture and therefore inherently moves more slowly and requires bigger motors with higher torque. Some moving yoke fixtures even have two motors for pan and two for tilt.

- More moving parts. Moving a yoke usually involves gears and belts, adding to the parts count in a fixture. The more parts a machine has, the more likely it is that something will fail.

- Higher cost. Added parts and bigger motors usually lead to higher manufacturing costs, which are, of course, passed on to the end user. (See Figures 23-1A–23-1I.)

Moving Mirror Fixtures

When the automated lighting industry took root, Vari-Lite all but locked up moving yoke technology with patents. And they proved their willingness to defend their intellectual property by pursuing litigation against Summa Technology, Syncrolite, Morpheus, High End Systems, and Martin Professional. But several lighting manufacturers avoided trouble by manu-

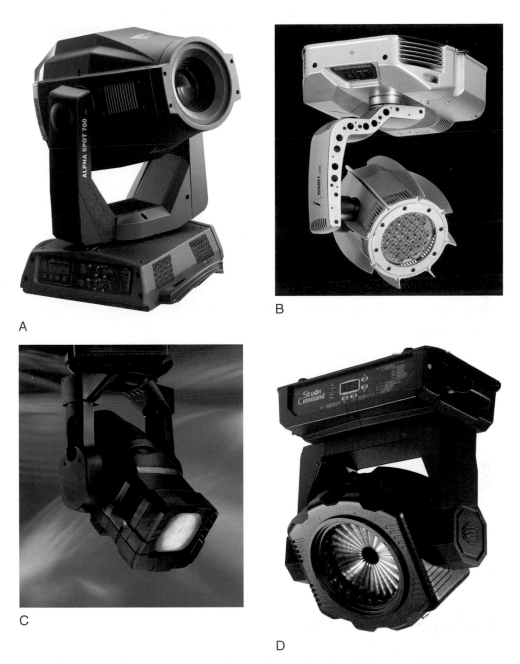

Figure 23-1 (A) Clay Paky Alpha Spot 700; (B) Coemar iWash LED; (C) ETC Source Four Revolution; (D) High End Systems Studio Command; (E) Martin Professional MAC 700; (F) Robe ColorWash 250AT; (G) SGM Synthesis 700; (H) Vari-Lite VL500; (I) Zap BigLite 4.5.

E

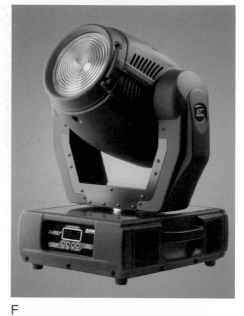

F

G

H

Figure 23-1 *Continued*

Figure 23-1 *Continued*

facturing moving mirror fixtures. As it turns out, there are advantages to moving mirror fixtures as well, including the following:

- Faster movement. The mass of a mirror is only a fraction of the mass of a moving yoke. Therefore, they can move much more quickly and require smaller motors with less torque. For that reason, moving mirror fixtures are more popular in certain applications such as night-clubs, where fast movement is a priority.

- Fewer moving parts. Most moving mirrors are coupled directly to the pan and tilt motors, which requires fewer parts and is inherently more reliable than a belt drive moving yoke.

- Lower cost. Fewer parts and less complexity result in lower manufac-turing cost and lower sales price.

Of course, there are disadvantages as well. They include:

- Smaller range of movement. The maximum pan and tilt range for a typical moving mirror fixture is 180 degrees of pan and 110 degrees of tilt. If a moving mirror fixture is rigged on the upstage electric so that it can target the cyc, it will be unable to target any downstage positions and vice versa.

- Longer optical path, resulting in bigger fixtures and higher transport costs.

- Rotation of the image as the image pans. Some fixtures such as the High End System's Cyberlight deliberately rotate the gobo in the opposite direction as the unit pans to counteract this.

- Difficult to program straight line moves because of the rotation introduced by the mirror. (See Figures 23-2A–23-2E.)

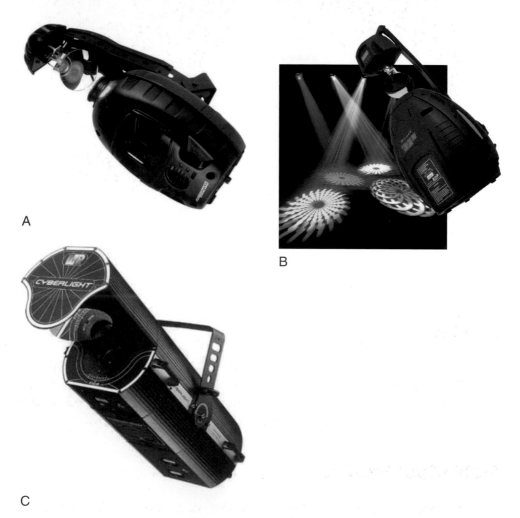

A

B

C

Figure 23-2 (A) American DJ Fusion Scan 250; (B) Elation VisionScan 575; (C) High End Systems Cyberlight; (D) Martin Mania SCX500; (E) Meteor KLS Club Scan.

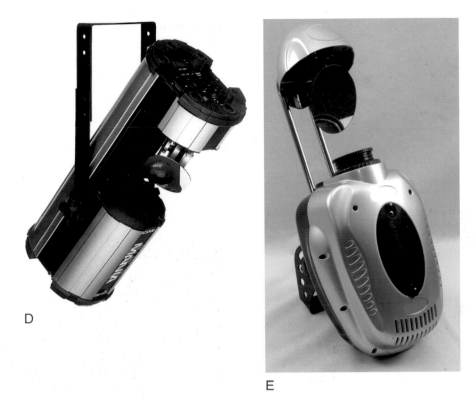

D

E

Figure 23-2 *Continued*

Hybrids

The orbital mirror head developed by Wynne Willson Gottelier (WWG) is a double mirror head that enables the projection of light in an area 250 degrees by 360 degrees with no image distortion. It has been used on the Coemar NAT (Figure 23-3) and the High End Systems Catalyst.

Profile Spot Fixtures

Just as in the conventional lighting world, an automated profile spot luminaire is a hard-edge fixture that can project an image by using a gobo. It can be used to control light spill or to project scenery or graphic images.

Figure 23-3 The orbital mirror head as shown on this Coemar NAT was designed by Wynne Willson Gottelier as a means of providing the range of a moving yoke fixture combined with the speed of a moving mirror fixture.

Color Wash Fixtures

An automated color wash luminaire is a soft-edge instrument with color-changing capability used to wash a set in colored light or to project colored beams. It may be a color-mixing luminaire with CMY color-mixing capability or it may be a color changer with a color wheel and a discrete number of colors. There are a few different types of automated color wash fixtures that can be classified according to their field characteristics.

Fresnel Fixtures

An automated color wash fixture with a Fresnel lens is the most common of the wash fixtures. It produces a soft light that blends well with other color wash fixtures. Some of them, such as the SGM Giotto Wash 1200 and the Martin MAC 2000 Wash, also have automated barn door units.

Plano-Convex Fixtures

Automated color wash fixtures with a plano-convex lens are soft-edge instruments with a beam that lies somewhere between a profile spot and a Fresnel. It produces a slightly more focused field than a Fresnel, but it still has a soft edge.

Cyc Lighting Fixtures

In the late 1990s, an Italian manufacturer of automated lighting named Studio Due patented a rectangular reflector that they used to build a color-mixing cyc fixture called City Color. They subsequently licensed the reflector design to other automated lighting manufacturers, including Coemar (Figure 23-4), who used it to build the Panorama fixture. Fixtures built with this type of reflector are ideal for color washing rectangular surfaces like cycloramas and set pieces.

Exterlor Luminaires

In the early 1990s, Vari-Lite built an exterior color wash fixture as a way to expand their market for automated lighting. The Irideon AR500 was the

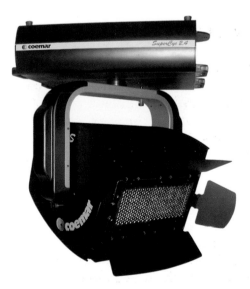

Figure 23-4 Coemar SuperCyc 2.4.

first automated color wash fixture designed for outdoor use. Since then, a number of other automated lighting manufacturers have followed their lead and offered exterior color wash fixtures (Figure 23-5). Alternatively, there are a few manufacturers who offer weatherized housings, some permanent and some temporary, for the use of nonweatherized fixtures in an outdoor environment.

IP Ratings

A weatherized fixture or housing intended to be used in the elements should be IP rated. The International Protection Code, or IP Code, is a rating for "degrees of protection provided by enclosures" as published by the Commission Electrotechnique Internationale (IEC) in 1989. The international standard describes how well an enclosure protects against the ingress of foreign objects such as dust, dirt, and moisture.

An IP rating comprises a two-digit code with optional suffixes. It is always preceded by the code letters "IP," which stand for "international protection."

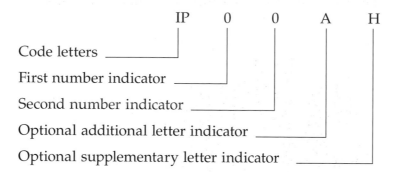

The two-digit numeric indicators are coded as follows. The first number after the code letters indicates the degree of protection against the ingress of solid objects such as dust, dirt, bird feathers, fingers and hands, etc. It can range from 0 to 6, and it indicates the diameter of the smallest object that can get into the enclosure, as follows:

0: not protected
1: ≥50 mm diameter
2: ≥12.5 mm diameter

3: ≥2.5 mm diameter
4: ≥1.0 mm diameter
5: dust protected
6: dust tight

The second number indicates the degree of protection against the ingress of water. It can range from 0 to 8, and the highest rating is 8. The numbers are defined as follows:

0: not protected
1: protection against vertically dripping water
2: protection against dripping water at up to a 15-degree angle from the vertical
3: protection against water spray at up to 60-degree angle from the vertical
4: protection against splashing water from all directions
5: protection against low-pressure jetting water from all directions
6: protection against a powerful jet of water from all directions
7: protection against temporary immersion in water less than 1 m deep
8: protection against continuous immersion in water at a specified depth

Figure 23-5 PR-Lighting Design 150 exterior color wash luminaire.

The first optional letter indicates the degree of protection to personnel and tools. It ranges from A to D, and the letters are defined as follows:

A: protection against contact with back of hand
B: protection against contact with finger
C: protection against contact with tool such as a screwdriver
D: protection against contact with wire

The supplementary optional letter indicates the degree of protection specific to four items as indicated below:

H: protection against high-voltage apparatus
M: enclosure was in motion during water testing
S: enclosure was stationary during water testing
W: protection against weather

For example, if a fixture has an IP rating of 65, then it is dust tight and rated for the protection against jetting water. The IP standard also provides for specific means of testing enclosures. A dust-tight enclosure, for example, is tested with talcum powder sifted for specific dimensions with a specific density of powder in the chamber. More information about IP ratings can be found in IEC publication number 60529. The document can be purchased from the IEC website (www.iec.ch).

CHAPTER 24

Automated Lighting Applications

Light makes photography. Embrace light. Admire it. Love it. But above all, know light. Know it for all you are worth, and you will know the key to photography.—George Eastman

When automated lighting became widely available in the 1980s, some people thought it was a novelty that wouldn't last; others thought it would eventually replace conventional lighting. But throughout the history of theatrical lighting, rarely has any single technology totally replaced another. Instead, the lighting designer's toolbox grows as a result of the introduction of new technology. Such is the case with automated lighting.

Most lighting rigs today make use of both conventional and automated lighting. The ratio of conventional lighting to automated lighting used depends on the application, but in many instances, automated lighting is playing a greater part, both in terms of percentage of the overall lighting and in terms of the size of the rig. This is most likely due to the abundance of automated lighting and its easy accessibility. In the first couple years of production of the High End Systems Intellabeam 700 (the first model was a 400-watt fixture with 60% dimming) in the early 1990s, there were approximately 10,000 units sold worldwide, which was unheard of at the time. Many people thought the market was saturated, and some predicted the demise of automated lighting manufacturers because there were no untapped markets—all were chocked full of automated lights. But in a short time the next big thing in automated lighting, a new product with more light output and new features, hit the market and despite the fact that the market was "dead," it sold just as well. The lesson is that there will always be a market for innovation and novel applications of new technology. Worldwide fluctuations in economic conditions likely have more of an effect on the lighting industry than the saturation of markets, but economic downturns have proven to be short lived and isolated to certain regions. But as long as the industry keeps providing products that offer something new, the market will absorb them.

This trend continues today. For example, it was rumored that during the first 2 years of production of the Martin MAC 2000, there were approximately 17,000 units sold worldwide, and the numbers are still growing. So much for the saturation of markets.

Along with the abundance of automated lighting comes the opportunity to apply it in more and more situations. Couple that with a hypercompetitive market in which manufacturers search every dark corner for niche markets to fill, and the result is a growing number of automated lighting systems with features to suit virtually every application—"silent" fixtures for theatre, incandescent lamp sources for video and television, low-cost entry-level fixtures for high school theatre, incredibly bright fixtures for auto shows and high ceiling applications, framing shutters for spill control. . . . The list goes on.

Another very important factor in the application of automated lighting is the growing sophistication of consoles and networking. What used to be an incredibly complicated task is being made simpler by the power and ability of automated lighting consoles. They have enabled the growth of automated lighting systems beyond the practical limits of a decade ago. The growing use of networking has made possible multiuser programming sessions that are taming large systems that used to be unmanageable.

All of these factors are working to make automated lighting more commonplace and accessible to more people and productions. Lighting designers are usually very creative people, and each one has a unique approach to automated lighting. To categorize the uses of automated lighting is to limit and confine it, so any attempt to do so should be taken with a grain of salt. But we can, however, discuss how these fixtures have been used in certain applications without limiting them to a specific use.

Key Light

There was a time in the not-too-distant past when automated lighting systems were the exclusive domain of rock-and-roll tours and nightclubs. They were used primarily as effects lighting for beam projection and color wash. But the abundance of automated lighting and the introduction of features like framing shutters and incandescent lamp sources are changing the lighting production landscape. Although it's still cheaper to use conventional lights, it's much faster and less labor intensive to use automated lighting for key light. Consequently, it is used as such very often when the cost of production time is high and labor costs are high. For example, the North American International Auto Show in Detroit runs for over 2 weeks in a hall with a very high ceiling. In order to refocus a light, a rigging crew has to be called and they have to use a manlift, both of which are very expensive. Therefore, the vast majority of lighting at the show is automated. Television shows often have very tight production schedules that don't allow for refocusing lights. Therefore, many productions use a full rig of automated lighting in order to save time should the lighting need to be refocused.

In the design of an automated lighting system, the lighting levels vary. If there is a video or film crew involved, then the expectations for the key lighting with regard to the illumination and color temperature are likely to change. Most of the time, anywhere from 860 lux (80 footcandles) to 3228 lux (300 footcandles) is requested. New cameras are much more sensitive and require less light, but they still produce less grain and greater depth of field with higher light levels. It's a good idea to design the system for about 125% of the maximum desired illumination to account for lumen maintenance of the lamps and other contingencies. Once you know the target illumination, you can then calculate the illumination based on the throw distance and trim height (Figure 24-1). Sometimes the manufacturer supplies an easy-to-read chart with the illumination and beam or field diameter for a set of given throw distances.

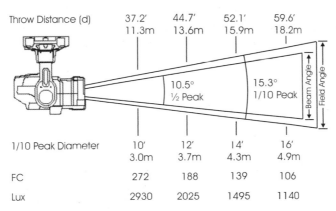

Figure 24-1 Photometric data chart for an ETC Revolution showing the illumination and beam angle at a given throw distance.

Alternatively, if you are given only the luminous intensity in candelas, you have to calculate the illuminance using the inverse square law. The inverse square law says that for a given amount of luminous intensity, the illuminance is inversely proportional to the square of the throw distance.

Illuminance (lux or footcandles) = luminous intensity (candelas) ÷ [throw distance (meters or feet)]^2

For example, if the fixture you plan to use for key light produces 250,000 candelas and you want a minimum illumination of 1614 lux (150 footcandles) on stage, then by using the inverse square law, you can calculate the maximum throw distance.

Illuminance (lux or footcandles) = luminous flux (candelas) ÷ [throw distance (m or feet)]^2

Throw distance = square root (luminous flux × illuminance)

Throw distance = square root (250,000/1614) = 12.45 m (40.85 feet)

From the throw distance you can calculate the trim height using the formula for a right triangle using the Pythagorean theorem (Figure 24-2).

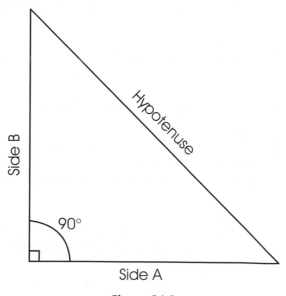

Side B

Hypotenuse

90°

Side A

Figure 24-2

Throw distance^2 = (setback distance)^2 + (elevation)^2

For optimal results, we want to maintain a maximum of a 45-degree angle from the horizontal of the stage. Otherwise there will be harsh shadows under the performers' eye sockets, nose, and jowls. For a 45-degree angle of projection, the elevation from the subject is the same as the setback distance. So we can call this distance X.

$$(\text{Throw distance})^2 = X^2 + X^2$$

$$(\text{Throw distance})^2 = 2X^2$$

$$\text{Throw distance} = \text{square root } (2X^2)$$

$$\text{Throw distance} = X \times \text{square root } (2)$$

$$X = \text{throw distance} \div \text{square root } (2)$$

$$X = \text{throw distance} \div 1.414$$

$$X = [12.45\,\text{m} \ (40.85 \ \text{feet})] \div 1.414 = 8.8\,\text{m} \ (28.9 \ \text{feet})$$

Keep in mind that most of the time the subject will be on a stage, so you have to add the height of the stage plus the height to the center of the target (Figure 24-3).

$$\text{Trim height (from floor)} = \text{elevation (from center of target)} + \text{stage height} + \text{height to center of target}$$

$$\text{Trim} = 8.8 \ \text{m} \ (28.9 \ \text{feet}) + 1.8 \ \text{m} \ (6 \ \text{feet}) + 1 \ \text{m} \ (3.28 \ \text{feet}) = 11.6\text{m} \ (38 \ \text{feet})$$

Once the throw distance has been determined, then you can calculate the beam or field diameter from the beam or field angle in the photometric data and you can determine how many instruments will be needed to cover a given area of the stage.

For example, if the beam angle of a fixture is 24 degrees, then you can use the formula for a right triangle to calculate the beam diameter for a given throw distance (Figure 24-4).

$$\text{Tan(beam angle} \div 2) = (\text{beam diameter} \div 2) \div \text{throw distance}$$

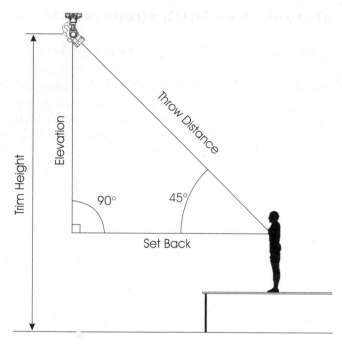

Figure 24-3 For a 45-degree projection, the elevation from the target is equal to the setback.

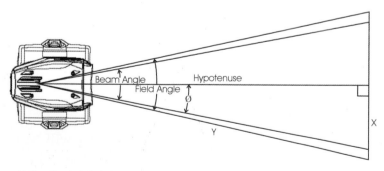

Figure 24-4 The Pythagorean theorem can be used to calculate the beam diameter of a luminaire at a given throw distance.

$$\text{Throw distance} \times \text{Tan}(12) = (\text{beam diameter} \div 2)$$

$$\text{Beam diameter} = 2 \times \text{throw distance} \times \text{Tan}(12)$$

$$\text{Beam diameter} = 2 \times 8.8 \times 0.2126 = 3.74 \text{ m (12.27 feet)}$$

Given the beam size, you can then calculate how many fixtures you will need to cover a given area of the stage. If the beam profile is peaked with a cosine distribution, then they should overlap at the 50% drop-off (as given by the beam angle) to get the most uniform distribution between the two beams (Figure 24-5). This is sometimes referred to as a blending distribution.

The width of the stage that is most uniformly covered by overlapping beams at the beam angle can be calculated with the following formula:

$$\text{Width of uniform coverage} = (\text{number of fixtures} - 1) \times \text{beam diameter}$$

If, in the preceding example, we have five fixtures overlapping at the 50% drop-off, then the width of uniform coverage is as follows:

$$\text{Width} = (5 - 1) \times 3.74 \text{ m} = 4 \times 3.74 = 14.96 \text{ m (49.1 feet)}$$

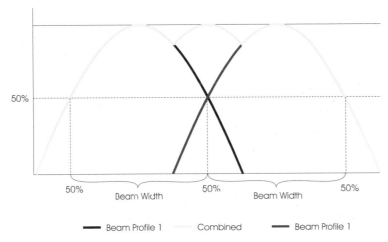

Figure 24-5 A cosine or mixing distribution has a peaked beam profile, which, when overlapped at the 50% drop-off with a like fixture, produces the most uniform wash between the beams.

On either side of the uniformly covered width, the light will fall off with a cosine distribution.

If the beam profile is flat, then the beams should overlap less. The amount of overlap in this case is a compromise between uniformity and coverage since they are round beams, not square beams.

Color Temperature and Balance

There are two particular issues to be aware of when using automated lighting for key light: the variation of color temperature across the fixtures and the color balance between green and magenta. Discharge lamps lose color temperature as they age. An MSR-type lamp will lose about 0.5 degree of color temperature per hour of operation and an HMI lamp will lose about 1 degree of color temperature per hour of operation. After 200 hours of use, an MSR lamp will have a color temperature of approximately 5500 K and an HMI lamp will have a color temperature of approximately 5400 K. Consequently, the more fixtures there are, the more likely they are to vary in color temperature from fixture to fixture. If there are five fixtures, the color temperature could vary quite a bit among them. If you are renting or hiring fixtures, keep in mind that some rental shops are very good about replacing aging lamps while others are not so conscientious. If you are doing an important video shoot it's a good idea to ask for fresh lamps when you're negotiating rates.

Also, some automated lights exhibit a color balance away from magenta and toward green. This is particularly problematic with certain lamps and luminaires and when video and film are involved. Sometimes the light may look white to the naked eye, but a vectorscope, an instrument used by video engineers to measure the color of a video signal, might indicate a bias toward green. During the setup procedure, the video cameras are focused on a white card illuminated by the key light and the video signals are displayed on a vectorscope. If the light and the cameras are balanced correctly, the vectorscope will show no bias toward any color, but a balance between them all.

The color temperature of a lamp is a measure of the balance between blue and red, but it doesn't take into consideration the balance between green and magenta. A lamp can have a high correlated color temperature and still have a high green content. Sometimes the gas mix, salt additives, reflector design, I/R filter, or a combination of any of these elements produces a shift toward green. When that happens, skin tones will look sickly and pale, particularly on camera. The video engineer can address the problem by balancing the camera away from green, but then the other sources will shift toward magenta. One way to address this problem is to use a green-absorbing gel filter designed to balance between green and magenta, such as a Roscolux Minusgreen. Tape the filter to the exit lens of the fixture so it will not burn or melt from the heat.

Fill Light and Back Light

It's hard to beat the economy and punch of a PAR can for backlighting, but given a sufficient budget, an automated color wash fixture with a Fresnel lens can provide a good fill or back light. Since it can be refocused with the press of a button, it can do double duty coloring set pieces when it's not occupied with its primary duty.

The calculations for finding the illumination, throw distance, trim height, and field diameter shown previously can also be used to determine the type and number of fixtures for the application, although the fill light and backlight level is generally about 50% less than the key light.

Image Projection and Beam Projection

Image projection and beam projection are two of the distinguishing features of automated profile spots. The eye candy that adorns cycs and set pieces and the well-defined shafts of light were two of the first applications of automated lighting. Advances in colored glass gobos, interchangeable gobo holders, and luminaire optics have helped keep them fresh and interesting (Figure 24-6). Projections no longer look cartoonish (unless that's the desired look), nor do they all look alike. There was a period of time when you could tell just by looking at the gobo pattern which brand of instrument was being used. Now with custom gobos and more automated lighting choices on the market, it's becoming more difficult to identify the instrument brand.

Color Wash

When Showco built the first Vari-Lite fixture, they were actually trying to build a color changer. Thus, they managed to popularize dichroic color

Figure 24-6 Advances in gobo manufacturing techniques and optics have vastly improved the quality of projections.

changing at the same time that they launched the first commercially available moving light. Since then, a number of automated color wash fixtures have become available, and they are ideal for washing large surfaces such as cycs, walls, columns, set pieces, and choir risers with color.

Most automated color wash luminaires use dichroic color changers with discharge lamps, both of which have some unique characteristics. Dichroic color lends itself to more saturated color than do gel filters, and the range of colors from a discharge lamp is somewhat limited compared to an incandescent lamp. Technically speaking, an automated light with eight-bit CMY color mixing has 196,608 unique color combinations ($256^2 \times 3$), but the visible differences are limited by the spectral distribution of the lamp and the characteristics of the dichroic color mixing filters. If the show is being broadcast or recorded, then the cameras and displays introduce another factor to the final outcome of the color wash. In the final analysis, the number of distinct colors is a few dozen at best.

"Architainment"

In 1993, Vari-Lite built the Irideon AR500, one of the first color wash fixtures made specifically for outdoor use in architectural applications. It spawned a new category of automated lighting for outdoor architectural use. Soon afterward, a number of outdoor enclosures and outdoor color wash luminaires hit the market in search of new customers. As a result, many landmarks around the world have become canvasses for color-changing light, including buildings, bridges, and structures, such as amusement park rides (Figure 24-7).

A

B

Figure 24-7 (A) The Sydney Opera House in Australia bathed with Coemar Panorama exterior color wash fixtures. (Photograph courtesy of Coemar DeSisti Australia.) (B) Place des Terreaux in Lyon's central square illuminated with 16 PIGI DDRA projectors during the Fête des Lumières (Festival of Lights). (C) The Theatre Royal New Castle lit by 20 Studio Due City Color color wash fixtures, seven Martin MAC 2000 Profile fixtures, 60 Source Four PARs, and four Philips Arena Vision fixtures. (Photograph by Louise Stickland.)

C

Figure 24-7 *Continued*

Using color wash fixtures to illuminate an outdoor structure works best with a white or light-colored canvas and low surrounding light levels. In order to make a building really "pop" with a color wash it should be lit to about a 10:1 ratio between the building and the surrounding light levels. Most buildings require from 15 to about 50 footcandles, depending on the absorption of the surface material on the building. Light-colored surfaces take light much better than dark-colored surfaces; therefore, dark surfaces require higher light levels. The photometric calculations previously discussed (see earlier Key Light section) can also be used to determine the number of fixtures required to cover a particular area as well as the setback (throw distance) of the fixtures.

Ingress Protection

When using automated lighting in outdoor architectural applications, there are several considerations outside of the normal considerations for theatrical lighting. Perhaps the most important is the luminaire's ability to withstand the weather and environmental conditions, as indicated by its IP Code. The system of classification for electrical enclosures is widely used to specify the suitability of automated luminaires for outdoor use. (See Chapter 23, Automated Luminaire Types, IP Ratings section.)

Serviceability

In addition to being able to withstand the elements, another important consideration for exterior lighting systems is how often they require service and how easy they are to service. While theatrical lighting systems typically benefit from the care and attention of a lighting professional, architectural installations often suffer from limited maintenance at the hands of personnel who are unskilled in the area of automated lighting. Therefore it's important to consider how easy it is to access the fixture for service and maintenance and design the system with that in mind. Choose a lamp source with the longest average lamp life available and plan for scheduled maintenance during the design phase. Any luminaire that accepts an MSR lamp will also accept an MSD lamp, which has an average life rating of approximately twice that of an MSR. CDM lamps, which have an average life rating of 8000 hours or better, are a better choice of lamp source than either an HTI or MSR.

CHAPTER 25

Automated Lighting in Production

Rage, rage against the dying of the light.—Dylan Thomas

The abundance of automated lighting and advances in automated lighting control have made them accessible to a growing number of users in a growing number of applications. Consequently, the demand for skilled personnel familiar with every aspect of automated lighting is constantly growing. Where can you find these jobs? Wherever automated lighting can be found. For the most part, automated lighting is a maturing technology with applications, to varying degrees, in almost every type of productions, provided there is the budget to support it.

Concerts and Touring

The concert and touring segment of the industry was one of the originators of automated lighting, and it continues to dominate the industry today. But while automated lighting was once the domain of big headliners with mammoth budgets, it is now commonplace among tours of all sizes and budgets. What's more, major headliners often tour with automated luminaires numbering in the hundreds. Some productions have grown to such proportions that they use a network on which multiple console programmers and operators work in a multiuser environment where the division of labor is the only way to meet the programming demands on schedule. Some of these networked consoles enable several programmers to simultaneously program portions of the show, which may be divided along the lines of hard edge–soft edge fixtures, stage lighting–audience lighting, and so on.

It's not unusual for tours of any size to be completely automated save for followspots at the front of house or in the truss. But more often a tour will use a combination of automated and conventional lighting. A typical mid-sized concert rig might have anywhere from handful to a few dozen automated profile fixtures, the same number of slightly more automated color wash fixtures, four-light or eight-light audience blinders for accents, perhaps some strobe lights, a number of PAR 64s with 1000-watt lamps, and followspots. The PARs may or may not have color scrollers, but they almost always have color, scrolling or otherwise.

The state of the recording industry shapes the touring industry because the record companies have traditionally been the source of seed money for most large tours. But the Internet and file sharing are threatening major labels, and the recording industry is in a state of flux. Consequently, there is more pressure on artists to tour more profitably, and some tours are responding by cutting personnel and traveling more efficiently with fewer trucks, buses, and expenses. But they aren't necessarily cutting back on the production. Instead, the crew is being asked to perform a variety of functions. A truck driver or rigger might double as a camera operator, and a stage manager might double as a lighting operator. In 2004, Hilary Duff toured with an automated lighting rig consisting of a few dozen automated and a handful of conventional fixtures, but only two lighting crew. They relied heavily on local crews for labor and the touring crew supervised the ins and outs.

There will always be the spectacle tours, like Britney Spears and Trans-Siberian Orchestra, whose shows carry upwards of 300 moving lights, as well as more moderate and smaller tours. The larger and medium-sized shows will increasingly rely on networked systems, and when ACN becomes a reality it will not be uncommon for large tours to travel with their own IT technician.

If you aspire to work with automated lighting, touring and live concert production offer vast opportunities for designers, programmers, operators, technicians, and stage hands. But it involves heavy travel and it's not for the faint of heart. The hours are long and the venues and hotels all look alike. It's not the life of glamour that some expect. In general, young people under 30 years of age are seeking ways to go on the road while those over the age of 30 are seeking ways of getting off the road.

Theatre

The more stringent requirements of the theatre have traditionally presented more hurdles for the early acceptance and widespread use of

Figure 25-1 The concert touring industry is changing in response to the Internet and file sharing. More tours, like this Hilary Duff production, are increasing efficiency by traveling with scaled-back crews and relying more heavily on local crews. (Photograph by Louise Strickland. Lighting design by Seth Jackson and B.K. Waggoner.)

automated lighting. The issues of fan noise, motor noise, color selection, and the lack of incandescent sources have been the main stumbling blocks for automated luminaires in the theatre. Only recently have manufacturers successfully addressed the market by building fixtures with convection cooling, noise baffles, reengineered cooling systems, color scrollers, and incandescent lamps specifically aimed at the theatrical market. As a result, many Broadway shows and touring theatrical productions are now using automated lighting (Figure 25-2), albeit in smaller numbers than a typical touring concert.

If you aspire to a life in the theatre, you should be ready, willing, and able to use automated lighting, but be prepared to go long spells between uses, unless you happen to specialize in automated lighting programming and you are not tied to one theatre. In addition, the hours are often long and sometimes grueling, and it's unlikely you will be greatly financially rewarded. But working in the theatre is richly rewarding in itself.

Figure 25-2 The use of automated lighting in the theatre is growing thanks to technology that addresses the specific concerns of the theatre, such as quieter fixtures, incandescent sources and color scrollers in automated lighting. This photograph is from *Jesus Christ Superstar* in the West End of London. (Photography by Louise Stickland.)

Television

In the world of television, automated lighting reigns supreme in awards shows and music shows. Several times a year one award show or another is vying for the 18- to 35-year-old demographic by emulating the spirit of the early MTV years with cutting-edge music and production, in which automated lighting plays a big part. In many instances, the "concert" lighting in these types of shows is completely automated because the limited preproduction time precludes the possibility of manually focusing lights. Therefore, these rigs tend to be heavily sprinkled with automated lighting (Figure 25-3).

Figure 25-3 Grammy Awards, 2005. Television awards shows are typically heavily stocked with automated lighting. Many of these lighting rigs rely on automated lighting not only for concert lighting effects but also because the short production time allows little time to manually refocus. (Photograph by Tamlyn Wright. Lighting by Bob Dickinson.)

Apart from award shows, beauty pageants, some cable comedy specials, and music shows, automated lighting in television is mostly limited to the occasional nightclub scene and special effects.

Industrial Shows and Corporate Events

Corporate events and industrial shows enjoy the luxury of relatively large budgets in proportion to the size of the show and the number of attendees, and lighting designers have come to rely on automated lighting to provide the pizzazz and energy needed to pump up the audience. Indeed, many corporate events are multifaceted affairs and often include a conference, breakout meetings, and live concert performances, sometimes with major headlining bands. Accordingly, the lighting rig sometimes does double duty as a conference rig by day and a concert rig by night (Figure 25-4).

Film

Lighting for film is still the exclusive domain of directors of photography and gaffers, whose concerns revolve more around film stock, film speed,

Figure 25-4 Corporate events provide an excellent opportunity to use automated lighting because they very often have healthy budgets. Many of them are multi-faceted affairs with conferences, meetings, and live concert performances. (Photograph courtesy of Herbalife and Scoop Marketing.)

and exposure values than the virtues of automated lighting. When they do call on automated lighting for special effects and the occasional nightclub scene, they typically call on production professionals outside of film production circles who deal with automated lighting on a more regular basis. They might bring in a lighting designer, an automated lighting programmer, and/or an automated lighting operator whose sole job is to oversee the automated lighting in certain scenes (Figure 25-5).

Houses of Worship

In houses of worship, automated lighting is quickly gaining in popularity as a medium that can help enhance the delivery of the message either dramatically or subtly. It appeals to the younger generation, a demographic that houses of worship are keen to reach, but its use is sometimes tempered to fit in with the more mature members of the congregation.

Modern houses of worship often use a blend of conventional and automated lighting for a variety of purposes, including Sunday worship, Christmas and Easter productions, special events, youth services, music

A

B

Figure 25-5 Scenes from the film *iRobot*. Film production rarely involves automated lighting except in the relatively rare event that special effects are needed or that a nightclub or concert scene is being filmed. Most film productions will bring in outside specialists when they opt for automated lighting. (Photograph courtesy of Q1 Productions.)

C

Figure 25-5 *Continued*

events, and more (Figure 25-6). The demands placed on the lighting are wide ranging. It is called on to increase visibility, focus attention to a specific area, create mood and drama, create ambiance, and enhance live music performances. Very often the Sunday service is lit for video, for image magnification, live or delayed broadcast, or both, which dictates much of the lighting requirements for lighting levels, uniformity, color temperature, color rendering, and fixture placement. The lighting rig has to be flexible enough to adapt to most any situation, including transforming the sanctuary into a live concert venue and accommodate touring music events. In all of these applications, the lighting rig is an amalgam of theatrical lighting, concert lighting, television lighting, and special event lighting.

Churches are an ideal training ground for anyone who aspires to work with automated lighting. In most situations, the operators are volunteers trained to maintain, operate, and sometimes program the lighting system.

Figure 25-6 Prestonwood Baptist Church in Plano, Texas. Automated lighting is gaining popularity in the modern house of worship. It is used for a variety of functions, including key lighting, special effects lighting, color wash, and architectural lighting. (Photograph courtesy of Brawner and Associates. Lighting design by Donnie Brawner.)

When the system is installed, the installation company often trains the staff on its use and operation, and volunteers are usually welcome to work with the equipment and learn how to use it. If the church is large enough, it might have a paid full-time or part-time staff member whose job it is to keep the equipment operating.

Nightclubs

Nightclubs are often the proving ground for young aspiring lighting professionals who cut their teeth on a nightclub lighting system and go on to bigger and better things (Figure 25-7). Many nightclubs that cater to a young demographic pride themselves on using cutting-edge technology with large lighting rigs. They sometimes use smaller, rack-mount controllers rather than a high-end console, but the basics of programming an automated light are the same. The installations are typically done by companies specializing in nightclub lighting, video, and audio installations,

Figure 25-7 Republik nightclub in Toronto, Canada. Automated lighting reigns supreme in large discotheques and nightclubs. Nightclubs often offer an ideal opportunity for aspiring lighting professionals to hone their lighting chops before moving into the world of professional production. (Lighting design by Howard Ungerleider.)

and they usually program the controllers with generic scenes and chases. The club lighting operator usually has plenty of opportunity to spend quality time learning and programming the lighting system between changing lamps and troubleshooting.

Cruise Ships

For the adventurer, cruise ships offer a great opportunity to work with automated lighting and travel for several months at a time. Today's cruise ships are enormous traveling entertainment centers, and they almost always feature a theatre with theatrical productions or Las Vegas-style reviews. The newest ships of the fleet are often outfitted with the latest in automated lighting and control. The need for lighting technicians, programmers, and operators onboard these ships is plentiful and growing. The caveat here is that on a cruise ship, practically everyone has dual roles in order to make the most efficient use of the crew. So if you plan to work as a lighting tech on a cruise ship, be prepared to swab the deck or do any other job that you may be assigned.

Retail

Most retail and architectural lighting is handled by boutique lighting designers who specialize in this area. However, there are the occasional lighting projects that involve automated lighting, such as the Forum Shops in Las Vegas, and the occasional color wash on a skyscraper project. Lighting designers who work on such projects are typically well trained and very often are professional lighting designers with credentials from the International Association of Lighting Designers (IALD, www.iald.org). There are, however, some lighting designers who cross over from theatre and corporate events into the retail and architectural realm.

If you aspire to work with automated lighting, there are many opportunities in a variety of fields that need good personnel. The key is to become proficient at your job; then the opportunities will present themselves. Once you have a few productions under your belt, and if you do a good job and are reliable and easy to get along with, then more opportunities will come your way by word of mouth. Often your personality is more important than your job skills, provided you can do your job sufficiently.

CHAPTER 26

Lighting Design Software

When Thomas Edison worked late into the night on the electric light, he had to do it by gas lamp or candle. I'm sure it made the work seem that much more urgent.—George Carlin

The increasing size and complexity of automated lighting systems are due in part to the ability of computers and software tools to design, manage, and program them quickly and efficiently. We have come to rely on these software tools so much that the industry would be paralyzed without them. Not only do they simplify and speed the task of designing and drawing a lighting plot, but they also save valuable time and money in the preproduction process.

There are a variety of software tools to aid in the design process, but they generally fall into at least three categories: computer-aided drafting software, previsualization software, and paperwork management software.

Computer-Aided Drafting

The advent of desktop computing has, for all practical purposes, made pencil and paper drafting obsolete. Not only is computer-aided drafting faster than drawing by hand, but it also allows you to build a 3D model, something that is virtually impossible to do on paper. It also makes such things as modifications, file sharing, printing, and keeping track of revisions much easier.

Computer-aided design or computer-aided drafting (CAD) is a means of creating scale drawings electronically using a desktop computer and an application-specific software package such as Autodesk AutoCAD. There are several CAD programs specific to the entertainment lighting industry that blend generic CAD techniques and drawing tools specific to the lighting industry. For example, most lighting CAD programs have a library of blocks, or predrawn 2D and 3D symbols, of lighting instruments and peripherals, such as truss and lighting consoles. These blocks speed the drawing process by eliminating the need to draw everything from scratch. You can simply find the block you're looking for in the library and drop it in the drawing. If the block is a symbol for an automated luminaire, then it often has lots of data attached to it, including the luminous flux, beam and field angle, power consumption, the number of DMX512 channels required to operate it, and its weight. Some programs attach more specific attribute data, such as bitmaps of the gobos and representations of the colors.

Once a plot is drawn and a virtual model is built, then you can display or print different views, including plan views (from above looking down), elevations (side views), and isometric views (from an angle) (Figure 26-1).

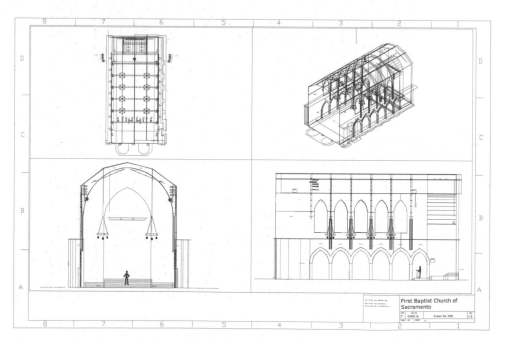

Figure 26-1 A 3D CAD drawing allows you to view and print a lighting plot from any angle.

Sometimes a drawing is created from scratch, and other times it starts from an architectural drawing taken from the architect. Most CAD drawings are in DWG format, which is the AutoCAD file format developed by Autodesk and which has become the de facto standard, or in DXF format (Drawing Exchange Format, also developed by Autodesk in order to exchange files between competing CAD programs). If you are starting with an existing DWG or DXF drawing, you may have to import the file, rather than simply opening it, depending on your application software. After you finish your plot you can create a drawing border and add pertinent information in the title block such as the name of the drawing, the date, the draftsperson, and so on (Figure 26-2).

Then you can e-mail the finished drawing or upload it to a reprographics service to have prints made. If it is to be printed you may need to either download a print driver to your computer or export it to a print file.

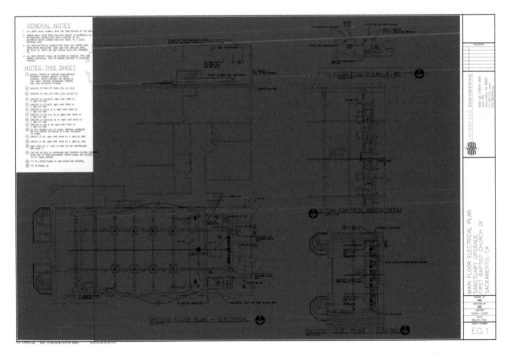

Figure 26-2 The title block in a lighting plot provides project-specific information, such as the name of the project, the date of the drawing, the revision number, lighting designer, and the draftsperson. Additional notes are sometimes drawn inside of the drawing border.

Rendering

One of the useful functions of lighting CAD software is to help sell a design. In the preliminary phase of a project, it may be necessary to draw a sample plot and create realistic renderings in order to convey your concept and win a design job. Alternatively, you might just want to illustrate how the end result will look. Either way, it can be accomplished with rendering software.

Rendering software is application-specific software designed to emulate the lighting and reflectance of materials in the model, providing a photo-realistic illustration of the lighting and set. Many lighting design software packages have rendering capabilities, but some lighting designers prefer to use stand-alone rendering software such as 3D Studio VIZ. In either case a 3D virtual model must first be drawn before it can be rendered.

Most rendering software has a materials library with bitmaps of various common materials such as aluminum and carpet (Figure 26-3). The materi-

Figure 26-3 A photo-realistic rendering closely approximates the end result of a lighting project. Lighting CAD software often contains a materials library from which materials can be applied to the objects in a 3D model of the lighting rig, stage, props, and anything else in the venue.

als can be applied to objects in the CAD model in order to approximate as closely as possible the behavior of the objects in real life. Once the materials have been applied, the lighting can be "turned on" in the virtual model to simulate a real-life scene. A snapshot of the scene can then be output as a common file type such as a JPEG or TIFF.

The point of view of the camera can be changed to show renderings from different angles. Each rendering can take several minutes to several hours to generate, depending on the size of the rendering, which is measured in pixels. If a rendering is to be displayed on a computer monitor, it only needs to be about 100 pixels per inch. But if it is to be printed, then it should be a minimum of 300 pixels per inch. An 8 × 10-inch print, for example, should be 2400 by 3000 pixels, which can take close to an hour to generate on a fast computer. For projects requiring intensive rendering there are rendering farms, which, for a fee, allow you to share their resources over the Internet. They provide specially built high-speed graphics computers designed to make quick work of rendering. You can upload your finished 3D model, then have them render it and send you the rendered file.

In addition to still life renderings, most rendering software allows you to create a movie, called a fly-through, with a moving point of view that looks as if you are flying through the set. It allows you to view a photo-realistic video representation of your design from various angles.

Visualization

One of the fastest growing areas of lighting software is that of visualization. Visualization software allows you to view a representation of the lighting, scene by scene, in real time. It uses wireframe cones of light, shaded rendering, or photo-realistic rendering to represent lighting projections, and it also displays gobo projections and color. It's intended to allow you to view your program in real time without having a direct line of sight or having any lighting instruments at all.

Visualization software has become one of the most important design tools in preproduction, where it is used for previsualization, or programming a show before the lighting designer ever sets foot on site. There are previsualization studios across the world that provide facilities and equipment to aid in preproduction with visualization tools. They offer high-speed computers, software, and display devices such as projection or plasma screens in the comfort of a studio. Lighting designers can bring their CAD files in on a disk and load them into the computer. Once they are set up they can begin to program their show by visualization. Most users report that they can program very accurately, with only minor position palette touching up required once they reach the show site. Using previsualization can save a production the cost of renting all of the lighting, truss and power distribution, paying for crew, hotels, airfare, and per diem, and the cost of renting a rehearsal facility.

The latest versions of visualization software allow you to import live video feeds and render them in your 3D model in real time. Some software also allows you to program moving truss and moving set pieces.

Lighting Paperwork

The third component of lighting design software involves managing the huge quantities of information associated with a lighting system. Lighting paperwork software is a sort of cross between a spreadsheet and a database management application (Figure 26-4). Its job is to keep track of each bit of information associated with each component of the lighting system. It becomes especially important with automated lighting, since each luminaire has so much more information associated with it.

A good lighting paperwork program makes it easier to keep track of information by storing libraries of information about luminaires that can be used repeatedly without having to research the information over and over again. It can help generate shop orders based on the lighting plot, help track inventory during load in and load out, and help facilitate set up and focus by providing such information as DMX512 charts and focus charts.

There are several lighting paperwork software packages on the market, some of which are integral to CAD programs and some of which are stand-alone programs. Most keep track of basic information such as instrument types, unit numbers, channel numbers, DMX512 addresses, power consumption, fixture weights, and accessories. Others add more detailed information, such as individual attributes of automated lights. If the software is part of a CAD suite, very often the information is linked to the drawing, and any changes made in the drawing space will be reflected in the paperwork. On the other hand, stand-alone programs are usually manually adjusted.

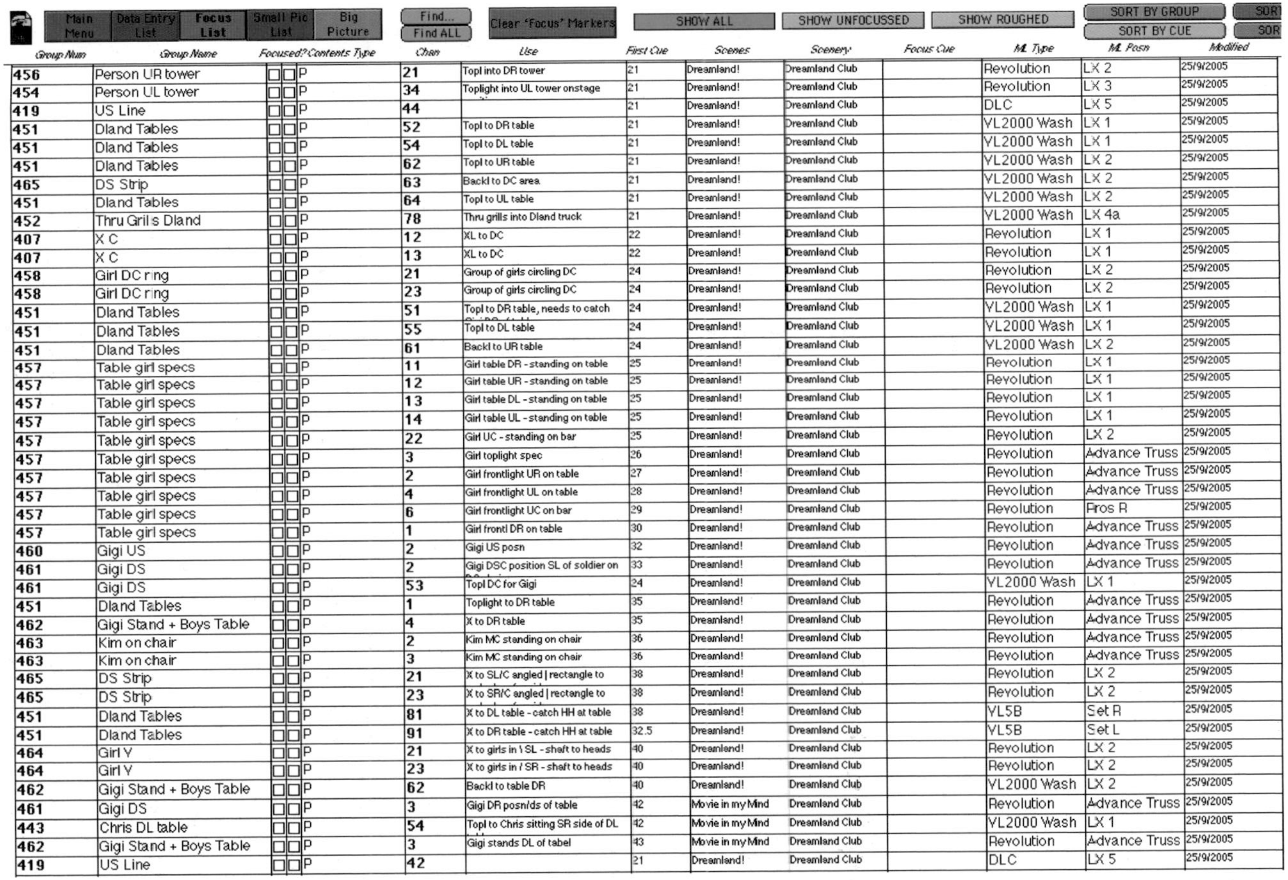

Group Num	Group Name	Chan	Use	First Cue	Scenes	Scenery	Focus Cue	M. Type	M. Posn	Modified
456	Person UR tower	21	Topl into DR tower	21	Dreanland!	Dreanland Club		Revolution	LX 2	25/9/2005
454	Person UL tower	34	Toplight into UL tower onstage	21	Dreanland!	Dreanland Club		Revolution	LX 3	25/9/2005
419	US Line	44		21	Dreanland!	Dreanland Club		DLC	LX 5	25/9/2005
451	Dland Tables	52	Topl to DR table	21	Dreanland!	Dreanland Club		VL2000 Wash	LX 1	25/9/2005
451	Dland Tables	54	Topl to DL table	21	Dreanland!	Dreanland Club		VL2000 Wash	LX 1	25/9/2005
451	Dland Tables	62	Topl to UR table	21	Dreanland!	Dreanland Club		VL2000 Wash	LX 2	25/9/2005
465	DS Strip	63	Back to DC area	21	Dreanland!	Dreanland Club		VL2000 Wash	LX 2	25/9/2005
451	Dland Tables	64	Topl to UL table	21	Dreanland!	Dreanland Club		VL2000 Wash	LX 2	25/9/2005
452	Thru Grills Dland	78	Thru grills into Dland truck	21	Dreanland!	Dreanland Club		VL2000 Wash	LX 4a	25/9/2005
407	X C	12	XL to DC	22	Dreanland!	Dreanland Club		Revolution	LX 1	25/9/2005
407	X C	13	XL to DC	22	Dreanland!	Dreanland Club		Revolution	LX 1	25/9/2005
458	Girl DC rng	21	Group of girls circling DC	24	Dreanland!	Dreanland Club		Revolution	LX 2	25/9/2005
458	Girl DC rng	23	Group of girls circling DC	24	Dreanland!	Dreanland Club		Revolution	LX 2	25/9/2005
451	Dland Tables	51	Topl to DR table, needs to catch	24	Dreanland!	Dreanland Club		VL2000 Wash	LX 1	25/9/2005
451	Dland Tables	55	Topl to DL table	24	Dreanland!	Dreanland Club		VL2000 Wash	LX 1	25/9/2005
451	Dland Tables	61	Back to UR table	24	Dreanland!	Dreanland Club		VL2000 Wash	LX 2	25/9/2005
457	Table girl specs	11	Girl table DR - standing on table	25	Dreanland!	Dreanland Club		Revolution	LX 2	25/9/2005
457	Table girl specs	12	Girl table UR - standing on table	25	Dreanland!	Dreanland Club		Revolution	LX 1	25/9/2005
457	Table girl specs	13	Girl table DL - standing on table	25	Dreanland!	Dreanland Club		Revolution	LX 1	25/9/2005
457	Table girl specs	14	Girl table UL - standing on table	25	Dreanland!	Dreanland Club		Revolution	LX 1	25/9/2005
457	Table girl specs	22	Girl UC - standing on bar	25	Dreanland!	Dreanland Club		Revolution	LX 2	25/9/2005
457	Table girl specs	3	Girl toplight spec	26	Dreanland!	Dreanland Club		Revolution	Advance Truss	25/9/2005
457	Table girl specs	2	Girl frontlight UR on table	27	Dreanland!	Dreanland Club		Revolution	Advance Truss	25/9/2005
457	Table girl specs	4	Girl frontlight UL on table	28	Dreanland!	Dreanland Club		Revolution	Advance Truss	25/9/2005
457	Table girl specs	6	Girl frontlight UC on bar	29	Dreanland!	Dreanland Club		Revolution	Pros R	25/9/2005
457	Table girl specs	1	Girl frontl DR on table	30	Dreanland!	Dreanland Club		Revolution	Advance Truss	25/9/2005
460	Gigi US	2	Gigi US posn	32	Dreanland!	Dreanland Club		Revolution	Advance Truss	25/9/2005
461	Gigi DS	2	Gigi DSC position SL of soldier on	33	Dreanland!	Dreanland Club		Revolution	Advance Truss	25/9/2005
461	Gigi DS	53	Topl DC for Gigi	24	Dreanland!	Dreanland Club		VL2000 Wash	LX 1	25/9/2005
451	Dland Tables	1	Toplight to DR table	35	Dreanland!	Dreanland Club		Revolution	Advance Truss	25/9/2005
462	Gigi Stand + Boys Table	4	X to DR table	35	Dreanland!	Dreanland Club		Revolution	Advance Truss	25/9/2005
463	Kim on chair	2	Kim MC standing on chair	36	Dreanland!	Dreanland Club		Revolution	Advance Truss	25/9/2005
463	Kim on chair	3	Kim MC standing on chair	36	Dreanland!	Dreanland Club		Revolution	Advance Truss	25/9/2005
465	DS Strip	21	X to SUC angled	rectangle to	38	Dreanland!	Dreanland Club		Revolution	LX 2	25/9/2005
465	DS Strip	23	X to SRC angled	rectangle to	38	Dreanland!	Dreanland Club		Revolution	LX 2	25/9/2005
451	Dland Tables	81	X to DL table - catch HH at table	38	Dreanland!	Dreanland Club		VL5B	Set R	25/9/2005
451	Dland Tables	91	X to DR table - catch HH at table	32.5	Dreanland!	Dreanland Club		VL5B	Set L	25/9/2005
464	Girl V	21	X to girls in SL - shat to heads	40	Dreanland!	Dreanland Club		Revolution	LX 2	25/9/2005
464	Girl V	23	X to girls in / SR - shat to heads	40	Dreanland!	Dreanland Club		Revolution	LX 2	25/9/2005
462	Gigi Stand + Boys Table	62	Back to table DR	40	Movie in myMind	Dreanland Club		VL2000 Wash	LX 2	25/9/2005
461	Gigi DS	3	Gigi DR posn/ds of table	42	Movie in myMind	Dreanland Club		Revolution	Advance Truss	25/9/2005
443	Chris DL table	54	Topl to Chris sitting SR side of DL	42	Movie in my Mind	Dreanland Club		VL2000 Wash	LX 1	25/9/2005
462	Gigi Stand + Boys Table	3	Gigi stands DL of rabel	43	Movie in my Mind	Dreanland Club		Revolution	Advance Truss	25/9/2005
419	US Line	42		21	Dreanland!	Dreanland Club		DLC	LX 5	25/9/2005

Figure 26-4 Lighting paperwork software makes it easier to manage huge quantities of information associated with automated lighting design and programming. This screenshot of Focus Track software shows cueing information associated with the moving lights in the show. (Courtesy of Rob Halliday, Focus Track.)

Many high-end automated lighting consoles are now packaging visualization software with the console, making it easier and more cost-effective to prepare for a show. Meanwhile, the falling prices of display technology and computers are making it cheaper and easier to set up a previsualization studio. Still, high-end graphics cards and high-end microprocessors will always be among the highest costing components of the previsualization system, even as "high end" is constantly being redefined. But the software continues to progress and the capabilities are increasing at a rapid rate. Today's visualizers are far more realistic than they were when they were first introduced a decade ago, and there is no reason to believe they will not continue to improve.

CHAPTER 27

Design Issues

Following the light of the sun, we left the Old World.—Christopher Columbus

Automated lighting has a certain appeal; its robotic movements and projection changing, color changing, and effects capabilities are irresistible to many lighting designers. Having all that power available at the tips of your fingers can be both exhilarating and overwhelming all at once. Even so, it is not a panacea for all issues in lighting design, nor does every situation call for every effect known to lighting. There are many pitfalls and situations to be avoided when working with automated lighting. There are also many good ways to use its power to maximum benefit.

Movement

One of the most common pitfalls of automated lighting is having too much happening at once, with little regard to composition, layering, tension, and release, or building a show and saving the best for last. When automated lighting was in its infancy it was easy to wow a crowd with automated lighting. Everyone was completely in awe of the synchronized movement of a group of lights. But for the current generation, who was weaned on a steady diet of MTV, television awards shows, and concerts, moving lights are no longer a novelty. It takes more than simple movement to make an impression. It takes thoughtful programming with the right movement at the right time. In fact, excessive movement or full-speed nonstop movement can be a distraction and detract from a show. There are times when slow, graceful movement is far more powerful than fast movement. Indeed, automated lighting doesn't have to move at all to be "moving," at least not while the shutter is open. As lighting designer Anne Militello once said, "Just because it can move doesn't mean it has to move."

There are other ways to convey movement than with pan and tilt. A shutter chase can move much faster than a moving yoke, and at times it can add a lot of drama to a show. A gobo or color wheel roll can also convey movement with a stationary beam.

The way a light moves, or doesn't move, is probably the single biggest factor in the quality of programming. When it's done tastefully with discretion, it can be a powerful effect. When it's done indiscriminately, it can be an annoyance and a distraction.

Color Consistency

As a discharge lamp ages it loses light output and color temperature. For every hour of operation, an HMI or HTI lamp loses about 1 degree of color temperature, and an MSR lamp loses about 0.5 degree of color temperature. As a result, the more discharge lamps that are in a lighting system, the more inconsistencies there are in the way they look. Some of the newer, more high-end automated lights have a variable color temperature feature to help address this problem, and at least one has a lamp and power supply that can be adjusted to match all the lights. If lacking those features, the only sure way to address the problem is to change all the lamps for important events such as a television or video shoot. Even then, new lamps can vary in color temperature. But in the event that color consistency is very important to a production, you should specify new lamps when negotiating a rental or hire deal.

Color Rendering

A discharge lamp does not have a continuous spectrum; instead, it is made up of bands of colors that approximate white when viewed together. Consequently, it doesn't render color exactly the same as natural light. Some shades of certain colors are minimized and others are not. There is not a lot of light energy in the red end of the spectrum of a discharge lamp, and it's difficult to render good skin tones and reproduce deep reds. Some discharge lamps commonly used in automated luminaires such as MSR/2 lamps have a very high color temperature and can make fair skin look pale and unhealthy. For that reason, some lighting designers prefer to use incandescent lamps over discharge lamps. There are a few automated lights with incandescent sources available, and there is at least one, the

ETC Revolution, with a gel scroller instead of a dichroic color changer. Incandescent lamps reproduce red better than discharge lamps, but they have less energy in the blue end of the spectrum. If deep reds are important to your production then you should consider an alternative to supplement or replace your discharge lamp sources.

Color Correction

Color correction becomes an issue mainly when television or video is involved in a production because the human eye is much more forgiving than a camera. It's easy enough to balance all the cameras to any color temperature, but if there is a mixture of lamp source types, then every lamp that is not the same color temperature as the camera balance will have to be corrected. The question is whether you should balance the cameras to the arc lamps and correct the tungsten lamps, or balance them to incandescent and correct the arc lamps. The answer is that there are trade-offs either way. If you balance to incandescent and then rely on color wash fixtures with arc lamps to paint the set, then the camera will emphasize the blue end of the spectrum and de-emphasize the red end of the spectrum, resulting in a video picture that differs significantly from the actual set. On the other hand, if you balance to the arc lamps, the higher color temperature will not flatter Caucasian skin tones—they will look sickly and pale under the lights, although they can look fine on video. These issues may or may not be important depending on whether there's a live audience and whether the lighting crew has its own video monitor to gage the video rendering (they should!). One alternative is to compromise and balance the camera in between 3200K and 5600K, like Primetime Emmy Award-winning lighting designer Jeff Ravitz sometimes does.

Magenta and Green Balance

We have already discussed color temperature and the balance in the spectral distribution between the red and blue ends of the visible range of light (see Chapter 13, Lamp Technology). But there is also an important balance between green and magenta. The human eye is very sensitive to green wavelengths, and if the spectrum has too much green skin tones will appear pale and sickly. For that reason, lamp manufacturers deliberately avoid green by targeting a balance that slightly favors magenta. They use MacAdam ellipses to define the tolerance for chromaticity variation in the

Indexing (Hysteresis)

One of the inherent problems with mechanical and electromechanical systems is that they sometimes exhibit properties that prevent them from accurately targeting exact positions in certain circumstances. The hysteresis in a system causes inaccuracies by behaving with slight differences depending on how it's being used. For example, if you were to program a focus position with a tight iris in order to target a prop, say a vase, and then you were to call up that preset from different cues, you would get different results depending on from which direction the beam comes. That's because the built-in tolerance or the "slop" in the gearing, the expansion of the drive belt (if there are belts), and the residual magnetism of the stepper motor combine to react to the situation in different ways. If the fixture is panning from the right, it stops at a slightly different place than if it's panning from the left. That is the hysteresis in the system. Some lights exhibit more hysteresis than others, so if accurate targeting is critical to a production, you should be aware of it and should practice your cues in circumstances as close to the show as possible to check the results.

Dimming

Since the advent of automated lighting, one of the persistent problems has been building a smooth mechanical dimmer. Incandescent lamps have a beautiful dimming curve because the intensity is a factor of the temperature of the filament, and that cannot change instantaneously; it can only cool off and heat up linearly. As a result, the dimming curve is extremely smooth. The trade-off is that the color temperature changes as the intensity changes. Arc lamps and mechanical dimming solve that issue, but they introduce two new issues: aberrations in the field and the equivalent of the jaggies in digital print media, steppy dimming.

In a mechanical dimmer, the optical path is partially interrupted by a shaped shutter in proportion to the dimming intensity. The dimmer is intentionally placed out of the focal plane so that it doesn't image, resulting in a general drop in intensity rather than a vignetted beam. But a mechanical dimmer almost always exhibits some nonuniformity in the field, particularly in the last few steps before a total blackout. It is particularly evident when an open beam is projected against a light-colored background, which is obviously a situation to be avoided for this very reason.

In addition to field aberrations, mechanical dimmers are almost always controlled by an eight-bit digital driver, meaning there are 256 dimming steps. Consequently, each step can be seen as a discrete level, particularly during a slow fade to black and near a total blackout.

Color Media

The vast majority of automated luminaires use dichroic color filters rather than gel filters. Dichroic filters have a unique look to them and tend to be more vibrant and saturated than gels, which is great if that's the effect that you're looking for. If you want more pastel colors, though, the caveat is that most off-the-shelf color wheels that are provided in automated lighting tend to have deeply saturated colors.

In the early days of automated lighting, color mixing was very rare, if not altogether nonexistent, and most automated luminaires used permanent adhesives to attach the dichroic color filters to the color wheel. When lighting designer Jim Tetlow was using Intellabeams for television production, he decided that the colors were too saturated for his purposes, so he began ordering custom color wheels with specifically selected dichroic filters chosen for their pastel qualities. These became known as Tetlow color wheels.

Today, many automated luminaires have CMY color mixing, which makes it much easier to attain those subtle colors that Tetlow was after. And those luminaires without color mixing very often have color wheels with interchangeable dichroic filters. Still, some lighting designers prefer to use gel filters because they are intimately familiar with their options. Either way, the lighting designer should be aware of the capabilities of the luminaire.

Fan and Motor Noise

Two types of noise still plague automated lighting to this day: the robotic whirring of stepper motors moving and the rushing-air sound of the cooling fans. In many applications the music or other noise drowns out the noise produced by automated lighting, but in other applications the noise of the automated lighting has prevented it from being used.

Fortunately, there are ways to avoid these problems. One way is to temporarily turn off or slow down the fans during quiet passages. Many automated luminaires have a control channel that allows the operator to manually control the fan speed or program a fan speed change in a cue. This is obviously meant to be a temporary fix. After all, the fans are there for a very good reason. And if the fixture starts to overheat, then the onboard logic will override the fan control and kick it back into maximum speed.

Another solution to the fan noise problem is to use any one of the special fixtures designed to reduce fan noise. Some of these fixtures are designated with Q, for quiet, as in the Vari-Lite version, or with SV, for studio version, as in the High End Systems version. They have specially designed baffles to muffle the fan noise and still retain the proper amount of airflow to keep the components sufficiently cooled.

The robotic noise problem is one that can be addressed in the programming and execution of cues. During a quiet passage, for example, is not a good time to change the focus positions of 300 automated lights. If it's unavoidable, then move them very slowly to minimize the motor noise.

Noise is a definable, albeit somewhat "squishy," quantity. Buildings are rated by their noise criteria (NC), which is the relative loudness of a space over a range of frequencies. It generally indicates the extent to which noise interferes with speech intelligibility (Figure 27-2).

Some automated lighting manufacturers will provide sound spectrum measurements for their fixtures in order to evaluate their relative contribution to the noise in an installation. To be completely unbiased, the data should be supplied by an independent testing laboratory, usually an acoustics engineer or laboratory. The fixtures are placed in an anechoic chamber and are measured with a calibrated microphone at a given distance, usually 1 m. They are measured from several different angles, and the results are plotted on a polar graph.

Because it is costly to undertake such testing, very few manufacturers offer the data. Sometimes for a critical application, such as a church, the architect or lighting designer will specify a maximum acceptable NC rating for a space, in which case the noise contribution from the automated lighting, along with the HVAC system, has to be evaluated.

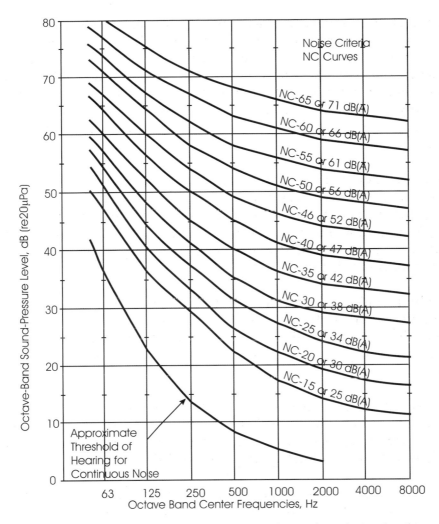

Figure 27-2 Noise criteria curves are used to evaluate the relative loudness of a space. The sound spectrum is plotted against the NC curves, and the lowest NC curve that is not exceeded by any component of the sound spectrum indicates the NC rating.

Heat

Einstein taught that energy can be neither created nor destroyed; it can only change forms. The light emanating from every luminaire starts out in the form of electrical energy and is eventually converted to heat energy— every bit of it. In new construction, the mechanical engineer in charge of designing the HVAC system needs to know what each and every thermal load in the building is as well as its contribution to the overall generation of heat in the room. If you have ever walked into a dimmer room you no doubt understand how much heat a rack of dimmers can generate. That's because electronic dimmers are not 100% efficient; they consume about 8% of the energy they receive and the rest is passed along to the lighting loads. That inefficiency translates to the generation of heat. The voltage drop across the junction of the electronic switching device generates current that changes to heat due to the resistance in the junction. Eight percent may not seem like a lot, but in a room with 96 dimmers it can get quite hot.

Now consider the efficiency of the average luminaire. In an incandescent lamp, only about 10% of the electricity flowing through the filament is converted to visible light. The rest changes to heat. A discharge lamp is more efficient, but it still loses about 65% of the energy to heat. And regardless of the efficiency of a luminaire, the light it produces is also converted to heat when it is absorbed.

What that means to the HVAC is that all of the lighting loads contribute to the heating of the building, and cooling capacity has to be added to compensate. How do you quantify the heat contribution due to the lighting system? Fortunately, the answer is a simple conversion formula:

$$1 \text{ kilowatt-hour} = 3412 \text{ BTU}$$

Thermal Load Calculations

In order to determine the heat load generated by an incandescent lighting system in the dimmer room and in the house, the electrical energy consumed by the dimmers and light sources must be converted to its thermal energy equivalent. By adding the energy consumed by the dimmers and the energy consumed by the lighting (in kilowatts) and multiplying by 3412, we can find the number of BTUs (British thermal units) generated per hour of operation.

$$1 \text{ kW} = 3412 \text{ BTU/hour}$$

Let's examine the heat in the dimmer room first. Since the dimmers are passing most of the electrical energy on to the lamp loads, only the inefficiency of the dimmers need be taken into account in the calculation. For example, if a 12-channel, 2.4 kW per channel dimmer is 8% inefficient, then the maximum energy loss due to the dimmer is 2304 watts or 2.304 kW (12 channels × 2400 watts per channel × 0.08 efficiency = 2304 watts). Using the conversion from watts to BTUs, we find that the 12-channel dimmer is producing 2.304 kW × 3412 BTU/kW = 7168.25 BTU for every hour of operation.

Once the thermal load is calculated, the amount of refrigeration in tons needed to dissipate the heat generated in the dimmer room can be calculated. The conversion from BTU/hour to tons of refrigeration is

$$12{,}000 \text{ BTU/hour} = 1 \text{ ton of refrigeration}$$

Therefore,

$$7168.25 \text{ BTU/hour} = 7168.25 \div 12{,}000 \text{ tons of refrigeration}$$
$$= 0.597 \text{ tons of refrigeration}$$

Example: In the example above, if there are a total of 12 1000-watt lamps connected to the dimmer in the house, one lamp per channel: (1) What is the thermal load generated in the house? (2) How many tons of air conditioning are required to dissipate the heat load from the lamps? A: (1) 12 × 1000 = 12,000 watts = 12 × 3412 BTU/hour = 40,944 BTU/hour. (2) 40,944 BTU/hour = 40,944 ÷ 12,000 tons of refrigeration = 3.412 tons of refrigeration.

Practice Problems

1. If a 1.2-kW 12-channel dimmer rack has an efficiency of 96%, what is the total energy consumed by the entire rack? A: 1200 watts × 12 channels × 0.04 efficiency = 576 watts.
2. If the 12-channel dimmer rack in the above example is driving 12 575-watt lamps, what is the total energy consumption of the dimmer rack/lamps combination? A: (12 × 575 watts) + 576 watts = 7,476 watts.
3. Given the above scenario, what is the thermal load of the dimmer/lamp system? A: 7.476 kW × 3412 BTU/kW = 25,508 BTU.

Remote-Controlled Followspots

Because one of the primary features of automated lighting systems is remote pan and tilt, it's easy to draw the conclusion that they would make great remote-controlled followspots. In the early days of automated lighting controllers, the joystick was the first means of controlling pan and tilt. As a result, many people, usually those who were not lighting professionals, assumed that you could grab the joystick and use it as a remotely controlled followspot.

The truth is, however, that the latency in the control system, the acceleration curve built into the firmware, and the orientation of the fixtures, which is not always the same as the joystick, make it extremely difficult to accurately follow a moving target with a moving light. There are, however, systems that are made for automatically following a moving target.

At the present, there are at least two different systems made to be used in conjunction with automated lighting in order to automatically follow a subject with the lights: the Wybron Autopilot and the Martin Lighting Director. Each system differs slightly, but the principle is the same. The subject wears a transmitter or receiver, and a set of receivers or transmitters are placed in the proximity of the stage. The signal emitted from the transmitter is then triangulated by the receiver–processor combination, which calculates its exact location in 3D space at any given time. The result is then converted to a control signal that is output to the automated lights, which then focus on the subject.

The systems work very well, but they have their limitations. One of the systems uses a radio frequency (RF) transmitter and one uses an ultrasonic transmitter. The RF transmitter requires relatively uncluttered airwaves with little interference from similar frequencies. The ultrasonic transmitter requires line-of-sight placement of the receivers. In both cases, the area that can be effectively covered is limited, although several systems can be matrixed to cover a larger area. When these systems are used they have to be recalibrated on a regular basis, especially when the lighting rig is moved.

One alternative to a completely remote-controlled followspot is to use the body of a moving mirror fixture as a manually controlled followspot by mounting it on a followspot yoke. That way, the operator can be charged with the responsibility of following the talent while the lighting director can remotely change the colors and control the dimming. This has been done on several productions, including a John Michael Montgomery tour that was supplied by Bandit Lites of Knoxville, Tennessee (conceived and designed by Dizzy Gosnell of Bandit Lites).

SECTION 10

The Future of Automated Lighting Technology

Toto 2006 World Tour with High End Systems DL2 digital luminaires. (Lighting and photograph by Andrew Doig.)

CHAPTER 28

The Evolution of Automated Lighting Technology

All evolution in thought and conduct must at first appear as heresy and misconduct.—George Bernard Shaw

Throughout the history of automated lighting, one undeniable trend has held true: year after year, automated lighting has become smaller, lighter, more efficient, and lower in cost. That's not to say there aren't bigger, heavier, and more expensive automated lights on the market, because there are. A 1200-watt luminaire is still bigger than a 575-watt light, and there are automated lights available with light sources up to 7K watts and higher. But if you consider the volume-to-output ratio, the weight-to-output ratio, the wattage-to-output ratio, and the cost-to-output ratio, then the trends become clear.

One of the first commercially successful automated moving lights was the Cyklops (see Chapter 2, The Foundation of the Automated Lighting Industry), built in 1972 by Stefan Graf and Jim Fackert for the band Grand Funk Railroad. It was basically a followspot body with a servo-driven moving mirror head. By today's standards it was very large—4 feet (1.2 m) long, a foot and a half (0.46 m) wide—and heavy. It weighed 80 pounds (36 kg) without the 150-pound (68-kg) remote ballast. And it was only a 500-watt fixture. Unfortunately we have no photometric data available on it, but we can assume that it was not the brightest star in the galaxy. If we use the size and weight of the Cyklops as a reference, then we can start to see how the automated luminaire has evolved over the years.

Almost 10 years after the Cyklops was built, Vari-Lite were building the VL1 and Cameleon was building the Telescan Mark I. The Telescan Mark I was a 1200-watt moving mirror fixture that was slightly over 3 feet long and weighed just over 100 pounds (45 kg). It was still very large and heavy by today's standards but clearly a step in the right direction. Not only was it smaller and lighter than the Cyklops, but it was also extremely bright.

The VL1 was less than half the size of the Telescan, but it produced about one-third of the light output.

By 1991, High End Systems were building and selling the Intellabeam and had begun working on the Cyberlight. A 1200-watt fixture that produced 8000 lumens, or almost seven lumens per watt, the Cyberlight started shipping in the middle of the decade. A few years later, High End Systems retrofitted the instrument with a Philips MSR 1200 short arc lamp and increased the light output by more than 50%. The result, the Cyberlight Turbo, produces more than 10 lumens per watt. At 44 inches (112 cm) in length, 13 inches (33 cm) in width, 12.5 inches (31.75 cm) high and weighing 101 pounds (45.8 kg), it's still a four-handed (two crew member) rigging job.

In 2000, Martin Professional introduced the MAC 2000, a 1200-watt moving yoke automated profile spot. The electronic ballast version produces 18,000 lumens or 12.2 lumens per watt, and it is 16 inches (40.6 cm) long, 19.3 inches (49 cm) wide, 29.3 inches (74 cm) high, and weighs 84 pounds (38 kg). As you can see, we're moving up the scale in terms of efficiency and down the scale in terms of size and weight.

Vari-Lite introduced the VL3000 in 2003 and bested the benchmark set by the MAC 2000 by producing 24,000 lumens in a 1200-watt automated luminaire. At 91 pounds (41.3 kg) and 31.6 inches (80.3 cm) high, 18 inches (45.7 cm) long, and 14.5 inches (36.8 cm) wide, it is slightly smaller but heavier, and produces 33% more total lumens.

Now we can start to see the trend: from the Cyklops to the VL3000, we've gone from a 500-watt 4-foot (1.2-m) behemoth to a 1200-watt dwarf standing less than 32 inches (0.81 m) high (Figure 28-1). And the light output is incomparable.

All the while, as automated lighting has become smaller, lighter, and brighter, the cost per lumen has come down and the feature set and quality of projection have grown dramatically. In 1989, a Coemar Robot had a list price in the United States of $4000. The 400-watt fixture produced about 4000 total lumens and had a basic feature set that included pan and tilt (about 180 by 90 degrees), a four-position color wheel, and a four-position gobo wheel that doubled as the shutter. Today, there are a number of 250-watt moving yoke fixtures that produce close to 4000 total lumens and cost less than $2500. And they do much more than the Robot did, including 540

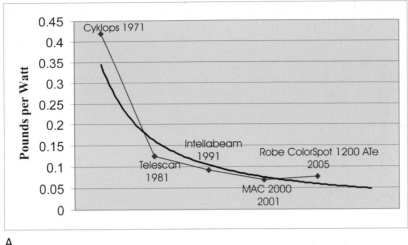

A

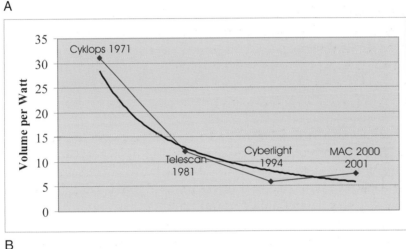

B

Figure 28-1 For more than 30 years, automated lighting has been getting smaller, lighter, cheaper, and brighter.

degrees of pan by 270 degrees of tilt (with position encoding), rotating indexable dichroic glass gobos, remote focus, full dimming, and rotating prisms.

Today, for just about the same price as the Coemar Robot a decade and a half ago, you can buy a 575-watt moving yoke fixture with at least twice the light output that is roughly half the size and weight, with more range of movement, far more gobos and colors, more effects, and greater reliability. Advances in just about every aspect of automated luminaire

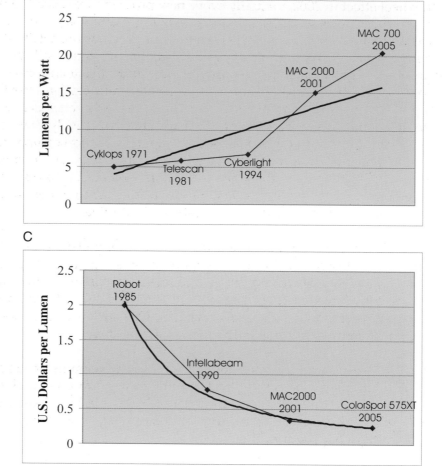

Figure 28-1 *Continued*

technology, from design to construction, have moved us far and fast. We have more efficient and reliable electronic switch-mode power supplies, improved lamps with greater efficiency, better optics with higher resolution gobos, better and lighter construction materials, and better design tools to speed products to market faster.

That's the good news. The bad news, if there is any, is that there have not been any new major developments in automated lighting effects, outside of digital lighting, in the last few years. Since Martin introduced the animation wheel effect in 2002, virtually every new product introduced to the market has been a new configuration of existing technology. The new products being introduced are smaller versions of previous models with a new combination of existing effects. To be sure, advances are still being made in size, weight, efficiency, and pricing, but innovative technology in terms of new effects is scarce. It's difficult to temper your elation over the quality and the quantity of products currently on the market because there are certainly some very good ones, some of which are relatively inexpensive. And that's good news for end users, designers, production companies, and productions, but it's a tough market for manufacturers. As a consequence, it's difficult for them to justify plowing money back into research and development to bring innovative products to market when profit margins are thin and their return on investment is limited.

Time will tell whether automated lighting has hit a long plateau or if it's just taking a short breather. But for the time being, some manufacturers will be content to reconfigure, repackage, and rerelease existing technology at lower and lower prices while others will look for new ways to innovate and develop new technology and new products. One such area of innovation that is just coming over the horizon is digital lighting.

Automated lighting control, on the other hand, is still developing at a rapid pace. Unlike luminaires, which depend heavily on hardware technology, automated lighting control is advancing due to advances in both hardware and software. And most of the software advances have come from the shifting paradigm of programming.

In the early days of automated lighting, console design and implementation were heavily channel oriented. If you wanted the ability to control an attribute such as a focus position or the speed of a rotating gobo, there was a channel for it. It was a paradigm borne from the analog model of control using a multifader console. But after years of experience, programmers and console designers are realizing that a fader that varies linearly from 0 to 256 or from 0 to 100% may not be the best way to control many attributes. It's fine for some attributes such as intensity; everybody understands what is meant by 50% intensity. But for other attributes, such as color, it makes little sense. After all, what is the meaning of 50% color? The fact is, the linear fader channel model requires human interpretation to decipher what is meant by 50% color. We have to know to which fixture we are referring and then we need a road map telling us what color the beam will be if we set the value of color fader to 50%.

In the real-world model, console design and implementation are less control channel oriented and more fixture attribute oriented. The control mechanism that is tied to a fixture attribute, either temporarily by the use of soft buttons or permanently by the use of faders, encoders, buttons, etc., is now configured and presented in real-world values that require no interpretation, deciphering, or lookup tables. Instead of adjusting a fader until it reaches the DMX512 value of the color we're looking for, we now select from a list of colors that corresponds to the color. Instead of assigning a channel to every attribute of a luminaire and then subdividing that control channel to modify its use, the control surface is being designed around the tasks to be performed and the logic in the console is left to decipher the channel assignments.

In the old model, pan and tilt were in percentages; in the new model, they are in degrees. In the old model, zoom was in percentage; in the new model, zoom is in degrees of beam or field angle. And so on.

With the advent of ACN, consoles will be able to discover on their own how many lights and DMX512 devices are plugged into the data network, what type of lights they are, which attributes they have, and the capability of each attribute. The system will virtually be "plug and play." Much of the work involving setting up palettes will be automated by the bidirectional communication link between the console and the luminaire.

How far can automation go? It's entirely possible that in the future we will be speaking to our consoles rather than punching buttons. As far back as the early 1980s, Tasco Starlite built a voice-controlled console. The technology is currently available, and it's a matter of time before someone invests the time and money to build another. (As of this writing, the author attended a private showing of a new console that is soon to be released and it is designed to have built-in voice recognition software.)

And if voice-activated control isn't enough, we could someday use telekinesis to control lights with our thoughts. If you find that hard to believe, consider that the Defense Advanced Research Projects Agency (DARPA) funded the successful completion of experiments involving telekinesis, according to author Joel Garreau in his book *Radical Evolution*. At a Duke University lab, an owl monkey named Belle was successfully trained to play a video game by rewarding her for playing it well. When she became proficient at it, researchers implanted sensors in her motor cortex, the part of the brain linked to muscle movements. The sensors converted the electrical impulses from her brain and transmitted them to a computer that was connected to a robotic arm. The signals were then sent by the Internet to a computer 600 miles away in a remote laboratory in Boston. That computer was also connected to a robotic arm. Then the researchers gave the monkey the joystick controller, except it wasn't hooked up to anything. When Belle moved the joystick to play the game, her thoughts were translated to electrical impulses, which then triggered the robotic arms. Belle was then able to play the game by *thinking* about playing the game. If a monkey can play a video game telekinetically, how far off can telekinetic lighting control be?

CHAPTER 29

The Digital Lighting Revolution

Every generation needs a new revolution.—Thomas Jefferson

If automated lighting is to hand over the mantle of cutting-edge lighting technology, then digital lighting will surely take it up. Digital lighting opens new avenues for production designers that they could previously only dream about. Its graphic and animation capabilities make gobos appear low-tech in comparison. The ability to create custom content to suit the production vastly increases the freedom of design and uniquely marks each production. Its scenic projection capabilities bring another dimension to productions that was previously unavailable.

Digital lighting is a bit more ethereal than "conventional" automated lighting with analog projection. While automated lighting can be defined as a light with remotely controllable attributes, digital lighting is a little harder to define. Is a projector on a yoke a digital light? Is a static projector, for that matter, a digital light? What about a static projector or an LED wall that is fed by a DMX512-controlled media server? What, exactly, comprises digital lighting? Is it the content, the light engine, the control mechanism?

There are those who argue that a projector on a yoke is simply a remote-controlled projector, not a digital light. Some purists argue that the Icon M is the only digital light to date because it has its own light source and DMD engine, yet stylized moving yoke housings with built-in video projectors are marketed and sold as digital lighting. Semantics aside, there is one distinguishing characteristic of all digital lighting, regardless of the hardware that is used to facilitate it, and that is the control method. Conventional video is operated by a director who uses a switcher to manually select a source and direct it to an output device. Digital lighting centralizes the control of video and lighting and puts it in the hands of a lighting programmer or director in order to harmonize the visual elements of a production. Digital lighting involves the control of the content being sent to a display device, whether that device is a projector, a projector on a yoke, an LED wall, or a quasi-video display device. It can be argued that a media server feeding digital content to an array of conventional automated lights whose CMY color mixers are under control of the media server is digital lighting.

Putting digital content under the control of the lighting designers, programmer, and operators is what is referred to in the lighting industry as convergence. Lighting and video are converging under the auspices of the lighting department to create a more cohesive design that coordinates the visual elements of a production. As a result, more and more lighting designers are taking on the role of production designer instead of the narrower role of lighting designer. In the future, it's likely that lighting programmers and lighting directors will become production programmers and production directors, respectively.

A production designer often designs the lighting and scenic elements, including the set and sometimes the video displays, which may be one and the same. For example, a matrix of video panels covered with Plexiglas might serve as a stage floor, or a sculpture of LED pixel modules might serve as a visual element and a video display unit at the same time. Or it could be as simple as a large video screen backdrop. The production designer might then be responsible for lighting the set and designing the content for the video displays, which affords the opportunity to coordinate the look and feel of every visual element of the production.

Digital Lighting Luminaires

Digital lighting is still in its infancy. At the moment, there are only a few digital lighting luminaires commercially available, and they are essentially video projectors housed in a stylized moving yoke chassis. They offer features such as zoom, remote focus, and an iris for a true blackout as opposed to video black. They are roughly three times the cost of a conventional automated light. Adding a media server, which is a necessity unless the luminaire has integrated media server capabilities, can more than double that cost. Alternatively, there are media servers available that are more economical, dual-channel media servers that can feed content to two digital lights, and digital luminaires with built-in media servers, all of which can help reduce the overall cost. As the technology matures and more manufacturers offer new products, the competition will put downward pressure on prices and these tools will become more affordable.

The currently available technology uses video projectors that produce about 4500 to 5000 ANSI lumens. In addition to the brightness, the contrast ratio is an important factor in the perceived brightness of a projected image. Texas Instrument's "dark metal" technology absorbs light on the DMD chip and has helped to improve contrast ratios in some projectors from about 800:1 to about 1100:1 or more. Projectors with these specs are sufficiently bright under the right conditions. But you have to use good lighting practices to ensure that the image reads well. That means that the projection surfaces should be light-colored with high reflectivity, and light spill from other sources should be controlled. The ambient lighting also has to be controlled, the image should be sized correctly, and the content should be optimized for live projection (Figure 29-1).

As the price, size, and weight of projectors continues to fall, digital lighting will gradually near the price point of automated lighting. Over the last 5 years since the introduction of commercially available digital lighting, the retail cost of entry has fallen from the range of about $60,000–$120,000 to about $30,000 *per unit*. According to an article by Jeff Sauer in the

Figure 29-1 Sheryl Crow's *Wildflower* tour (lighting designer Paul Guthrie) was an early adopter of the DL2 digital luminaire.

November 2004 issue of *Video Systems* magazine, in 2004 alone, portable projectors in the 10.1-pound to 15-pound range increased in brightness 20% over the prior year. Though not atypical, advances in brightness are not necessarily linear but rather take strides with new developments in technology. For example, when Philips discovered that by putting a mercury discharge lamp in an ultra high pressure environment they could shorten the arc gap, they increased the efficiency dramatically. The resulting lamp, the UHP, won the company an Emmy Award and it is now a common projector lamp. Ushio developed a DC version, the NSH lamp. Both are currently limited to no more than 250 watts, but when they solve the problem of managing heat more efficiently and break the 250-watt barrier, they will succeed in increasing the brightness in a whole new class of projectors.

But for now, digital lighting luminaires are still the dark horses of the industry, not so well known but very successful in transforming production as we know it.

Media Servers

A media server is a specialized computer with application software designed to store large amounts of graphics files, manipulate them, and "serve" them to a display device. The display device might be a projector, a digital luminaire, a video wall, or a quasi-video display. A media server typically has very fast processors, lots of memory and storage, and very powerful graphics capabilities. The architecture of the current generation of media servers is structured to work in "layers" or with "3D objects." Each layer or object allows the operator to build a look that can be mixed with other layers or objects, arranged on a background or cross-faded to another layer. The main difference between the layer approach and the object approach is that when 3D objects are used you can change the z coordinate, thereby changing the order in which the objects appear.

The power of the media server lies in its ability to generate effects on the fly or to program them into scenes (Figure 29-2). Most media servers have a wide variety of effects, ranging from manipulating the scale, position, and orientation to manipulating color, and much more. They often facilitate the mapping of graphics on 3D objects, and they offer a variety of manipulation tools for video such as speed control.

Figure 29-2 Media servers: (A) PRG Virtuoso EX-1; (B) Coolux Pandoras Box; (C) PRG Mbox Extreme; (D) Martin Maxedia; (E) High End Systems Axon 2.

Media servers are not new. They have been used in broadcast and live video reinforcement for a long time. What is new is that there are now several media servers with DMX512 control being manufactured by lighting companies and marketed in the lighting industry to lighting professionals. They have significantly altered productions by enabling the video to be integrated entirely into the lighting realm, transforming the way productions look and feel and how they are designed, programmed, and operated.

Content Development

If digital lighting is to be the nuclear reactor of the industry, then the content that feeds it is certainly destined to be the fuel rod of the industry. Without the digital content to supply the projection, there would be no digital lighting. It is the essence of the technology.

Content is what's in the "box." In a box of cereal, the content is the individual flakes of toasted corn glazed with crystallized sugar. In digital media, the content is made up of individual pixels containing information about the color of the pixel and how it changes over time. That's what's in the box. But the true essence of the content of a box of cereal is not the flakes of toasted corn glazed with sugar, but how they tastes in a bowl when you pour cold milk over them. In digital media, the true essence of content is how it looks and how it makes you feel when all the pixels come together and flash before your eyes. Art is the true essence of digital content.

Content can be sourced in a number of ways. There are several stock and custom content providers that can be located on the Internet. You can use them to select from a wide variety of graphic stills and video images to use as a starting point, or you can commission them to create custom content. Also, most media servers are provided with stock content—all sorts of graphic images and video clips—that can be manipulated to fit the needs of the production.

Alternatively, you can create your own content. The artists who create the content are part "technogeek" and part artisan. The tools they use to create content require knowledge of computer hardware and software, but the final product is a work of art. When the two come together in the right proportion then the results speak for themselves (Figure 29-3).

A

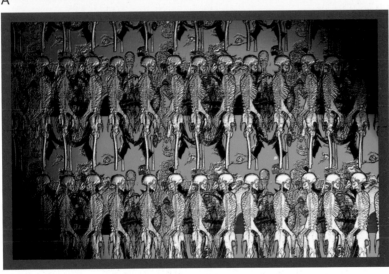

B

Figure 29-3 Michael A. Fink of Magical Designs created these digital works of art on the computer using several software programs. (A) SAUC; (B) The Last Dance Aids.

The tools of the trade for the content creator are acquisition tools and graphics manipulation tools. The acquisition tools can be a digital camera, a video camera, or a scanner. Alternatively, graphics can be created from scratch. There are a number of software packages, such as Adobe Photoshop and Illustrator, that allow you to create your own graphics, to acquire them, or to import them. The manipulation tools are the software packages that allow you to modify and manipulate the graphical content. For example, Adobe After Effects and Apple Final Cut Pro are just two of several popular software packages made for this purpose.

Digital content is formatted according to how a device creates, stores, and sends a picture to another device. There are a number of still-image formats, such as Joint Photographic Experts Group (JPEG), Tagged Image File Format (TIFF), and bitmap (BMP), and a number of video wrappers, such as Audio Video Interleave (AVI) and Quicktime (MOV), which combine many different formats into a piece of code. The formats can include the frames rate, the aspect ratio of the frames, the number of pixels in a frame, whether the frames are interlaced or progressive scans, the type of compression, and much more. (An interlaced frame is one in which every other scan line is displayed. It takes two fields, one with odd-numbered scan lines and one with even-numbered scan lines, to make a full frame. In a progressive scan, each frame contains every line and paints a complete picture.)

An uncompressed digital graphic is typically a very large file. In order to make more effective use of storage and bandwidth, digital images and videos are compressed for storage and decompressed for playback using a software module called a codec (compressor-decompressor). When data are compressed and decompressed, sometimes some of the original data are lost, but the final product is close enough to the original that they are virtually indistinguishable for most applications. This is known as lossy compression. If the compressed data can be recreated exactly as the original then it is known as a lossless compression. Lossy compression results in much smaller file sizes than lossless compression.

There are many different codecs, each with its own unique characteristics; some are more suited for fluid playback, while others are more suited for still image and color quality. One of the more important considerations in choosing a codec is whether or not you need random frame access to play still frames or for reverse playback. If so, then a codec such as MJPEG, in which every frame is individually compressed, is much better suited for the application. On the other hand, delta compression codecs such as MPEG2, which only store changes between frames, are designed to play video at its normal speed and only in the forward direction.

The compression algorithm of a codec balances the need for good quality graphics, the size of the compressed file, the minimum amount of data needed to accurately represent the original data, latency, and several other factors. Depending on the type of media server being used, some codecs might be more appropriate than others.

Regardless of the file format or the codec used with it, the content can be optimized for projection by manipulating the color saturation, contrast, intensity, gamma, and other variables. If a graphic is destined to be broadcast then it is subject to the requirements of the broadcast engineer and the format, but if not, there is a lot more freedom to manipulate a graphic as much as you like.

Display Devices

Part of the reason for the burgeoning digital lighting sector is the burgeoning number of new display devices. When live video reinforcement was first popularized in the 1980s, there were two main display devices from which to choose: projection and the Sony Jumbotron, which used vacuum fluorescent display (VFD) technology. The projectors were very large and expensive, and Jumbotrons were even larger and more expensive. The first LED wall was shown at the National Association of Broadcasters (NAB) trade show in 1996. It was built by a subsidiary of Cree, Inc. called Real Color Displays. The LED wall was popularized by the rock band U2 on their *Popmart* tour in 1997–1998.

Today, in addition to much smaller and more affordable (relatively speaking) front and rear projection and LED walls, production designers have many more video display and low-resolution or quasi-video display devices with which to enhance their designs (Figure 29-4). There are a number of new modular LED display devices, some as small as a single pixel each, coming onto the market that make it easy and affordable to build custom displays, giving the designer free reign with creativity and flexibility. They come in a variety of shapes and sizes. Plasma and LCD displays are also dropping in price, making them more attractive for use in productions.

As a result, most large-budget productions are making digital lighting an important element of the design (Figure 29-5). Designers are finding new and creative ways to enhance the visual impact of their productions, and

A

B

C

Figure 29-4 Low-resolution display devices: (A) Barco MiPix; (B) Barco MiSphere; (C) G-LEC Spaceframe; (D) Element Labs Versa Tile; (E) AC Lighting Color Web.

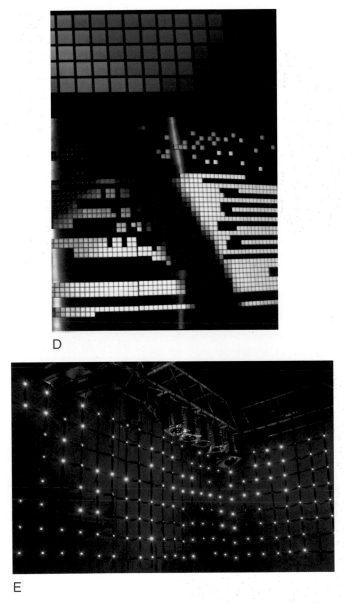

D

E

Figure 29-4 *Continued*

media servers are becoming more and more common in productions of
. every type. As this trend continues to develop, more opportunities will
present themselves for those who are willing to embrace the new technology and stay abreast of it. There will be a steadily growing demand
for content developers, media server programmers and operators,

A

B

Figure 29-5 (A) Journey with Main Light SoftLED low-res LED drapes, Barco D7 high-resolution LED panels (hanging), and Sony 10K ANSI lumen rear projection video (upstage), all fed by a Catalyst system. (B) Stereophonics with Barco iLite 12 LED panels fed by a Catalyst system (lighting designer Brent Clark).

computer- and digital lighting-savvy technicians, and designers who understand the technology.

Will digital lighting someday replace automated lighting? If history is any indication, then it's a safe bet that the two technologies will coexist in productions well into the future. After all, when automated lighting became available it didn't make conventional lighting obsolete; it served to enhance the designer's tools. Conventional lighting is still an important part of most every production, even though automated lighting is relatively cheap and plentiful. So there's no reason to believe that digital lighting will crowd out automated lighting or conventional lighting. What digital lighting will do, however, is enhance the creative palette and increase the size and power of the production designer's toolbox.

If we consider the first patent for a remotely controlled spotlight issued to Edmund Sohlberg in 1906 to be the genesis of automated lighting as we know it today, then 100 years has passed since its conception. However, the technology has advanced exponentially from its origin, and only in the last 25 years have we seen its true potential. Perhaps even more telling is a survey of automated lighting manufacturers conducted by *PLSN* magazine (www.plsn.com) near the end of 2005. A large sample of automated lighting manufacturers were asked for data on their latest products. When the data were collected and analyzed it was found that every one of the new products had two things in common: they all had remote focus capability and they all had replaceable gobos. What is remarkable about this is that in 1990, these were rare features. In 1995, they were features that only a few lights had. In 2000, more fixtures had them than didn't, and in 2005, they were more common than not. It's a telling example of how automated lighting is evolving.

Thank you, Edmund Sohlberg, wherever you are.

Index